Rave reviews for Julia Phillips's #1 Bestseller

YOU'LL NEVER EAT LUNCH IN THIS TOWN AGAIN

"Compelling. . . . What it means to be both at the top and at the bottom. . . . Names names, kicks ass, and kisses and tells about the various angels and devils with whom Julia Phillips has wrestled (and done drugs with) on the way up and the way down."

—Liz Smith

"One of the most honest books ever written about one of the most dishonest towns ever created!"

—*Boston Globe*

"A delightfully venomous Hollywood tell-all . . . fuel-injected dishing!"

—*Newsday*

"A confessional autobiography . . . an exposé of Hollywood . . . a manual on movie making. . . . A hell of a story!"

—*San Francisco Chronicle*

"The Hollywood memoir that tells all . . . Sex. Drugs. Greed. Why, it sounds just like a movie."

—*The New York Times*

ALSO BY JULIA PHILLIPS

You'll Never Eat Lunch in This Town Again

Driving
UNDER THE
AFFLUENCE

JULIA PHILLIPS

HarperPaperbacks
A Division of HarperCollinsPublishers

HarperPaperbacks
A Division of HarperCollinsPublishers
10 East 53rd Street, New York, N.Y. 10022-5299

ISBN: 0-06-101184-3

A hardcover edition of this book was published
in 1995 by HarperCollins*Publishers*.

A portion of this book appeared in modified form in the
August 1995 issue of *Los Angeles* magazine.

HarperCollins®, 🔥®, and HarperPaperbacks™
are trademarks of HarperCollins*Publishers*

Cover photograph by Chris Cuffaro/Edge

First HarperPaperbacks printing: January 1997

Printed in the United States of America

Visit HarperPaperbacks on the World Wide Web at
http://www.harpercollins.com/paperbacks

❖ 10 9 8 7 6 5 4 3 2 1

For my father Adolph. Best friend. Favorite teacher.
And my daughter Kate. Best teacher. Favorite friend.

We will now discuss in a little more detail
the Struggle for Existence.

CHARLES DARWIN
The Origin of the Species

Driving
UNDER THE
AFFLUENCE

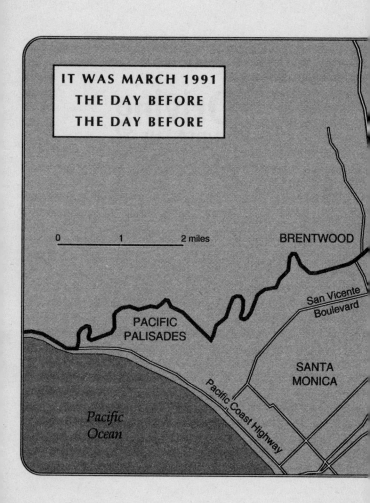

IT WAS MARCH 1991
THE DAY BEFORE
THE DAY BEFORE

Flick.
Pink.
For those girls.
Flick. Blue.
For those boys.
Ariel's French-manicured nails ting against the edges of the table in the corner of my bedroom as she pastes alternating post-its around its border. Color-coding guests.

"I'm not sure I even wanna *do* this, Air!" I whine and sweeping my arms expressively I knock the *Scientific American* from which I've been reading aloud to the floor. It stays open on THE SEARCH FOR THE TOP QUARK. The most elusive of the postulated subatoms whence all matter in the Universe springs. All universes, for that matter.

I've been extrapolating from the learned poop, condensing the six quarks (up down top bottom strange charm) to three (sabrina kelly jill).

Framing a hypothetical pitch for one of the few executives in town still speaking to me. A series.

Tentative title *Three Quarks for Muster Mark.*

Think *Charlie's Angels of The Cosmos,* I'll tell him and he'll reply, it's TV. *Three Quacks for Mister Mack.*

Translation: Forget it, Jools, it's Chinatown.

Ariel tosses the magazine back and shoots me a scowl.

Ariel, my assistant, is six feet tall with long blonde hair and a not-bad-for-a-girl dunk shot and I don't argue with her.

I *do* call her Air which always makes us laugh.

"I can't be bothered to hear that," she says evenly and presses on.

Flick. Pink. Flick. Blue.

First-draft seating for the debut of my book *You'll Never Eat Lunch in This Town Again*. The cognoscenti who sneaked each other bootleg xeroxed manuscripts this past Christmas when Desert Sturm and Drang was a mere condom dubbed it *YNELITTA*. I couldn't figure how to pronounce it but I liked its look on paper.

YNELITTA had been a pain in the ass to write. Pain in the gut more precisely, as I pretty much puked my way through the process, particularly if my period and the full moon were imminent and I was on a roll.

Puke. Roll. Puke. Roll.

Salt. Sweet. Salt. Sweet. Puke. Roll.

Safety Safety Safety and drink plenty of water.

Sometimes, weeping on the floor of the bathroom after a particularly wrenching episode I'd remind myself that David Byrne had confided he threw up before each Talking Heads concert. And years ago I'd seen an interview with Bill Russell, center for the Boston Celtics, in which he confessed to vomiting before every game.

I suppose writing is akin to rock 'n' roll or sports in its Go-fuck-yourself/Okay-I-will overtones but the performances are for the smallest of rooms.

And the sound of one hand clapping is silence.

Bulimia had never been my drug of choice and it stopped the moment legal requirements (which had taken a year) were fulfilled. Just in time for shipment a week ago of *YNELITTA*'s first printing: 70,000 copies.

Not too much not too little, what with the recession.

Like my advance, meted out in dollops over the three years it's taken to bring the tome that was my life to market.

YNELITTA's release coincides roughly with an upcoming birthday. Forty-seven. Four and seven is eleven. Eleven is a Master Number. Double ones. Ones mean new beginnings.

To solve old tax problems? One can only hope.

My IRS collector E. McGuffin, who has me on the top third of her shitlist, would no doubt be thrilled. I've fantasized from the imperious tone of her letters — threatening to take the house the car the kid — that her files on me have been confused with her files on someone named Julio Phillippe, an irresponsible negligent Hispanic-speaking person.

I've been in a financial fiasco since the crash of '87, when I ran out of old money. Then I earned enough new money to cover bills and loans but there was nothing left for taxes. By 1989 I had a high-five-figure debt to E. I couldn't make a dent in. Interest and penalties have accrued exponentially into the low-six-figure realm.

Yo tengo un tax problema!

Pink. Blue. Pink. Blue.

The color-coding is an empty activity, something else to fill the spaces between each opening night jitter. We've already polished the silver and Ajaxed the porcelain in the bathrooms and kitchen. In the good old bad old days we'd have rolled a joint and glided through the neighborhood hills in my late-seventies silver SLC.

Last year, though, I attended a party off Mulholland Drive where one of the guests' cars blazed to the ground and damn near ignited the surrounding trees.

"Was it secured with a Club?" LAPD asked and the owner said, Yes how did he know?

"Most likely gang kids from The Valley," a fireman said, glancing at an empty gas can on the shoulder of the road. "When they can't steal it, they torch it."

"Gang kids from The Valley?" I said. "I thought they skateboarded to the mall . . ."

"Nope, we got white homeboys all over The Valley," LAPD said philosophically. "Maybe it's from the smog . . ."

Nobody of the female persuasion glides anywhere this hour of night anymore anyway.

This hour of day either.

Times being what they are and all.

I try not to remember that when I was just a little girl, seven maybe, I rode the subway at dusk to and from dance classes at the Brooklyn Academy of Music, which was in a rough neighborhood, but I can't help myself. I remember everything, including the phone numbers of dead people.

"Where's Kate?" Air asks, switching pinks and blues, referring to my seventeen-year-old daughter who's been charging in and out of my room all night agitated with midterm-exam anxiety. I've reminded her that since she's in her second semester senior year these tests won't count. Presumably the colleges where she's applied have made their choices by now.

Every four years or so I have to steer my baby through a maze of applications for the next step in her upwardly mobile education and steel her for possible rejection.

At least I don't have to go on the interviews, as I did for lower and upper school. Now that I don't consume massive quantities of foodstuffs at power lunches I don't really own any Republican-looking clothes. Kate probably does though, and would surely lend them to me as she has a generous spirit, her flirtation with Conservatism notwithstanding.

For a year there, as she was leaning further and further right, tormenting me with cheers like "I like Jesse/He's so sexy/I love Newt/He's so cute," I feared I might arise one morning to discover that my one and only progeny had transformed into Richard Nixon during the night and insisted I replace her hip little backpack with a briefcase for her school papers.

Which would have killed my mother, Tanya, if she were still alive. My mother couldn't utter Richard Nixon's name in neutral: richardnixon.

She spat it between tightly pursed lips, eyes sparking, body jiggling with suppressed rage: RITCHErrrd. NICKS! Unnn.

RitcherrrdNicks!unnn was the personification of everything about The United States my mother detested.

Populist fundamentalism and concomitant anti-intellectualism and the paranoid pettiness of the Self-Made Man. Which led inevitably to molestation and mutilation and murder, personal and professional.

In The Gospel According to Tanya RN was the enemy of freedom, democracy and goodwill. The Antichrist. She died before the ascension of such other likely candidates for the job as, say ... Arnold Schwarzenegger ... Michael Jackson ... Oliver North ... Arsenio Hall ...

"Wrapped warmly in the arms of Morpheus on the other side of the house, I hope," but I hear Kate's telltale mac-and-cheese preparations rustling in the kitchen nearby.

We snicker knowingly.

Flick flick flick go Air's nails and they meld with a heavy tick tick tick from the timepiece across the way.

A novelty item that runs on a single Eveready C.

The clock is a one-foot white-faced square framed in plain black wood. A thin black circle within the square.

Black hour and minute hands. Black numbers.

1 2 3 etc. is what they say.

"Where are you?!" Air asks sharply.

"Reminiscing about a present from an ancient inamorato . . ." I smile. We both know that by the time I celebrated my thirtieth birthday I had injested imbibed or inhaled sufficient doses of tofu toxins and THC for my neuroceptors to induce FLASHBACKS at will. Without my permission. Makes my life feel like an endless renegotiation between the conscious and the guide.

"Uh-huh . . ." Air shrugs casually.

Flick flick flick.

Discards in a cosmic game of chance.

The gift giver — Greek curiously — was one of the last to live here before I recused myself from the futile search for the perfect orgasm, which was about as rewarding as the search for the perfect jeans.

"You know he understood nothing about me . . . save my relationship to minutes seconds hours . . ."

Air laughs. Shuffles. Deconstructs. Reconstructs.

The Penelope of Party planners.

1 2 3 etc. originally had a second hand pushing forward in urgent stop-stop-stop motion.

A temblor epicentered in The Desert dislodged it New Year's Day more than a decade ago. 1979. Maybe '80.

A reminder from an orderly universe.

Or.

Chaotically random whatever.

Thank-you-and-have-a-nice-day-and-fuck-you. Love God.

Kindest personal regards. Mother Nature.

I was in the shower washing off the night's sins, which weren't near what they used to be, and rolled with it and thought, So Earth is a dog. And we are . . . the fleas?

The Greek understood plenty about Kate, still single-digit age.

"She's a grown woman," he smiled at me wickedly as she writhed in his arms, howling as if possessed by psychic indigestion from Eve's verboten snack.

I took her to the doctor.

Flu, he diagnosed and overprescribed antibiotics, Tylenol, fluids, bed rest and TLC chez Mom.

Home. Sanctuary.

Whilst the car idled furiously at the longest light in Beverly Hills Kate glazed out the window to focus for a moment on the first Caucasian Female, Homeless, lingering at the Santa Monica Boulevard Fountain.

"That's so sad, Mommy," she murmured then turned to me with a demented grin. "You remind me of a man. . . ." she muttered hopefully from the side of her mouth as we pulled into traffic. We'd been snookering each other into this game since she could talk.

"What man?" I smiled and accelerated onto Canon Drive; into the flats, where people lived in $2.5 million estates on 125-running-foot lots. Point your blow-dryer in the wrong direction and you ruined your neighbor's new perm.

"The man with the power!" Kate squealed delightedly.

"*What* power?!"

"The power of voodoo . . ."

"Who do . . . ?"

"*You* do . . ."

"I do *what*!@#?"

"*Reeemind* me of a man . . ."

Ah honaaay, sometimes you ask too much . . .

Later, camped out in my bed, laughing and sparkling from high fever Kate rubbed her hands longingly across a Ouija board The Greek had purchased that afternoon for our amusement.

"What do I do?" She smiled, then coughed with the deep
gelatinous resonance of a tubercular denizen of South Side,
U.S.A. White woman at Santa Monica Fountain for example.
Kate hocked up a sizable brown mass. Just like everyone in
L.A. does every morning. Even the nonsmoking.

If all that viscous goo could be remolecularized into clean-
burning fuel or microconductors for the interactive highway
Southern California would bounce from its recession in a hurry.

Yo, chip this!

"A Breakfast of Champions," I kidded, worried.

"Eeeuuuoooow," she grimaced and tossed the offending
snot-rag toward a wastebasket. "C'mon Mom. Let's play."

"Okay we hold it on our knees equally and keep our fingers lightly on the pointer. No jostling, no guiding. Got it?" ·

"What are the letters and numbers for?"

"Well if we rouse the spirits with some YES/NO we can
pose more complicated questions. Which require more spe-
cific answers." Kate frowned seriously and aimed fiery brown
eyes on the board. I half-expected a red laser beam to emanate
from her forehead.

"C'mon Mom . . ." We positioned ourselves. Khrushchev
and Kennedy. Bobby Fischer and Boris Spassky.
"Concentrate!" Martina and Chris. "Mooom . . ." Death and
the Archbishop. Archie and Veronica. ". . . ask a question!"

"Are there any spirits in this house?" I said. "Hello hello
are you out there?"

Nothing.

Then the pointer moved. By itself. Cross my heart.

Our hands flew inexorably to YES.

"Are you a good spirit?" Kate asked, so young so sweet so
free.

The pointer whoopdedooed and curlicued.

YES.

"Phew," Kate said and wiped her forehead dramatically.
"How old are you?"

The board wobbled a bit and the pointer got busy.

1-1-0-0-0 Y-R-S.

"Girl? Boy?"

G-I-R-L A-N-D B-O-Y.

"Oh right, you're a spirit after all."

YES.

"What's your name?" Kate asked, talking normally to the Talking Board, which wasn't normal at all. Sniffing at the air she scoped the room with feral alertness.

V-I-R-G-I-L-I-A.

"Too long . . ." Kate said dreamily, vibing vapors in the middle distance. "What about VTG? For Virgilia The Good . . ."

YES.

"Kate!" I interjected sharply, "I think we should stop . . ."

"Nooooo . . ." she wailed. "No no no no no . . . VTG, where are you from?"

R-O-M-A.

"VTG, are there other spirits here?"

YES.

"Good spirits?"

NO.

Then the bed torqued and our eyes locked, less frightened than surprised and the power surged. Soundtracked by a tiny roar, like a platoon of trucks passing by at fifty miles an hour.

The board jackknifed from our knees onto the spread and the pointer lay cantilevered like the tongue of a dead woodland animal.

GOOD BYE.

Good-bye yourself.

"Aftershock," I informed my overstimulated offspring; packed up Robert Fuld's Talking Board and pointer in their Parker Bros. box and stashed them permanently under the bed before she could protest.

The shaker was 3.2 on the Richter scale and knocked some sense into me.

So I got rid of The Greek.

Sent him away.

Just in time.

One two three etcetera . . .

Flick. Pink. Flick. Blue. Pinkblue. Pinkblue.

"What about Yellow for the sexually confused?!" Air quips.

"The whole table would be Yellow. Except for a Green or two . . ."

"Green?!"

". . . for the uncommitted." Air laughs.

"Then there's the Red and the Black. Red is for the alienated and *Black* is for —"

Suddenly all three phone lines spark into service and the lights and radio flutter stutter and die and the canyon where I live — the one that looks like AlmostColorado — gets dark.

Very dark.

And silent.

Sooo silent.

"Eeeeeek!!!" Kate screams from the kitchen.

"Oh shit!!!" Air explodes.

"Oh fuck!" I exclaim ritualistically and reach for the flashlight in the middle of the table where the cigarettes and tissues are.

Oh fuck is what I say when the power goes.

More and more come to think of it.

Especially since that 3.2 on the New Year's Scale.

Breakdown of the Infrastructure right here in Sanctuary. Good old $3500 to $4200 a month.

Depending on Alan Greenspan's serotonin uptake.

Pastorally but unpropitiously situated in the crotch of intersecting networks.

"Who can give a shit for the quarks when she's got no lights?" I say and find a Sportman's Lamp.

POWER ON

Air sighs with relief.

I wend to the kitchen and guide my daughter into the bedroom.

Who among us likes to be alone in the dark, the . . .

"Black — your color — what's the black for?" Air fiddles with her Post-its, her Deck of Lives.

BAAAlllummmmm.

Lights. Sound. Speeeed. Action!

A movie set coming to life.

"Thank you," Air says to the ceiling, addressing her Higher Power and I turn off the Sportman's Lamp.

"I'm a hydroelectric hiccup at the weakest link in the grid," I declare, looking for a laugh.

Air obliges me with a reluctant chuckle.

I puff out my chest, feisty. "I'm The Black Jewish Surge."

Kate cackles. She knows what's coming.

"I'm their worst nightmare. The Other . . ."

"She's the man with the power of voodooo," Kate says solemnly.

"The Top Quack, Ritcherrrd Nicks!unnn!" I brag.

Then every bulb and appliance in Sanctuary flashes and strobes violently . . .

POWER OFF

. . . and we plunge into dark laughter.

THOSE GIRLS
THE MANICURIST

Mommy was a tramp and Papa was a rolling stone but she says she loves them anyway. She doesn't stay in touch.

She performs miracles for the moneyed:

Acrylics — virtual fingernails — that appear actual.

Feet that are groomed if not precisely pretty, but how many pretty feet are there really?

She stocks great colors. Purveys spectacular dish.

She still captures the imagination of those younger boys with good makeup, good luck and good lighting but she rarely pays attention anymore. Sometimes she passes one off to an A-list client.

You're kinkier than I am, she shrugs and smiles mysteriously although she suspects that's not true.

If the moon is full over a weekend one of her ex-Significant Autres arrives early in the morning or late at night, brandishing a gun.

It scares her but she is not afraid of him.

She's putting her son through junior college which is nobody's business but her own.

Every once in a while *I Love Lucy* makes her cry for hours. She's positive it's from the fumes at work.

She knows how to keep a secret.

And how to invent one, too.

Back.

Forth.

Mara paces angrily in my bedroom and I bob my head tennis-matchish to follow her.

Back. Forth.

It's days after the release of George Holliday's video of the beating of Rodney King and Mara's still beside herself.

Backforth Backforth. Backforth Backforth.

Since I'm the one imminently traveling by nonsmoking air to New York PR Hell I've counted on *Mara* to be the laid-back calming one so I'm pooh-poohing her.

"Duuude are you surprised? Don't you think this goes on in every town in every city in every country in every world? Isn't that why those boys like to be cops? So they can beat other people to a pulp with impunity?"

I smack my hand against my current light-reading emphatically. Another *Scientific American* piece: VIOLENCE AND ECO-LOGICAL SCARCITY.

"Mara," I imprecate, "you *know* it's bigger than Rodney King. As in: We create the toxins that mutate the cancer cells whilst we ravage the forests that grow the lichen that contain the cure for the cancer cells . . ."

The SCARCITY diatribe reminds me so much of a write-up on a Harvard stress experiment overcrowding rats I read some thirty years ago in the same periodical I wonder why I still subscribe.

"*You're* just upset that you have to watch it repeatedly on your teevee." Mara laughs.

"No, I'm relieved that *everyone* has to see . . . *and* pissed . . ."

I channelsurf dramatically. Intercut with relentless replays of the beating are day-after shots.

The whole depressing display reminds me of the week Century Cable was offering "new" movie channels: HBO, SHO, TMC, DIS.

Showcasing *Raging Bull* in syncopated rhythm.

Click. You fuck my wife? Click. You fuck my wife?

Click. Click. Click. You . . . fuck . . . my . . . ?

I learned channelsurfing in the midEighties from Victor, whom I've known since I was fifteen and he was seventeen, cutting my mother's hair at Bendel's. Before all those boys got fired for purveying weed between heads. Or was it performing head between weaves?

Victor — VS — is not always my nearest-and-dearest but he is surely my longest-running friend, the only one who knew me when I was a virgin.

I was in New York for some meeting or other about some project or other at some studio or other that didn't pan out. Still pretending to be in movies, phone-romancing The Stone into writing/directing *The Vampire Lestat*.

Our conversations were soundtracked by Vietnam, as he was rushing *Platoon* to its prearranged release date. Movies, organized backward. With story lines dictated but not read by marketing mavens, those boys who liked to brag they just delivered the asses to thc scats.

Pretty soon BigScreen offerings would be about Absolutely Nothing and cost minimally a hundred mil.

And break even because you can fool all of the people all of the time.

Oliver did.

VS kept me company in a dark Park suite at the Sherry Netherland all rainy New York afternoon whilst I engaged in hotshot exchanges with Oliver. Finally, in a carefully worded statement I imagined him reading he said he was sort-of in. I saw the fine hand of his CAA agent, Paula Wagner, penciling his lines.

Background walla throughout: cluster bombs and high-pitched screams.

"I just gotta tell Richard and we're outta here," I assured him because VS was wandering around the suite. Picking up ashtrays and matches and depositing them somewhere else.

Checking out the weather. Bored.

"Ucccchhhh! He's traveling through the Third World. It'll be hours. Days maybe. Who knows . . ."

He flapped his arms nervously, opened the teevee cabinet and picked up the remote.

BAAAlllluuuummmmm . . .

POWER ON

Victor paced, occasionally stopping dead in his tracks to zap the boobtube with his bopgun.

Click.

"Second! He's in the Second World . . . stop that, you're making me tense and we're talking minutes here!" I protested and dialed the operator, an old friend who'd been contacting very-more-important-than-me persons in portions of the globe where most white men feared to tread for almost two decades.

Richard Gere was on a spiritual segue through Honduras but I reached him right away, first try, because he was a movie star and movie stars always got the best available wherever they went, even if it was merely minimally reliable telecommunication.

Richard had been the conduit through which the material reached Oliver, had brought him in so to say, and we'd cleaved in the course of a couple of afternoon meetings on my patio as Oliver consumed whole bottles of tequila in a single quaff, it seemed, then sweated it out as we tossed him our most seductive pitches.

I considered Richard-as-Lestat my eighties gesture and not a grade-A eighties gesture at that.

But Oliver was a Grade-A. Gesture.

I didn't know why I was so convinced about Oliver from *Salvador* but I was. Maybe because he made the James Woods/Belushi characters, quintessential scumbags, sympathetic? Heroic even? He'd just have to take tiny little baby steps to Lestat, I figured.

In preparation for a meeting with him I made Anne Rice watch videotape on a large-screen monitor in the bedroom.

Her soft scribe's body lay strewn across my spread.

"He does violo-porn!" she exclaimed enthusiastically as I rewound and I thought, Like you . . .

Victor found a roach. Puff puff. Click click.

After sort-of congratulating Richard through static I hung the phone up forcefully, irritated.

Click click click.

"It's like you're whacking off by remote control!"

"All my girlfriends say that. It must be a guy thing." Victor laughed his soft laugh. "Poor Oliver," he added cryptically.

"Poor Oliver? Do tell," I said, perking up.

"I used to hang out with his mother," Victor smiled. "Jacqueline. Jjjock-leen. Very French, married to Lewis Stone, Wall Street icon . . ."

"Yeah yeah I know about his father . . ."

"I used to hit Studio 54 with Jjjock-leen. She loved to dance! I had a friend who was a pharmacist on the West Side, used to give me industrial-strength vitamin B over the counter . . .

"Jjjock-leen'd call me all afternoon if we were going out that night: 'Veectore, don' forget zeee Beee. Veectore, don' forget zee Bee-eee-eee . . .'"

He laughed softly at the memory. Click click click.

"So why poor Oliver?"

"Ooooh I think Jjjock-leen was an overbearing woman who loooved too much. Being so French and all . . ."

"See if that's true he's even better for this project than I thought.

Mais pauvre petit Olivier . . ."

We cracked up and Veectore dropped the remote. It fell to the floor end over end in extreme slow motion.

Instinctively, we checked the screen to see what fare Divine Providence had chosen. Birds. Perfect.

I retrieved the remote and cranked the volume.

Rapacious birds, the announcer voice-overed in that smooth mundane monotone affected by nature shows, who killed their second chick upon birth.

Like a lot of people I know, myself included, these birds had the capacity to raise only a single child.

Victor and I witnessed the painful sixty-second life span of a second chick transfixed.

When it didn't expire quickly enough the parents nipped it to death.

"Saves a lot of pain in between," I joked uneasily.

"You always were the results-oriented one . . ."

"I'm the second chick," I said.

"No *I'm* the second chick!"

"No, *me*!"

"You're the oldest sibling. I'm the second!"

"In my family we were both the second, but okay, you . . ."

Victor was the one after all with Kaposi's sarcoma on the roof of his mouth, which — he'd been informed after a battery of tests by a wheelchair-ridden great and famous specialist at New York University Hospital — was due more to his New York Italian genealogy than his New York Italian homosexuality. When I've asked Victor if his medical uncertainty has caused him to alter lifestyle he's said, Sure, now instead of cruising a hundred thirty-five guys a week, I cruise a hundred thirty-five guys a year.

Victor favored denial as a primary survival tool.

Me too.

Rodney probably called upon it a couple of times the night of March 3.

Click. Wow! Click. POW! Click. ow-Ow-OW!

Rodney's looking very second-chick.

"You have to call this number at the mayor's office to protest," Mara says, fishing in her purse with one beautifully manicured hand whilst the other frets in high-strung circles above her re: the Rodney King of it all.

"We've been protesting since birth. For all the good it ever did." Mara fights a laugh with pursed lips.

Mara and I were reasonably young and crazy together. We got over it. Sometimes I wish we were back then but the way we are now so we could make the best use of our youth.

Duh.

But Jeeez, où sont Those Girls d'antan?

"Just give me the paper," I insist; Mara's dyslexic and I never really believe the names and numbers she imparts. "So whaddya think?" I say, "the pinstripe?"

We glance at a chair in the color-coding corner piled high with Norma Kamali spandex and Gaultier jackets and a twenty-year-old pinstripe suit.

Armor.

"Well of course the pinstripe," Mara snaps. How dare I worry about what to wear when the world is . . . ?

Because.

Sooner or later I must go to New York for *YNELITTA*'s final publicity. No matter how dyspeptic I become from the process.

Morph into a tantalizingly sharp-edged morsel for . . .

The InfernoTainment Soft Machine.

Act grateful for the bookings and try not to be gummed to shreds by its masticating maws. Dress neutral and smile for the camera.

Times being what they are and all.

I have pulled a few items from my closet, my disgusting secret portrait. Designer drag, tags still dangling from some sleeves randomly stuffed cheek by jowl along too-tightly-pressed racks. Shoes and belts and bustiers strewn rampantly across the floor, forming an obstacle course I'm almost sure has carpet underneath.

I've funneled all my anxiety about *YNELITTA*'s release into the question of what to wear to The Soft Machine, even summoned Janet from Maxfield's, who took one look at the designer detritus and the ancient pinstripe with a sharp Are-you-kidding? downturn of her mouth.

"This is a wonderful suit," she said. "You should take the

black and white Gaultier cutaway, too, though . . ." Then smiled and hurried off with her advance-copy first-edition *YNELITTA*.

I strode bravely into the closet, which I sometimes thought of as The Cabinet of Dr. Caligari, to retrieve Le Gaultier. I bought it a couple of years ago to wear over a short black Romeo Gigli two-piecer before my American Express card imploded.

Wendy Stark was throwing a dinner party that night for Tina Brown, the editor of *Vanity Fair*, and had cornered me into an affirmative RSVP.

"Must I?" I whined to Wendy, trying to wriggle out of attending in an A.M. phone call.

"Honey, you have to meet her," Wendy said firmly. "She's very interested in your book. Besides, I wanted to provide you with an opportunity to take one last swipe at these people."

"Including Daddy?"

"Including Daddy most of all . . ."

Suddenly insecure, I called Janet who happily informed me, Private sale — Come on down . . .

"How old are you, fifty?" Big Daddy Stark smarmed at me that evening, swathed in nouveau Gaultier. Adding a few years to put me at ease.

He smiled his yellow-toothed smile.

"Forty-five," I replied, whirling my fingertip around my glass of vodka at Mach 1.

"Do you remember when we were almost in business?"

"Mmmm, sorta, but not really. I wasn't at my best just then . . ."

"You blew the deal over a bathroom," he smirked and the whole incident came back to me. Yeah I wanted a bathroom to smoke my drugs in. Wendy was right. I haven't been here twenty minutes and I'm getting material.

She seated me between Guy McElwaine and Mike Medavoy so I knew I'd be chatting up myself mostly. At Tina's ICM dinner. Medavoy, however, filled in a blank or two on *The Sting* and Guy McElwaine made repeated Joe

Eszterhas remarks, emphasizing each reference to his hot new client with such a familiar shooting of cuffs I experienced small portions of three FLASHBACKS before dessert.

For example:

Mortons. Fall 1989.

My editors Joni Evans and Julie Grau and I discuss *YNELITTA*'s legal notes (a twenty-three-page single-spaced essay) over dinner, finally break from the extreme agro they cause to dish about the recently disclosed much ballyhooed Eszterhas rendition of his final explosive meeting with Mike Ovitz.

I'm leaving you!

My-foot-soldiers-will-march/Blow-your-brains-out!

Etcetera.

Count on Those A-List Boys to define a business dispute as a pitched Beverly Hills battle in The War of Wilshire Boulevard.

They'd be silly if they weren't so powerful.

Amusing if they weren't so dangerous.

Me: Soooo Joni, these notes . . . are you looking for the names and places? The truth? Or the gist?

Joni (a beat, thinking): The gist.

Me: Then I have an idea. Inspired by the Eszterhas letter. Little movie scenes: He/She, She/Me. Maybe the whole book is a movie . . .

Julie (hopeful): That's too clever by half. But it could be a solution.

Me: I'm just wondering, girls, when the gist isn't the truth anymore . . .

Joni: Not for a verrry long time . . .

What is truth? said gisting Pilate and did not stay for an answer . . .

After coffee I found myself in Wendy's front hall attempting chitchat with Alana Stewart.

Alana's most compelling credits were her ex-marriages to George Hamilton and Rod Stewart.

She was the prototype of a subspecies found only in the three Bs — Brentwood, Beverly Hills, Bel Air — whose cachet accrued from arcane sexual prowess, I presumed.

Infinitely more acceptable to the men in this room than I was and she certainly wasn't beleaguered by financial insecurity. Grrrr. . . .

"That's a hell of a jacket," a familiar voice whispered and relieved, I turned to come face to chest with Clint Eastwood. Tall. Lean. Grizzled. Large leonine head blanketed by a fulsome tract of movie-star hair.

The Last Big Boy.

Most leading men were so short that even I (who knew that about actors) was shocked when I met them offscreen.

"Thanks." I smiled and we started to small-talk about his current obsession *White Hunter Black Heart*, when Medavoy's wife, Patricia Duff Medavoy, cut in. Her self-esteem depended greatly upon ejecting me so I eased off and searched for Tina Brown, who was the job I'd come to do.

I found her in the living room.

I was taken with her Princess Diana good looks (older shorter heavier) and her porcelain English skin, but I was most impressed by her steamroller approach to conversation and I found myself interior-riffing throughout our dialogue on alternative definitions of the verb To Do:

To Accomplish. To Fuck. To Kill . . .

Tina did me for ten minutes, then moved on and I split.

A couple of days later I wore Le Gaultier over jeans to Adriano's.

"Nice jacket, honey," Linda Guber cooed as I passed her table. "How's the book comin'?"

"Just about done. It's pretty strong stuff ya know. I don't think Those Boyeez are gonna be happy about it . . ."

Including your husband, PeterPeterPetersEater . . .

"Darling," Linda smiled, "we've all been waiting . . ."

Will I fold? No I'm bold. So my Gaultier is old . . .

• • •

The pinstripe's a present from Mike Maday.

A Brioni Carnaby Street custom-made. The only one he ever owned, Southside Chicago Polish-American Survivor-Stress-Syndrome Viet Vet that he is.

He was the man on point and outlived his entire platoon. Inadequately trained and fresh from boot camp, he misdirected them to their demise in a failed search and destroy mission. He never got over it.

When we gave up freebase together just before the Ascension of Ronald Reagan, Bob's BigBoy/Goytoy, he bestowed The Suit in a ceremonious recycling gesture.

"This'll never fit me again," he said, eyeing the pants' twenty-eight-inch waist sadly. "It's yours . . ." The sleeves are an inch too long as are the slightly belled pants but whenever I wear it I'm showered with compliments.

Most significantly, the long jacket completely conceals two fatty deposits on a part of my hips where no one I've personally met has anything but bone. I've carried them, albatrossish, since college when I was too young to know you pay endless dues for excessive living.

I added and subtracted twenty-five pounds to my delicate frame not once but twice. The second diet was successful in all aspects but the hideous points.

"Julia's dewlaps," my father called them.

"Dollops," I'd reply haughtily, making them sound prettier I thought.

Me and Fifi Thatcher, who liked to be called Feefff, gained and lost the weight together.

Feefff was a wild rich gentile girl from the Main Line.

Too hip and gay before her time.

"Teach me how to swear in Yiddish teach me how to swear in Yiddish," Feefff would demand when she had too much to drink, which was — by junior year — just about always. Like if you were Jewish, you knew Yiddish. Not in my generation.

"Feefff wants to swear in Yiddish. Got any suggestions?" I

asked my parents one Sunday, sweating out a marathon call in the tiny Mead Hall phone booth.

Mount Holyoke College. South Hadley, Massachusetts.

They had been communicating in Yiddish over the heads of my brother Matthew and me since we were wee. When they wanted us to know that they didn't want us to know.

"How about 'Oy gevalt, meshuggener shvartzer'?" my mother said dryly.

"That's the same voice you used when you told me gefilte fish came from the west bank of the Hudson," I said. Cracking wise like she taught me.

"Exactly," Tanya said. "It means, 'Oh God, crazy nigger . . .'"

My mother was a Stevenson Democrat and raised Matthew and me under the liberal aegis of the Laws of Equality and Justice; never to say "colored" or "nigger" but "Negro."

When we reached our late teens, though, she started saying "nigger." As if now we were old enough to hear it.

I choose to believe that she was just overreacting to H. Rap Brown's nightly six-o'clock-news appearances:

Beep beep/boom boom/um-gowwa/black powah!

I have a friend who claims that when he was sixteen his father, instead of the requisite man-to-man about condoms, told him, "Son, I gotta admit it to you . . . this God stuff? I don't believe a word of it."

Which must have been as confusing to him as the question of how to refer to my darker brothers was to me.

"That oughtta satisfy Feefff."

"Indeed," Mom laughed and we hung up on a good note.

For a change . . .

"Boy look at that motherfucker struggle," Mara says.

Referring to the imminently InfernoTainmently celebrated oy gevalte meshuggener shvartzer, aka Rodney King.

Mara plops into a chair. "Phew that wore me out. How do you do that all the time?"

"Hey babe, yo tengo un tax problema."

Mara laughs.

"Oh I brought you this nail polish," she says, fishing again. "Ballet Slippers." Pale. Sheer. Soporific. We once sported jungle red but then we realized the real world was red enough.

I have convinced Ruby, who works in a white-on-white Beverly Hills salon, she must indulge me with a house call.

Ruby is a pretty talented painter-slash-manicurist.

Manicurist-slash-friend.

Everyone in L.A. is a hyphenate:

waiter/actor;

limousine driver/screenwriter;

producer/dealer;

actress/model/whatever

Stomp. Thomp. Whomp whomp whomp.

Police Chief Daryl Gates has floated the hypothesis that Rodney was high on PCP but the tests reveal zilch. Officer Powell, on the other hand . . . if he's *not* high on something what's *his* excuse?

Rodney's hands are *cuffed* behind his back.

"He's trying to get away," I say. "Remember that girl from the Palisades who was murdered Graduation Night last year by the private cop-slash-psychokiller?"

Everyone in L.A. is a hyphenate in every way.

"*She* was handcuffed and *she* tried to get away . . ."

"How do you know . . ." Mara challenges.

"Because Kate's friend Bronwyn's mom, Peg, is representing the parents in a civil suit against the security service for hiring him. He had a record of mental illness and arrests. She told me the flesh on the girl's wrists was torn down to the bone."

I feel pilloried for a moment by an involuntary flashback to Peg Garrity's ferocious azure glare: She fought to the end, Julia.

She'd have ripped her hands off to escape, Peg said.

"Uh-huh-hughghghhh . . ." Mara shudders, as do I.

Mothers of Daughters.

How is it we worry only about *them* as potential victims, not ourselves?

"Rodney King is lucky he's alive. Although from the way he looks right now I don't think he'd agree."

"I'm gonna split on that happy note. When do you depart?" Mara says, gathering her bag and two signed advance copies of *YNELITTA*. Mara knows I have a hard time committing to flight.

Worse since Reagan busted the air traffic controllers' union.

"Mmmm. Uncertain. I'm stalling."

I'd rather go next week than this week. *YNELITTA*'s gathering momentum and the InfernoTainment part of me knows I'll have more cachet — notoriety? — next week.

The deeper part is that even though I have always known *YNELITTA* will cause a firestorm I've kidded myself that The Fourth Estate — a lower life-form nicknamed The Press — will embrace it.

Instead Those Slugs have come out slugging.

Particularly the locals.

Duh.

"Richard Dreyfuss is quoted as saying that first you committed suicide with drugs and now you're committing suicide with this book." Jim Brown from the *Today* show had slipped in yesterday. Pretaping for next week.

And then asked me to sign his copy!

Bon Appetit! Love Julia, I wrote.

Eat this. Choke on it.

"Oh I don't know" I smiled my see-how-I'm-smiling smile. "I haven't felt this alive since Nixon resigned" That morning, eyes straight through the lens, I responded, ". . . since Johnson didn't run for a second term," to the same query from CNN, who'd pleaded for the interview.

I've read the quote, attributed to Dreyfuss by David Geffen in a hostile *Los Angeles Times* CALENDAR piece by Nina Easton, who didn't like me on a hastily arranged phoner a couple of days before.

David Geffen has decided my book — which displeases him in the extreme — is about him. As far as I'm concerned my book is about me and his cameo appearances aren't nearly as unflattering as I could've written them.

A month ago just before shipment, Joni Evans, publisher/editor/girlfriend stopped the presses and messengered him a repro.

The Geff called me within an hour to protest.

"What does this mean?" he said: "'Is he restraining me?'"

I stayed silent, sooo silent.

"Look," he continued, "I have my position in the community . . ."

Oh you boys and your positions in the community.

Why don't you try *this* position?! In the community.

"I don't want to talk to you anymore. I don't want to see myself in another book of yours . . . or in a magazine article," he went on in a quivering voice.

You mean you don't want to see yourself in a book or article you don't control.

I was at a loss, really, what the tone of my reply should be so I opted for impudent.

"I'm glad you agree I have a future as a writer," I said. My voice was calm but I felt queasy I'll admit.

"Well you certainly don't know how to be a friend! And there's certainly no more to say!" he spat and slammed down the phone.

"A friend?!" I said to thin air. Maybe just a tad guilty. Which isn't saying much because any Jew can summon guilt for any thing at any time.

Probably all goes back to killing Their Lord.

I guess this is our last call, I thought.

Oh please! We are by no stretch of the definition friends. Not even Hollywood friends.

Although we had our last lunch together almost a year ago at his house.

Unforgettable, as it was preceded by a gnarly POWER OFF night and a moribund exercise session by dawn's early light.

It was May Day 1990, and the only thing that held me together heinous nanosecond after heinous nanosecond was that Gorbachev was having a harder time than I was and The

Republicans had been busted for embezzlement of HUD funds.

Still, alone in the dark, it was hard not to fixate on my dissatisfaction with *YNELITTA*'s denouement.

A set piece at Mortons, ShowBiz's CEO commissary.

Worried about ending on the too Didionesque line: Mortons, she said. I'd been searching for months for an ensuing coda that would leave the reader more exhilarated! if not precisely hopeful.

11:30 A.M. Just as I thought, So first Those Bohemian Boys cut the low-cost housing budget and then they stole the paltry billions left, every appliance aroused itself from slumber. Noisily accompanied by the prosaic Protestant undertone of Mr. Rogers emanating from PBS:

> *It's a beautiful day in my neighborhood*
> *A beautiful day in my neighborhood*
> *A beautiful day in my neighborhood*

Grrrr . . .

I jumped in the shower for a quickie, toweled off and within minutes I was blow-drying, tearing at my two-inch-long hair, power-perusing *The New York Times* laid out on the counter — quartered like the guys on the subway do it — sweating under the unforgiving fluorescence of my bathroom.

When the phone rang I feared another DWP deprivation but then the answering machine kicked in.

Blow-dryer OFF. Julia ON.

"Hi, it's Julia. You've reached 555-5555. If you'd care to, leave a message and I'll call ya back reeeal soon. I promise . . ."

I loved the insincerity of the real-soon-I-promise closer. Hell, it was a triumph just to record the message; I often broke new techno-toys with a glance. Made me wonder if I'd been misplaced in the wrong century, i.e., too soon.

Beeep.

"Julia, it's Michael Levy. Wanted to know if you'd talked to David Geffen yet."

Mike Levy, my last partner.

Who had a nasty tendency to address me in the abusive tone he'd spent half a career perfecting on his secretaries.

I couldn't even remember how we hooked up on *Interview With The Vampire*, which Levy called *Interview With A! Vampire*. Levy was preposition-insensitive but Levy didn't attend a Lit. Crit. lecture in college where a professor began: Henry James was a verrry careful writer. In other words, girls, it matters that he called it *The! Portrait Of A! Lady* . . .

Over six years the relationship had evolved into I'm-the-outside-man-and-Levy-pushes-me. I was certain he despised his job as much as I did mine.

Later for Levy.

But I picked up the phone in the bathroom anyway, which didn't disconnect the machine in the bedroom so the light kept flashing like he was on hold: MikeLevyMikeLevy.

"So here's the deal . . ." I purred without preamble and smiled to keep impatience from my voice. Over two decades of talking to those boys I'd trained myself to be The Cheshire Cat on the phone. I kidded myself that the other party would see bare bicuspids in my voice, a harsh and raspy baritone from smoking and running lines with myself.

Verbal intercourse with guys like MikeLevy required such heavily committed smiling I'd often have charliehorse of the face by the time we finished a conversation.

"Tell me the deal," MikeLevy chuckled seriously.

"He says we have no contractual rights in *The Witching Hour*. He says he's free to do as he pleases, which in this case is to make a deal with Dick Donner and Lauren Shuler-Donner. He says he won't let them produce if Donner doesn't direct. He says that because he's such a nice guy he'll go for a verbal agreement that we're in second position after the Donners. He says I'm welcome to come to lunch at the beach to say yes or no, not negotiate . . .

"He says, 'That's the deal.' And that's the story. In a nutshell."

I felt like I'd just delivered an encyclical on behalf of the Pope, translated from the Latin.

How did guys indulge in this for ten, fifteen hours and think at the end of the day they really busted their chops?

Feel good about themselves?

"I've never met a man so comfortable with himself," I'd heard George Shultz say of Ronald Reagan.

As far as I was concerned the self-esteem movement had made entirely too many deficient people think they were just great.

"We're being fucked," MikeLevy said disconsolately.

"Welcome to the wonderful world of Geffen."

"Well go have lunch with him. He likes you . . ."

"I *hate* that idea." I'd already hated soliciting the sixteen-hundred-page manuscript directly from a reluctant Anne Rice — who wanted to know in a plaintive voice why I even cared now that I was a writer — read it over a weekend and engaged in a high-decibel rights fight with Lynn Nesbit, who was Anne's agent. And mine.

Lynn and I had known each other more than twenty years and never had so much as a spat.

It was too bad we had this contretemps the day I called to inform her excitedly that with Julie Grau I had finished recutting my manuscript and FedExed it to Joni. Julie's boss. My boss too, strictly speaking.

We started as old friends.

Then Joni became Publisher/Random House.

And I became Writer/Temperamental.

I was about to tell Lynn how gratified I felt that the page count, 954, was 18 which reduced to 9 — the number of completion — when she ripped into me about meddling in *The Witching Hour*.

Personal considerations aside, I wasn't enthusiastic about *The Witching Hour* anyway as the book hardly translated handily to film.

Its most compelling conceit was a five-hundred-page detour that would surely be cut and I had already told Anne that if she could squeeze a million dollars out of David Geffen I was too well-bred to present a problem.

I'd get rid of myself. Send myself away.

Who was I to separate a writer from her score?

Her one two three etc. . . .

MikeLevy's partner, that's who.

And LevyLevy's manners were more rough-hewn than mine.

"Look Julia, he likes you go talk to him you have to do this," LevyLevy said tiredly.

"I know, but I want you to understand I'm very uncomfortable with a person-to-person confab with David Geffen right now."

Breaking bread with him, no less.

His bread. Moreover.

Less is more, Tanya said, removing my strand of pearls Prom Night. Milwaukee. Wisconsin. 1961.

The beginning of the End. I thought it was the beginning of The Beginning with Kennedy elected and all.

You look beautiful, my father added. You're Daddy's Little Girl.

Daddy's little girl grew up in an environment perpetually gray with the stormclouds of complexity that form in homes where nothing is definite, where everything is negotiable, or at least Socratic-dialogueable, and so she yearned for nothing less than The Absolute.

Daddy's little girl spent the better part of her matriculations assembling revising and reworking long lists of people places and things, herself included, under the headings GOOD and BAD.

The lists and Daddy's little girl changed and grew and changed again.

Good. Bad. Good. Bad.

Over the years Daddy's little girl developed a penchant for people places and things that were bad bad bad . . .

Harumph. Imagine feeling conflicted about David Geffen, the epitome of egregious Eighties Empire-building.

Who was sooo comfortable with himself he felt fine brushing LevyLevy and me aside on something to which we had at the least a moral claim.

And he didn't have an inkling what I'd written about him yet, so he wasn't even angry.

He behaved this way as a matter of course.

Ahh but his is business. Yours is personal.

Bullshit, his business is all personal.

And vice versa. More? Or less. Good? And bad?

Ah Jeeez, when will World War II be over already?

I fiddled with my *New York Times* whilst LevyLevy prat-
tled on about how we were being screwed and how I must
drive to the beach to bond with The Geff. And I agreed, coo-
ing and shmoozing, smiling mightily, because even though I
occasionally plucked a long white eyebrow I was Daddy's little girl after all and I wanted to be good Good GOOD.

Finally LevyLevy released me from his desperate greedy
grasp and I returned to the burning issues of how much Mudd
to coat my hair with, and which Rena Gallay bicycle suit to
underdress in for my uptight beachfront déjeuner with The
Sun God of Hollywood.

That après-moi-le-déluge guy.

The Geff.

The man with the power.

As I sped along Pacific Coast Highway, I flashed reflexively on my first pet with Michael Phillips, my first-and-last-
ex-husband. Our practice-child. A cat named OJ after the only
Heisman Trophy winner who caught my attention, he was so
fast and so handsome.

OJ because she too was fleet of foot, had an orange nose
and Michael had threatened to call her Michael Steven
Phillips Junior if I didn't come up with an alternative.

We brought OJ with us when we immigrated to Los
Angeles for a better future than the one we'd have in New
York and she was run over in the middle of the night shortly
after we arrived. Probably by a high-speed truck as her body
was flattened and her eyes expunged from their sockets when
we found her Christmas day . . .

Devastated by the memory I almost flew through a Stop! I
jammed my brakes to the floor and damn near impacted the
Beamer idling in the lane beside me.

The driver glared at me with such intensity I hoped he

didn't carry a gun. Californians commanded as much fire-power as any Third World country. Sometimes I imagined I was the last unarmed person in the entire state.

I Russian-rouletted, glared back and he turned away.

When I first arrived here in 1970 and the danger was still beneath the surface, a pimple that hadn't come to a head, cruising and scoping were common.

Nobody dared anymore.

It was all eyes front now.

An L.A. version of a New York walk.

I pushed in a tape. Soundtrack for *Performance*, a great ahead-of-its-time failure. Like me. I thought its themes hit too bull's-eye for Those Big Boys: the ones who pushed the buttons that pushed the buttons.

I always wondered if maybe it was suppressed. Like me.

My engiiine's pumping steel
And I was ridin' at you hard and fast

Randy Newman wailed to Ry Cooder sliders and I eased into my seat with mere minor lower-back twinge, punched the accelerator and left the Beamer in a wake of dust.

The Geff's house was in a section just south of The Malibu Colony where million-dollar houses were stuffed tightly against each other's borders along prime eroding beachfront property. I checked the piece of paper with his address.

So many twos. Two is a fear number.

What was The Geff afraid of? Something. Like me?

Victor's friend Barry was always regaling me with cute-Geffen-from-high-school stories. "Whenever we'd go to a concert he was always in the backseat conducting," Barry laughed at dinner one night. "Jools, he was so cute!"

"I'll bet . . ." Still was.

Which didn't make him any less-is-more a monster.

Although years back when Elliot Roberts's Malibu house was under IRS siege, with red stickers on the gate, The Geff settled the problem one afternoon with a $300,000 check he messengered in a plain brown envelope.

"He said I could pay him back whenever," Elliot said, his rheumy blue eyes dreamy with wine-soaked reverie.

Elliot was The Geff's management partner — the one who really nourished Joni Mitchell, Crosby Stills Nash and Young and Tom Petty in the beginning.

"I don't think he should have expected you to repay him."

The way I saw it, David Geffen could have spared the three hundred thou as a ThankYouElliot gesture but Elliot didn't want to hear that. Elliot had survived the experience with the helping hand of Denial.

The house of twos was studiously minimalistic and unpretentious. White and small and easy to pass by but I turned in the open low-profile gate just as Mick Jagger snarled "Memo from Turner":

I remember you in Hemlock Road in 1956
You're a faggy little leather boy
With a smaller piece of stick
You're —

POWER OFF

A diminutive middle-aged Filipino woman in maid-white stood at the open door. She smiled but she didn't mean it.

"This way," she said and stood aside for me to pass then stepped in front. "This way please," she repeated with the casually cynical inflection of a person who'd run the place for years.

I was immediately accosted by two rambunctious love-starved purebred puppies who tripped over their outsized paws competing for who tongued my legs first.

David Geffen, boxers-clad to reveal an adequately rippling hairless bare tan chest and legs that wouldn't be requiring silicone implants any time soon, followed close behind. He reached across a chasm of canine exuberance to kiss air in the vicinity of my right cheek.

I reciprocated and recoiled.

He presumed it was the puppies. Sure, why not?

"You wanna drink?" The Geff offered and I said, Yes thank you, vodka on the rocks would be nice.

Third World Woman nodded and disappeared into her domain and the puppies and I followed The Geff through his house and along his deck to a glass-enclosed terrace on his beach.

"Why do you even have these puppies?" I asked.

Global Geff had just been acquired by MCA/Universal and had just acquired the old Warner mansion. He seemed far too busy to be adopting puppies.

Check that, *acquiring* puppies.

"I'm looking for love . . ." The Geff tossed over his shoulder, soooo cute!

"Aren't we all?" I said with a smile, wiping the lie from my lips and he turned around and laughed.

Somewhere in the vast interactive decade-and-a-half between the invention of a Neanderthal video game called *Pong* and *Mortal Kombat* there was a trifle, *Pac-Man,* in which dozens of creatures who most strongly resembled half-moons with shark's teeth devoured each other. Kate played with such superior hand-eye coordination I wanted to give up.

David Geffen's unfulfilled appetites and voracious hunger always reminded me of *Pac-Man.*

Which made me want to give up even the *pretense* of ShowBiz.

But not until after lunch.

He led me to a table set for two in the corner of the deck. Tablecloth, napkins, fresh-cut flowers, verrry tasty. I had the sensation I was being seated in the best location at an exclusive/cozy bistro by the snootiest maître d' in Los Angeles.

The Geff shot the puppies a commanding look and they retreated to more hospitable environs inside the house.

Suddenly, a piercing SQUAWWWK AWCK AWCK AWCHECK-CHEKCHEK and a large overwrought black and purple bird crashed against the bars of his cage, affixed definitively to the rafter overhead.

"Poor thing," I said too quickly. "He wants *out!*"

"Rare African parrot. Cost a fortune. He's just a baby," The Geff sniffed. "He wouldn't survive half a day if he weren't in his cage."

"Still, it must be very frustrating for him to be at the edge of the wide open Pacific and be locked up . . ."

The Geff pursed his lips, conversation-over, and sat down, back to the right angle of the transparent walls, where I'd sit ordinarily, if it weren't for the view.

Beyond protective glass the ocean roiled hypertensively and the wind whipped in nervous sporadic gusts.

Behind the cumulonimbus cloud cover was the promise of a blazing ultraviolent sun.

I panned up for one more look at the parrot.

He pouted soulfully, ruffled his feathers and settling down, surrendered to his incarceration.

"Is he another piece of the looking-for-love puzzle?" I needled.

The Geff played with one of the lilies on the table.

"Y'know, I was with a boy last night, maybe twenty-five, a flower —"

"I was with a boy last night — nineteen, tops — a weed . . ."

I grabbed his flower, clamped it between my teeth.

It broke in half so I stashed it behind my right ear.

The Geff didn't miss a beat:

". . . who knew more about love in his little pinkie than I will ever know with my whole being . . ."

". . . who knew less about anything in his whole being than I knew in my pinkie . . . when I was born . . ."

Sometimes, Daddy's little girl's gotta say what Daddy's little girl's gotta say. Even if she's just kidding . . .

"I'm serious . . ."

Oh please, that's your problem. You're too serious.

"Me, too . . ." I said.

The Geff threw me a quizzical look; I formed the sign of the cross with my forefingers, Vampire/InfernoBiz bonding.

"So is Mike Levy happy?" he asked, opting for the biz part of the moment.

"With second position? He's not happy, but he probably knows it's a step up for him . . ."

The Geff cracked up and Daddy's little girl smiled thinly. Oh and do we think I should be your court jester? The female Howard Rosenman, as it were? Isn't Fran Leibowitz already cast in that part?

And what am I, her fucking understudy?

"Where do you think Mike Levy would be if I didn't like you?" The Geff said slyly.

"Gone . . . toast . . . history . . ." Might Daddy's little girl have considered your invitation to the High School Prom?

"Right . . ."

"So that means he should be thrilled about second position?" Perhaps. Why not?

"Exactly . . ." Actually, I don't think so.

"But what about me what about me what about me?" I exploded.

The Geff howled and the parrot stirred for a brief harmonious moment.

David Geffen will be looking for love for a long long time, I thought and glared up at the parrot.

You think I'm joking?!

NO.

The maid brought lunch and my drink and a large bottle of Evian. Two Rock Cornish hens on rice. Side of steamed vegetables.

"Thank you," I said and reached for my vodka whilst The Geff, wordless, attacked his food in a manner I imagined his puppies attacked theirs.

My first-and-last-ex-husband shoveled food into his face similarly. He lived in a castle on Coldwater Canyon surrounded by art and buddhas and leftover progeny from failed marriages. Just another rich guy. Not as rich as David Geffen — but who was? —with too many trappings and not enough grace. Just another rat struggling to stay abreast in the Hollywood Stress Test.

On the other hand Michael wasn't suffering my financial difficulties, so who was I to be so snotty?

"All roads lead to Arnold," he'd said philosophically at our most recent get-together regarding Kate's upbringing and bills accruing thereto.

I did the upbringing and he did the bills.

Referring to The Terminegger, and I brainsurfed:

If Madonna and The Schwarzenator spawned offspring would they be little Madonnaneggers? Schwarzenonnas?

The Geff cleaned his plate and licked his fingers.

Directing attention to my Cornish hen I wondered how the parrot above felt about our dining on his relatives in plain sight.

Happy you're not the second chick?

YES.

"So do you have heart palpitations with every up- and down-tick of MCA stock?" I smalltalked.

"Mmmm, nah, not anymore . . ."

"Cool. So is it enough?" I looked up at him and reached for my water. I really wanted to know.

The Geff frowned and crossed his chest with folded arms: How dare you ask such an impertinent question?

He looked away from me to the ocean, turned back and took a deep breath.

"Enough," he said confidently, but his arms remained clamped across his chest so I didn't believe him.

"Except of course for the old Warner estate . . ."

The Geff relaxed and smiled and leaned onto the table.

"Oh y'know Sandy and I passed that gate on Angelo Drive a thousand times and one day after I closed The Deal, he said, 'Let's just go in and take a look . . .' and Barbara happened to be there and showed us around herself.

"That afternoon, for the hell of it, I offered forty-seven million dollars. I think the asking price was fifty-two."

"The difference equals two decent mini-manses in Bel Air. Aaahhh maybe only one and a half."

"So I get a call from the real estate agent. Barbara wants me to have the house. She'll give me all the furniture, all the mementos — which includes eight Oscars — for the forty-

seven million. I took a deep breath and said, 'Fine.' I got the
house and the next day I sold Warner Bros. all the scripts all
the furniture all the Oscars for three —"

"All the Oscars?!"

Shocked, I inhaled too sharply and nearly choked on a bone.

The Geff frowned and covered his chest with his arms
again.

Uh-oh. And we were doing so well.

"Why would I want somebody else's Oscars? See you
have one of your own. You don't understand . . ."

"Please, I do. I feel like mine's borrowed half the time . . ."

"So how's the book coming? Done?"

"Mmmm-hmmm."

"What's it about, your drug experiences?" The Geff asked
condescendingly, uncrossing his arms.

"Oooh nooo, it's about all of it!"

"What do you mean?"

"Oh you know. The up and the down the bottom and the
top. The strange charm of it all. Right up to . . ."

This lunch if it's material.

Consider yourself forewarned, Geff. Forearmed.

The Geff smiled, disarmingly dismissive. Sooo cute.

"Is this a movie? Should I be making you an offer? Is this
something people will be bidding on?"

"Only if they want to suppress it." I took a sip of vodka
while The Geff didn't react. Silence. Nothing. "Look, it's
clearing up . . ."

"Let's go sit in the sun . . ."

We repaired to some chaises poolside. I used to think that
people at the beach with pools were being a tad conspicuous
in their consumption, but now that there was no beach and
what was left was polluted 89 percent of the time, they
seemed like innovative investors.

I could remember when carphones were a luxury, too.

I checked The Geff. His eyes were closed and his breathing had the peaceful rhythm of slumber. Sure. Right. I'm the
one who's exhausted and he's the one sleeping.

Does he feel that comfortable with me?

Or that superior?

Back twinge. Back twinge.

Moral conflict.

I pulled the flower from behind my ear and twiddled it in my fingers. I lit a cigarette, swigged some water and squinted at the horizon.

Tiny 3-D orange and purple and red dots squiggled around, struggling to form a hologram atop the rough sea.

Uh-oh. I feel a FLASHBACK coming on . . .

Hollywood loooves to say it with flowers:

Hey Babe, it's your birthday!

And the deal's in negotiation.

Darling. You got married and the deal's almost closed.

You had a baby?

Then the deal's in renegotiation, Baybee.

You got the big job and the deal is closed.

Your first divorce *and* fired? You have no deal.

Over forty? I'm gonna deal you out.

You're dead, big deal.

The final deal, as it were.

I used to send flowers.

One year, my business manager presented me a faux-deed to a place called Julia's Flower Farm for Christmas.

Stated purchase price: fifteen grand.

"Did you get fifteen thousand dollars of goodwill for all the flowers you sent to people this year?" he said sternly when I called to ask the meaning of his gift.

I knew he meant did I get deals, money back.

"I didn't send the flowers for *that* kind of goodwill . . . not always . . ."

"Then why? This is a lot of money for flowers . . ."

"I hate shopping. When an occasion calls for a present I let my fingers do the walking, i.e., call the florist and *charge it* . . ."

The day after that unsettling exchange, Kate and her nanny Jackie and I took off for the Kahala Hilton. Oahu. Hawaii. We ran into Jeff Wald, whom I call Mr. Wald, checking in. Mr. Wald took us to dinner that night and sent me a grand arrangement of posies the next morning.

I assumed they were the commencement of a negotiation for which I had zero inclination.

He insisted they were a gesture from his heart.

We repaired to a raft fifty yards into the waveless water off the private beach, raked clean every morning and every night by a silent staff of Orientals, to continue our discussion supine. Eyes closed.

Sucking in those rays. Sucking up to God.

Sucking on our third joints of the day.

Striving for stupor.

"Y'know maybe you're right," Mr. Wald said after a while. "I used flowers to torment Totie Fields when she was opening for Helen in Vegas. In a loving way, I swear."

Mr. Wald was referring to happier times, The Seventies, when his soon-to-be Ex-(I Am)Woman, Miz Reddy, sang for quazillions a week.

Happiness was cash flow, as far as Mr. Wald was concerned. If he had it to do over again, Mr. Wald said, he'd forswear a career in personal management and go into Telereligion instead.

Nothing but tens, fives, ones — oodles of 'em . . .

"Torment?"

"But she got me in the end. You'll love this . . .

"I send her flowers Opening Night and she lets me know right away that she hates those Vegas arrangements that are spray-painted and look like hats.

"Of course this is a challenge, so now I send her an arrangement daily for the run of the show.

"Her dressing room is wall-to-wall hideous flowers . . .

"She never says a word . . .

"Cut to months later. I'm giving a fancy dinner. Mayor Bradley, Prince Charles I think, and Totie and her husband, among others. That afternoon, United Parcel delivers a huge carton from Totie.

"I open it and it stinks like the heaviest perfume ever. It's all the dead petals from the Vegas arrangements.

"And the note reads:

"'If you're so fuckin' rich, how come your flowers died?'"

Brrring brrring.

The phone purred.

I shook remembrance of fucks past from my shoulders and my whole body shuddered violently into the moment.

The flower fell from my hands to the ground.

The Geff startled awake and reached for the receiver.

"Calvin!" he exclaimed happily and settled into velvet-voiced dish with another of The Gang of Four.

I picked up the lily and found a bathroom where I spent an unconscionable amount of time pulling at my hair then washing the Mudd from my hands. Interspersed with a spectrum of line readings into the mirror.

If you're so fuckin' rich howcum your flowers died?

Howcum your flowers died? Nah nah nah.

I tossed the browning lily into the swirling water of the soundless toilet and when I emerged The Geff was chasing the parrot, who'd escaped, around the deck.

"Looking for love?" I quipped as he shooed the addlepated bird to its destiny.

The Geff laughed and locked the parrot in the cage.

"What about the flower?" I taunted.

"Ah," The Geff said philosophically, "he wilted . . ."

It was the end of lunch.

"Thanks for the yummy food and the blazing rays and the second position . . ."

"Stay . . ."

"Nah, Kate'll be home from school soon. And it's changeover day from the other house . . ."

The phone rang again and we kissed air.

"Good-bye . . ."

"Good-bye . . ."

GOOD BYE.

Good-bye yourself . . .

I hung a right onto Pacific Coast Highway, accelerated into the turn and wondered: Why does interacting with David Geffen always make me yearn for redistribution of the wealth? Why does David Geffen always remind me of Ritcherrrd Nicks!unnn?

Probably because The Geff was driven most strenuously by deep insecurities and extreme pettiness.

That he kept an enemies' list.

That if he were president he'd install Swiss Guards outside the White House. Just like King Richard.

Who considered 1600 Pennsylvania Avenue his castle and also had no charm.

> You're the gray gray man
> Whose daughter licks policemen's buttons clean
> You're the man who squats behind the man
> Who works the soft machine . . .

The Mick crooned and I experienced an epiphany.

I understood completely why communism was invented.

Count on me to get it just as it's over, I thought, and sped past the beach house where it was rumored Don Simpson had exceeded the limits of good taste socializing with a Mafia Princess during a MoversAndShakers July Fourth bash.

He had to go underground for six months, the story went, before an overweight Hollywood Fixer persuaded her father —who'd ordered Simpson terminated with extreme prejudice — to rescind the hit.

When I got home I turned the computer's POWER ON and fiddled restlessly with the ragged post-its alternating around the edges of a nearby coffee table whilst waiting for The Creature to warm up.

Pink for Those Girls with the blues.

Blue for Those Boys in the pink.

Yellow Yellow Yellow.

Seating for another birthday commemoration, a failure that ended at 2:00 A.M. when I caught a fiber of celery on my glottis and it took ten seconds less than 911 for anyone to figure out it was Heimlich maneuver time.

Whoop-de-doo.

Another year closer to dying and I didn't.

Nah nah nah . . .

I scowled into the novelty mirrors lining the wall behind The Creature and typed in a file name.

Stop! I told my reflection but I was glad too, as anger was a wonderfully efficient clean-burning writing-fuel.

As opposed to the fossil-like I-need-MONEY-barbeque, which burned dark and dirty.

If you'd just behave, The Geff might Elliot-Roberts you with a single stroke of the pen, I remonstrated, but I scrolled through the file anyway. Fuck it. If the power is terminated-with-extreme-prejudice for nonpayment I'll have my integrity to keep me warm.

I'd already placed The Geff in the last scene of *YNELITTA*. I just needed to add Enough?/Enough!

Maybe it would inspire me, lead somewhere.

Scroll Scroll Scroll

"Mortons," she said. Mmmmm.

I scoped the screen.

Go-fuck-yourself. Okay-I-will.

Mortons she said she said she said . . .

Within a week of our final phone call, King David of Geffen's attorney Bert Fields hits ICM (nominal agents for Phillips/Levy) with not one but two notices terminating our services as producers on *Interview with the Vampire*. Which I had personally steered to him after years of shlepping from corner office to corner office with Anne Rice.

"You're not gonna believe what they say in this second letter," says Stuart Kleinman, the ICM business affairs tyro assigned to the case.

"Failure of fiduciary responsibility?"

I've read some lawyerspeak in my time.

"Yeah," Stuart says with a baleful tinge of admiration. "You divulged the contents of confidential meetings."

"I don't remember being asked to sign any pieces of paper."

"Well it's a crock . . ."

"I know."

"This letter is not up to Bert Fields's usual standard . . ."

"Ooooh Big Bad Bert. I'm trembling."

"You need to retain outside counsel," Stuart says in a tone I'm supposed to take seriously.

"Can't you just send a letter on my behalf reserving all my rights etc.? I don't have the cash just now to plunk down a retainer, but maybe — who knows — in just a couple of weeks some mouthpiece who wants or preferably *has* profile will take this on contingency."

I have in mind Pierce O'Donnell, who's representing Art Buchwald and Alain Bernheim in their *Coming to America* lawsuit against Paramount.

I'd really hate letting The Geff get away with firing me for free. *Nobody* in Hollywood gets fired for nothing.

I know boys who net perfectly respectable annual incomes getting fired from one project to another.

I bet they don't have a tax problem.

Okay. All right. I picked the fight but The Geff escalates to open warfare and makes himself uncharacteristically available to the press. I think his negative quotes are making me more important than I am. They sting for a minute but I also know every time he opens his mouth I go into another printing.

Personally, I'd have played it another way.

If I were David Geffen dealing with me and my book, I'd throw me a party at Mortons . . .

Can I help it if my clock — my 1 2 3 etc. — like Talleyrand's, runs fifteen minutes fast?

Before it's chic, *YNELITTA* excoriates The Eighties.

I've worried about being ahead of time as I don't think a decade ever really begins until the third or fourth year.

I know plenty of culturally literate people who think of the murder of four students at Kent State University by the National Guard as a late-sixties event.

I've forgotten the press is — or more precisely *wantstabe* — part of The Establishment.

I can tell by their questions they haven't grasped how definitively *that* particular era of American excess is just another part of our prurient past. Christ, though, the troops *are* returning from Desert Sturm und Drang.

Surely Those Bohemian Boys' last bellicose belch.

"I hope this fucking war is over soon," Joni had snapped over grilled vegetables at the corner table inside Orso's during a short hand-holding trip some weeks ago. Referring to the difficulty Random House Publicity was having booking *me* for promo instead of the latest WASP foray into global jingoism.

Cool colors on teevee though. For a minute.

"It'll be over in time," I said, because one thing of which I was sure was the quick pulse of the American heart.

YNELITTA has taken so long to bring to market that Joni's held three jobs during its gestation period.

First, she was going to start an imprint at Random House. Then she became Publisher, Random House.

Now she's back to starting an imprint, Turtle Bay Books.

Maybe that's why she's cranky.

Her replacement is Harry Evans, who's married to Ms. *Vanity Un-Fair*; I confess that in the privacy of Sanctuary I've occasionally referred to him as Mr. Tina Brown.

Tina Brown had told Lynn Nesbit she didn't like the voice of *YNELITTA* when she rejected its first serial rights.

This from a woman who seemed most susceptible to the siren songs of The Geff and Barry Diller.

Joni keeps reassuring me that she is *YNELITTA*'s active publisher but I can't help but worry I'll be suppressed by another boss at Random House. Here I am. Me and my book.

Caught in the conflagration of networks intersecting.

• • •

YNELITTA arrives in L.A. bookstores over a rare rainy weekend. I bop around my house wailing the Mamas and the Papas' *It Never Rains in California* whilst friends, family and neighbors leave excited messages and send missives regarding sellouts. Brentano's. B. Dalton. Doubleday.

Suzanne Wickham, Random House's West Coast PR lady, swings by to pick up one of my precious boxes of complimentary copies. Book Soup has run out.

The writer part of me is thrilled.

Then the producer part wants to know how quickly the empty shelves will be restocked and why supply expired so quickly in the first place, Mr. Brown.

Hey! Yo tengo un tax problema.

I listen to piled-up messages on my answering machine and return a few calls.

I leave Dick DeBlois, my downward-mobility business manager, for last. Dick is one of those boys who likes to keep you at bay with his bad temper but I was brought up by a family of bad tempers so I'm not intimidated.

I just find interacting with him depleting.

He comes on the line immediately and his voice is trembly. Uh-oh.

"The IRS seized all the money in your OD account at City National Bank today."

Bon voyage, Jools. Break a leg . . .

Ooooh noooo.

My last $2500. Out of ten grand Arnold Stiefel's lent me. He's perused *YNELITTA*'s proofs; appreciated them.

Arnold's a long-not-strong friend. I've known him twenty years at least. Since the salad days in New York, when as Bantam's PR guy he squired Jacqueline Susann and Irving Mansfield around.

"Lunch is not enough!" we'd kid him.

Arnold and I enter and depart each other's lives every five to seven years.

We don't know each other well, but we wish each other well.

The first time he called with words of encouragement he'd just left a Sting concert. He couldn't stop laughing and I was compelled to ask what could possibly be so amusing about Sting, surely one of the more dour rock 'n' rollers extant.

"Oh darling, Queer Nation was outside chanting, 'We're here/We're queer/And so are some of you.'

"People were just flyyyyying past them.

"I got out of the parking lot at the Arena so fast!"

Arnold made me promise I'd tell *no one* he saved my ass.

"That would turn my career into toilet material."

"If I know anyone with job security it's you."

Arnold represented Rod Stewart, among others, and had just been offered $5 million for Rod's services serenading Happy MacBirthday to an eccentric Scottish laird.

"Geee," I said. "Marilyn did it gratis for a president. Is he gonna do it?"

"Goddamn right! He knows it's a recession and besides, I've gotta fix the hill behind my house. Which is falling into my carport because my neighbor built a gazebo and shifted the hill above me.

"I'm gonna have to take him to court but in the meantime I've gotta get the hill off my cars!"

"At least you can throw money at the problema."

"Honey, don't be upset. It'll all be fine. You are going to have a huge best-seller! Trust me I know."

"You're gonna have somewhere between fifteen and twenty-five percent of five mill-i-on dollars.

"Happy birthday. I'd rather be you."

"No you wouldn't. Belieeeve me," Arnold said in his singing-for-supper voice and I knew it was true. I wouldn't. "Guess who has to go to Scotland with Rod in the private jet who hates to fly in those little things. Hey I work hard for my money."

I try not to obsess on Arnold's 15 to 25 percent of $5 million.

That would settle my bills my debts *and* my tax problem.

Ten percent would do it. But who's counting?

"I thought we had the matter frozen," I say to Dick DeBlois, my short-fused business manager.

"So did we! We have a letter from E. McGuffin to that effect."

"I guess E. woke up on the wrong side of bed today, hunh?"

"They weren't supposed to do this. It's a computer fuck-up . . ."

You're a computer fuck-up! I think but don't say.

There's a lot I don't say lately.

PR. Detente. Deflection.

I wrote a brutally honest book and now I get to fib about it all the time. In The Suit.

I feel like a Republican. Ronald Reagan. George Bush.

The men who made the world safe for hypocrisy.

"Mmmmm I'm just a tiny glitch in some giant program," I intone more calmly than I feel. I feel so suddenly dizzy in fact, I plop myself onto a worn wicker chair.

Kate wanders in to discuss dinner.

"What about Ruthless?" I ask. Referring to my corporate entity, christened when I was still smoking half an ounce of coke a day. Junkie jocularity.

"They didn't take anything out of that. But there wasn't much there," The Dick says with the defensive edge in his voice that always tuckers me out.

"I'd better rustle up some cash right away," I reply, finessing the Why-was-my-money-in-the-wrong-account? question. I cut him off as quickly as Joni does me.

I'm nothing if not a quick study.

"What was that?" Kate asks, communing with her mirror-self decked out in Le Gaultier.

"The IRS just wiped out my last tiny money."

She whips around, brown eyes alarmed and sympathetic.

"You can have my money, Mommy."

I shake my head and brush away angry tears.

I have seventy dollars in cash and one card working.

With maybe four hundred dollars left to the limit.

Memo to Tanya: less is not more.

My heartbeat reverberates in my brain.

Panic? Excitement? Material?

Kate embraces me tightly which lowers my blood pressure an iota. I take a couple of deep breaths.

"I'll ask Joni to help out, go to New York, hit the list, get them to advance some royalties . . ."

"You know you always pull it out at the eleventh hour, Mom."

"Try five minutes to twelve."

"Jooools, it'll be fine."

"You realize I was Mommy Mom and Jools in a single conversation?" I have told Kate that I'm Mommy when she's feeling small and weak, Mom when she's a snotty adolescent, and Jools when her ancient omniscient soul is ascendant.

"Must be a sign! Let's go to Hamburger Hamlet," she says brightly and we do.

The sojourn provides temporary relief.

By the time I'm back at Sanctuary though, rocking on my bed, I get pretty worked up over back-to-back hostility-laden New York interviews/IRS wipeout and with Rodney and The Gates Gestapo on MUTE for inspiration I call Joni at home.

The more I watch Rodney the more I *am* Rodney.

And the cops are The State/Fourth Estate.

Method Acting:

I have measured out my strife in Stacy Koons.

I burst into tears and tell Joni my IRS setback is a straw breaking my back, I'll be smoking freebase by the end of the week if she makes me come now. I haven't smoked freebase for more than a decade and wouldn't dream of a single ecstatic puff but Joni, whose experience with The Life is more limited than mine, doesn't know that.

More to the point, Joni hates a woman crying as much as any boy so she lets me off the hook immediately.

Says she'll FedEx a personal check for $2500.

The blessings of a regular job.

Thank goodness Joni has one. I calm down.

"Besides the bookings'll improve. You'll see . . ."

"I hope so," Joni says doubtfully.

"I was right about Desert Strom Thurmond, wasn't I?"

Joni ignores me. She hates the puns and anagrams.

Stop showing off! she's told me.

I'm *not* showing off. It's the way I think!

"I'm gonna tell you what Nancy Collins told me the first time *The New York Times* ran a nasty front-page story about me. People don't remember what was said. They just remember you're famous, they saw your picture in the paper . . ."

"And I'm doing so well in that department!"

"It's getting better . . ."

"I've got it figured. If the piece is nasty the picture's okay. If the piece is nice the picture's hideous."

"You're gonna have to adjust to the fact that you're famous!"

"Not like Gorbachev's birthmark!" Joni humors me with a comme ci, comme ça, heh-heh-heh. "Besides *that* person is Julia Phillips. *That* person is not me! Jools. The oppressed Jew with a tax problema."

"I know," Joni sighs. "Get over it! Get used to yourself."

"And I don't think that now is the time, Joni, to invoke Nancy Collins!"

Joni laughs and hangs up quickly.

We all have one improbable friend. One what's-wrong-with-this-picture in our photograph album. Mine is Corey Haim, who at nineteen (less than half my age) has already starred in more than double the movies I ever made.

Sometimes, with *Humpty Dance* emanating loudly from his black Testarossa's top-of-the-line speakers we take off for an adventure and I worry what I'll tell a cop should Corey be pulled over for exuberance.

When people wonder aloud what might possibly attract me to him, I explain that my psyche most resembles that of an eighteen-year-old boy. With homosexual tendencies . . .

I suspect Nancy Collins is Joni's improbable friend.

I met her telephonically, actually, when I called Joni in the country and Nancy the Houseguest answered.

Nancy, who'd absconded from *Today* and was reinventing herself as a print journalist, didn't converse with me. She conducted an interview. I hung up too slowly and had to shower immediately, I'd perspired so heavily.

I met her at Joni's request almost two years later.

She was winging to LaLaLand to interview Sophia Loren for *Vanity Fair* and had cadged a Q&A assignment with me for *Mirabella*.

When she opened the door to her room at the Four Seasons Hotel I saw she was suffering.

"Root canal," she explained in response to my raised eyebrows. "And no painkillers."

"Well that's dumb," I said before I thought, Who's to account for blonde ambition? That's not fair. Maybe she's got a tax problem. Nancy laughed. "I can't believe you got on a plane. Let's go downstairs. I know what to do."

We found a corner couch in the bar and I ordered scotch and aspirin for Nancy, a martini for me.

I taught her the Old Wives' trick of holding a pill on the tooth whilst swilling the alcohol, which rendered her functional if not painless within fifteen minutes.

Julia's helpful drug hints.

Nancy's questions irritated annoyed and angered me. Explain backtrack explain backtrack explain explain explain. Like she was picking at scabs. I had no idea she was this good. Pick pick pick, but after an hour I acclimated to her rhythm and relaxed. Big mistake. To paraphrase Joan Didion: She who treats a member of The Press like a friend deserves what she gets — deceit and betrayal.

"Julia, do you think you're hard to love?" Nancy ambushed, pinning me with a root-canal psychostare.

I sprouted profuse anxiety back-sweat and my skin bonded painfully to the leather banquette.

Rehearsing for Sophia? Not likely.

"Isn't everyone?" I said. Smiling prettily over grinding teeth.

Not as hard as you, Nancy.

Not as hard as David Geffen . . .

• • •

"The Polo Lounge has given the *New York Times* permission to shoot a photograph of you. Aren't you having lunch there today?" Suzanne Wickham sounds shaky.

"This is my one human-being endeavor before I leave," I whine. I'm dining with Christine Cuddy, my lawyer/friend, and Doris Bacon, a reporter. They've been connected for years through the Ahn family of Korea to whom Christine is multiculturally related.

Doris, who interviewed both me and Kate for *People* magazine, has had to pull her managing editor out of a staff meeting to change the prose in their piece on me.

The writer, whom I've never met, despises me.

"She thinks you're punk because of your haircut," Doris said in an exasperated tone one dank winter afternoon just a week ago. Doris describes the writer as a frustrated middle-aged type in a raincoat and hat who commutes daily between her tiny apartment and her tiny office.

This woman doesn't know we're on the same side.

I run her name by Joni and she laughs.

"She's submitted at least five outlines to me and I've turned them all down . . ."

More critical than a friendly meal is an anticipated drop-in by Frankie. Christened Francine. Joined SDS and became Francesca for a minute. Ron Bernstein introduced us at a National Book Awards fete in the late sixties.

We were both in leather.

One night in a ladies room, after years of fighting like sisters, we agreed I'd call her Frankie, she'd call me Jools and the names stuck.

Frankie dabbles. Film one year. Art the next. Jewelry design. Fashion. Frankie is my only close friend who still meanders through the movie business. We never discuss it, but I'm sure she finds the process less fun than it used to be.

I had Kate four years before Frankie, after repeated

miscarriages, delivered her daughter; Frankie came west before me, just in time to experience The Big One in 1971.

The Sylmar Quake.

Frankie is generously digging deeper into her savings account to deliver a thousand dollars in cash whilst I pose and dine, which brings my bill with her up to ten grand.

I accede to Suzanne's request even though I get palpitations from a photo shoot, particularly one where I'm not protected by professional makeup and lights. It's been drizzling for two days and nothing I do sops the shine from my forehead.

Plus I believe — deeply — that those prehistoric tribes indigenous to places like New Guinea who fear the camera-shutter steals one's soul have a point.

The photographer, a nice middle-aged guy, says he knows the father-secondwife/mother-secondhusband joint-custody parents of Jaime, a close friend of Kate's. To put me at ease I suppose, like somehow we're related.

I'm reminded of an interchange I overheard years ago at a Christmas party I threw at Sanctuary.

"Oh I know you!" The Wife of Nobody said to Barbra Streisand.

"Noooo you don't know me," came The Barbra's measured reply, in the spirit of what I call The Vulnerable Season. "You know who I am . . ."

The Vulnerable Season commences the day after Halloween and lasts until a week after New Year's Eve.

Assuming the Moon isn't in Void or Mercury in Retrograde or Saturn trined with anything.

It's characterized by impulsive purchases liaisons and suicides, compulsive eating drinking fucking and murder, and reconciliations that don't last.

An older friend, Phyllis Levy, who mentored both Joni and me, once said, "There's a family in Queens where the sons and daughters saved their pennies all year to afford the bus trip home. The clan, happily reunited, gather together Christmas Eve with little but the discount tree and a sad string

of lights and a lean turkey and their love for each other and
it's what the season is all about . . .

"But they're the only ones and we're not related to them!"

A quarter century ago Phyllis awakened me with a 5:00
A.M. phone call to sob that Bobby Kennedy had been shot in
California.

"They got him," she said and I knew exactly what she
meant and wondered if she ever slept at all.

I'm older now than she was then and I never sleep either . . .

The rain is letting up, replenished stockpiles of *YNELITTA* are
selling out, and I'm afraid to leave my house.

Yesterday I trundled down my driveway to pick up my
*Times*es and a bearded fellow in a black Cherokee screeched
to a halt, vaulted from his car and requested I autograph his
YNELITTA.

I'm not a morning person and with my hair rising at a
forty-five-degree angle from my head like Gumby I felt distinctly disadvantaged.

The more my picture is in magazines and newspapers, the
more I hear I'm the talk of the town, the more I'm abed.

Surrounded by a sea of sartorial selections.

Clickclickclicking my REMOTE.

By the time Those Boys suggest a celebratory nightcap at
Mortons I can't wait to escape Sanctuary.

Now *there's* a splendid idea. Time to say GOOD BYE.

A moment for those boys. They are:

Todd, 24: Shy dark and sensitive with a fighter's broken
nose and tight muscular body. He started life in Hollywood as
a dancer and though he's moved on and up he's retained a
dancer's nonverbalness. Todd thinks I should be prouder of
my writing/accomplishment than I am.

"If I'd written a book," he said, eyeing an unopened box of
complimentary copies, "I'd be clasping it to my heart for at
least a day or two . . ."

Stuart, 35: Smart, high-strung, ambitious but also compas-
sionate. An unusual combination. Free-falling on the

Hollywood Roller Coaster for a couple of years, but now that his management firm is up and running and he has an older girlfriend he seems more stable. Thinner, too.

Brooke, 26: Athletic, blond and blue-eyed, he was a hot young model in New York when he was fourteen.

One of the legion of Omar's Men.

Omar, a black Panamanian who started as a model himself, can prevaricate/negotiate/manipulate in at least seven languages and he revolutionized the model-look in the eighties.

Found multicultural street kids, cleaned them up.

Put them to work.

I'll make you famous, he said, and billed them later.

Brooke crossed over from mannequin to matinee-idol-in-waiting as a *Lost Boy* but that was a few years back and nothing's come of it.

He'd make a great rock 'n' roller if he had the pipes.

And Corey. Little Corey's been acting in movies since he was ten. He's smart and knowing, particularly about ShowBiz and Hollywood but he's also unread undereducated and overtelevisioned. Recently, viewing a C&C Music Factory video together, I'd asked him if he was at all disturbed that Zelma was lip-syncing Martha Wash.'s voice.

Nah, he'd smirked. Why'd he wanna see a three-hundred-pound black mama if he could watch a fox instead?

I adore Corey like a prodigal son but he's so ignorant he frightens me.

Todd picks me up.

Stuart, Brooke and Corey will meet us there. It's only 10:30 P.M. and the place is nearly empty but we bump into Suzanne de Passe and Howard Rosenman leaving as we enter.

"I hear the next Dorothy Parker," Suzanne smiles insincerely.

"Darling, you're getting so famous," Howard swoons.

Howard was one of the people who saw *YNELITTA*'s galleys for legal purposes. He claimed to be knocked out but I sometimes wonder if he's responsible for siccing Le Geff on me.

"Thanks. I think . . ."

". . . therefore I yam what I yam . . ." Howard says, quoting my twisted rendition of Descartes from a Popeye POV.

"I think therefore I'm poor," I crackwise to Todd on the way to the big round table in front where Brooke and Corey are already lounging, and he guffaws.

Howcum I get my biggest laughs when I'm my most serious and where the fuck is Stuart? Count on Stuart to be last, i.e., most important. Even at my celebratory drink.

I grind my molars noisily and pop a bridge.

I shove it into place and a laser beam of pain shoots through my right brain.

I excuse myself and sprint to the single-stall nouvelle ladies room. Rinse and wedge and try to recover from the schizophrenic aspects of semi-fame and antiquated dental work.

This is nothing compared to, say, *Madonna*, but still . . .

How can she embrace this?

I'm so relieved Stuart has materialized I don't notice the bearded boy with prominent ears and dirty hair lurking in the corridor outside the bathrooms until I bump into him.

"Julia?" he says in a vaguely familiar wobbly Southern inflection.

"Mmmm . . . yes."

"Don Henley."

"Love your music . . ."

"Maybe you needed to embellish your book, but my partner and I can't remember ever doing cocaine in your house . . ."

What?! What?! I open my mouth to respond, I'll just *bet* you can't! and my bridge flies loose again. I stick my hand in my mouth, jam it hard and quicken my pace.

"You got a problem, have your lawyers speak to the lawyers at Random House," I garble over my wayward bridge.

How dare you ambush me! Grrrr . . .

"What goes around comes around," Don says pointlessly. I accelerate and he drops away in my wake. It already has. Come and gone. Gone and come. Around and around. When I reach the table I lecture those boys for not protecting me.

"That was Don Henley?" Brooke smiles, surprised. "I saw him and I thought, He's waiting for Jools. I didn't recognize him. I figured he was some agent or video director from the old days. He looks terrible."

"He doesn't remember doing coke at my house," I smile. "Too busy being arrested in his own house with a naked teenage girl. Stashed between his stash . . ."

"If I'd known I'd have said, 'Hey Don, the Eagles were somethin' in their time.' But that was twenty years ago, man," Corey offers.

"Aaaah, it bums me out a little. Politically me and Don Henley are on the same side and I *like* the Eagles . . ."

"Out of the business," Stuart says churlishly. "He's lucky you mentioned him at all."

We laugh and order Stoly Cristal vodka martinis all around. Rocks for me who's a girl, Todd who's a beer drinker and Corey who's underage. Up for Stuart who's tough and Brooke who's gentile.

Doug, the maître d', pockets a tip from a departing customer and joins us.

"Jeez honey," he says appreciatively. "Your book is all anybody's talking about and it's sold out everywhere. Where's my signed edition?"

"Duuude, it's not like it's a thin little volume one can tuck discreetly under one's arm."

I'm saved from whining by the requisite discussion of Rodney King's beating, which is in such heavy rotation even vidiot Corey's seen it often enough to be appalled.

He leans over to say something that just occurred to him as our drinks arrive.

"Hold that thought," I say.

"A toast?" Stuart suggests and we raise our glasses. "To Number One," Stuart says, ever the results-oriented personal manager.

"To Number One," Brooke and Todd and Doug chorus.

"Number One. Ladygod," Corey says. Taking his moment.

"To our last drink at Mortons," I say.

And we drink to that even though none of us has a clue what I might mean.

"What were you gonna say?" I whisper to Corey.

"I forgot. It was too long ago." Corey smiles, slithering down his chair to a more comfortable position.

"At least thirty seconds," I snort. "There is no fucking hope!" Corey laughs.

"I hate this call. I hate making this call . . ." Rick, Mortons' Monday through Thursday maître d'. He of the stentorian tones and the twenty-five extra pounds. Nervous.

"What's up?"

"I've been instructed to tell you that we can't honor your reservations here anymore," Rick stutters.

I am stunned. But I am also smiling.

Rick continues like he's reading from prepared text. "I mean I love you, you know all of us here love you, but a number of our most important patrons are just infuriated by your book and . . ."

I chuckle. This is cheering me up.

I haven't really expected to be *banished* from Mortons.

I have in mind a loose plan called I DON'T THINK I'LL BE DINING THERE TONIGHT.

I haven't been *banished* since The Brownies.

No — check that — since *Close Encounters of the Third Kind.* My most obsessive production.

No — check that — since the Hollywood Women's Political Committee. Which I helped to invent.

"I get the point! You delivered the message. Nice of Peter to have *you* deliver the message by the way. Listen, I'd enjoy chatting but I think I can just reach Joni in New York. She'll love hearing this."

I call Joni.

"Waitasecond Julie has to hear this . . . Julie!"

I tell the tale of my exile.

I have the brief sensation I'm reporting in to Adolph and Tanya Sunday from the phone booth in Mead Hall.

Mount Holyoke College. South Hadley. Massachusetts.

They gasp. Then silence.

"What? You don't believe me?"

"Nononono, I believe you . . . I don't believe . . . *it*!"

Their voices chorus/overlap.

You . . . fuck . . . my . . . ?!@#

"You don't believe those petty assholes acted precisely as I described them?! I.e., like petty assholes!?

"Nothing more important going on in the world! Than our positions. In the *community*! We'll banish her from Mortons!"

I laugh. This is *really* cheering me up.

"I can just catch Liz Smith. Liz Smith, don'tcha think? Shit! Julie, did Liz Smith get a copy? I gotta go." I can see that Joni smile. The one she gets when she smells blood and money.

"Yeah, I figured . . ." I say to the empty line.

Call-waiting. Deeper-than-*my*-Deep-Throat.

"Jools. I just heard . . ."

"Banished. Exiled! Did they really think I was gonna hang out there on a regular basis after the book was released?"

"Now I wanna read it and it's sold out everywhere. Can I come up and get a freebie?"

"Who called Peter?"

DMDT thinks for a moment.

"Geffen. He called Peter vacationing in Hawaii . . ."

"Weird, huh? I thought they'd be grateful for their fifteen pages!"

Fame.

Most everyone thinks it's reeeally something, no matter what they say.

I did too. In my first career.

It was my fatal flaw.

"Duuude. You must be loving this!"

"I'm hating this but that's because I'm oppressed by financial problems. I have this fantasy twelve-step program.

"Financial Fuck-ups Anonymous. FFA.

"'Hi, I'm Julia and I'm a financial fuck-up!'"

"'Hiiii Julia . . .'" DMDT laughs.

"Hey, it keeps you honest," DMDT says.

"That seems to be a big problem right now."

"What about integrity?"

"I've got enough of *that* for an entire slate of alternative movies."

"I'm on my way."

Liz Smith runs two items.

The first starts with one of the more controversial passages from the book: Writers and women are the niggers of Hollywood. A daring choice for a gossip column.

I talk to her a couple of times.

Screened by her assistant, a deep-voiced intimidating Southerner called The Saint.

"She's in her room reading your book with the door closed," The Saint confides the first time we speak. "She even took it to the dentist for root canal."

Mortons denies the story, what a surprise.

Joni calls delighted.

"I don't care what they say, Jools. Everybody reads her column."

I can see that blood and money smile.

"Weird. All this stuff going on out there and we know the real deal. I can't really call to mind any other middle-aged Jewish women who've been carted off to prison and wiped out by the IRS within a month. Back to back, as it were."

Joni cackles.

"Neither can I," she says.

"I understand why communism was invented."

Joni laughs ha-ha even though she knows I'm not joking.

"Don't underestimate that support," Arnold Stiefel pronounces re: Liz Smith.

Open Mercedes window to open Mercedes window.

His license plate says A S and mine says 329WOE.

I've considered arguing WOE with the State of California

but given my problems with The Authorities I figure now's not the time to draw attention to myself.

Or my WOE.

We've spotted each other at the turnoff from Alpine to Lexington. The one with the burned-out mansion that used to stop traffic with its anatomically correct nude painted statues along the curve at Sunset.

Half a year ago, 4:00 A.M., I was hanging out on this very corner with Those LAPD Boys.

GO DIRECTLY TO JAIL.

DO NOT PASS GO.

DO NOT COLLECT $200 . . .

"Darling, I was at this party the other night, chatting up Alana Stewart and Don Simpson and he couldn't stop talking about your book.

"'Unputdownable,' he said.

"But then I said, 'And what about the writing?! Really somethin' hunh?'

"And he said, 'I won't give her that.'"

"Like it's his to give."

"Darling, exactly . . .

"I want you to know I made a reservation for a large 8:00 P.M. party at Mortons last night and called at a quarter after to tell them I'd just heard they exiled you and I was canceling in protest.

"That's the effect your book had on me.

"Made me, y'know, aggressively honest.

"They denied it of course."

"Of course . . ."

THOSE BOYS
THE BARTENDER

Mommy said Three No Trump and Papa rolled a stone (a four-carat diamond engagement ring) into her first trick.

The Scion of The Family, The Senior, drowned in full view of the final fifty inebriated carousers attending the Annual July Fourth Shenanigans at The Clan's compound.

The Senior was performing inspired cunnilingus on his secretary, McCoy, under the deck jutting from the house to the shore when a monstrous wave amplified by an unpredicted riptide swept him away.

He had never bothered to learn to swim.

Mrs. Senior, slender body swathed in sequins, led the guests to water's edge.

Three times The Senior waved for help. Three times the guests waved back. Last quarter: Rah. Rah. Rah.

Escaping the party under the deck, The Junior bore witness to McCoy's multiples, achieved long after Daddy died.

He doesn't acknowledge or celebrate Independence Day.

He doesn't imbibe.

His Patrons have too much fun and say too much.

He has too many secrets of his own to think of Theirs.

Recalled he had fun once.

Started with The Real McCoy.

Daddy's Little Girl.

A Spontaneous Expedition with Todd.

In anticipation of No-More-Mortons we've scoped some younger hipper cheaper eateries and settled on the Olive, an alternately trendy/outré dive hard by the Farmer's Daughter's Motel on Fairfax, which is about as far east as I like to go.

Times being what they are and all.

"You just missed Madonna," Don, the aristocratically chiseled maître d', informs us and throws us into the third booth on the left, the one he holds for the unexpected friend-of-Jon-and-Sean, the owners.

The place vibrates with the peripatetic beat of the Hollywood Hustle, alternatively choreographed. Indie prods and rappers, cosmetics heirs and girls-who-don't-intend-to-stay-in-development-for-the-rest-of-their-lives-thank-you, mini-movie-stars and middle-aged managers.

Cigarettes smoking and martinis straight up.

We order and shoot odds and evens for who goes to the bathroom first. Todd may be the only person I know who pees as often as I do. I win.

Yuppies stop me on my way to the bathroom: I loved your book! Which is nice, I'll admit, after the pounding I've taken from The Press.

In the tight little alley where the phones and bathrooms are Omar yells long-distance into the receiver.

In Portuguese, I think.

"Dahhlling," Omar smiles. "You look goood . . ." Omar is sooo charming he can look you up and down and make you feel you've received a compliment. "I loved your book," he says. "Inspiring. Makes me want to write a book too."

"Omar, you're entirely too busy to write a book." Omar has seven offices globally speaking, and is currently on a world tour releasing Joop! Parfums with the owner, a handsome hard-faced Kraut who hovers nearby.

"Well dahhling, I've got a title."

"It's a start. Tell me."

"*I'm Not Ashamed . . .*"

En route to my table I bump face to midsection into a corpulent black man with a goatee and a beret. Sooo Fifties but he is, "Heavy Dee!" I blurt, "Where's those boys?"

He smiles.

"You're Julia Phillips aren't you?"

I nod, nonplussed. We are so mutually shocked to be recognized by each other we actually chat for a moment.

"Whowazzat?" Todd asks with a slight grimace of racial distrust when I return to the booth. Not his fault.

He's descended from a long line of cops.

"Heavy Dee sans The Boys . . ."

"What is it with you and black guys?"

"Oh please. *Any* white woman and black guys."

"Nah Jools, it's not like they're comin' on or anything. They like you."

"I'm a man of the people," I say solemnly and he laughs

and excuses himself. I hear him through the noisy chatter, laughing all the way to the bathroom.

We're loitering curbside awaiting 329WOE when a bunch of those nastyboys in a passing car scream, "Julia Phillips sucks cock!"

Todd and I mime the line for reconfirmation.

Other people hang out watching, waiting. This stinks.

"Not in a reeeally loooong tiiiime," I vamp and get a supportive laugh just as the car arrives.

"When the PR is over I'm going home and I'm not coming out for a year," I tell Todd as he merges into traffic and he doesn't disagree. I pull down the visor to check my look, apply some lip gloss, squint for focus. "Let's go to Steve Antin's party, what the fuck . . . ?"

Club Louie's in the black part of town. There is in fact a large toothless street guy who watches 329WOE for five bucks, which I hand him now.

Rob, a hardcore roughtrade leatherjacketed combatbooted sport with four earrings on the left and one on the right, smiles and waves us in.

"You just missed Madonna," he says.

"I've been missing her all night," I josh, smile too widely and the air from the tight little bar in front whooshes into my throat with a blast. Todd slaps my back sharply so I don't choke and guides me to the back room where the party is.

On the dance floor a sea of extras from a Fifties Roman movie.

Hot house music. Boom and throb.

Beautiful boys, heartthrobthrobs. Omar's men.

Some girls, either beautiful and gay, or big fat faghags wearing too much makeup and too few clothes.

Zero throbs.

This has to be the only club in town where there's never a line for the ladies room.

The VIP room is crowded with well-wishers. I run into Howard Rosenman squiring Tarlton, Peter Morton's wife.

"I just want you to know I had nothing to do with it!" she exclaims, referring no doubt to my banishment from her husband's restaurant. "I read the book in thirty-six hours," she says. "Released my endorphins. I'm gonna go circulate honey. In search of . . . magic . . ."

"Does she know what sort of place this is?" I laugh and head to the bar for some fortification, chat for a minute with Steve's mother Brenda who keeps telling me how brilliant I am. As in: Brilliant! B+. Or, Brilliant! Pass. The old I-think-therefore-I'm-poor syndrome.

"Here's The Birthday Boy," she says and I turn to proffer Happy Birthday air kisses.

"Jools, y'know Barry and Sandy showed up but they left when they heard you were here."

"Oh honey, I'm sorry."

"You kidding? I don't need that crowd trolling my boyeeez . . . gotta go circulate, honey . . . in search of magic . . ."

"Jools!" I turn. The Other Jools, tall and gorgeous wearing her trademark knotted pearls.

"Hey Jools . . ."

"So Those Big Boys left on accounta li'l ol' you . . ." she grins. "Y'know what Steven calls them?"

"What?"

"The two-blueberries-and-a-peanut crowd! Hah! Gotta go circulate . . . I'm searching . . ."

". . . for magic?" I whisper to Todd and check the room.

There's a boy leaning against a support beam, sort of handsome but his hair is dyed harsh dark-brown and he's plastered it into a widow's peak that threatens to collide with the bridge of his nose.

"Who's that vampire over there?" I ask Todd.

"George Michael sporting his new look." Todd laughs.

We sidle over, introduce ourselves and chat for a moment, an arduous task since he's both shy and snotty, a difficult combination.

"I'm straining all my social skills," I aside to Todd, "and they're not working."

"Let's dance!" he exclaims, and we head to the outer room reverberating with a heavy beat.

And boom and throb
And boom and throb and boom and throb.
And crash and bang
And ring my chime and pull my chain!
And bam and thrash
And scratch my nose and kiss my ass!

"I feel like we've got ringside seats at The End!" I exclaim happily and then it is that second before it is time to leave when it is time to leave.

"They're jumping the pub date by a week. It's a biggie on the third page and there's a headline on the front page," Joni chirps tentatively, referring to her advance copy of *The New York Times Book Review*.

"Oh yeah? What's the headline?"

"HOLLYWOOD CHAINSAW MASSACRE . . ."

"Ah Jeez . . . who wrote it?" I ask.

"Steven Bach."

"The man who presided over *Heaven's Gate* and lived to sell the tale . . ."

"Well you're gonna outdo *Final Cut*." Joni sounds frustrated. "Lemme just read it to you."

It's clear after the first paragraph the review's a pan.

"Notice anything familiar?" Joni laughs midway.

"'We soldier on?'"

"It's weird, but it sounds to me like he's trying to imitate your cadence."

"Then why couldn't he be flattering?"

"Jealous."

"So you're telling me that wordsmiths are worse to each other than movie stars?"

"Mmmmm I never thought of it that way. Prob-ab-lee."

"I know it's meant to be negative but it's just gonna sell more copies . . . like David Geffen . . ."

"Why?"

"Because *YNELITTA* is undeniable. Inevitable."

"Like you?"

"You too."

"I guess they decided you shouldn't have dinner either."
Brooke lounges in the color-coding corner and leafs through
Time. I've just finished a short No-More-Mortons/Liz
Smith/Gates's Gestapo précis for Brooke and Corey and Air,
who's accompanying me to New York.

She's brought *Time*, *Newsweek*, *People*.

I'm in all of them and for once the photos don't suck.

Although the picture of me and Kate in *People* is captioned: "'It was the mood swings,' her daughter recalls."

And grazing the *Newsweek* article I've noticed David
Geffen describes me as "a sociopath."

Look at the pot calling the kettle meshuggener shvartzer.

There are folks in this town who'd give anything for a
break like this. Even for murder.

Air works The Program diligently and she can't bear hanging around Brooke and Corey. "My sobriety is very important
to me," she's said more than once; usually when she doesn't
want to put in overtime. She takes her leave.

"Duuude," I say, "did they really think I was coming
back?! That after putting in those long years of research there
I'd ever want to see their pasty faces again? The pinstripe,
right? I'm booked on Donahue and Larry King Radio-not-
Live . . ."

I'm going through final wardrobe check with Brooke.

"But you knew. You said, 'To our last drink at Mortons.'
See that's why you're Ladygod!" Corey says, holding The
Suit aloft.

I check the *People* article, can't figure what Doris Bacon
was so worried about but that's probably because I've gotten
used to myself/over it.

The only piece that's pierced my heart is Jean Vallely's
review in Sunday's *Los Angeles Times* where I've debuted at
Number Three on the best-seller list.

The last time I saw Jean Vallely was at a wedding reception I threw at Sanctuary for her and my then-assistant David Parks. Jean and David ended in nasty divorce. Maybe my portrait of him was too positive for her taste.

She's called *YNELITTA* trashy and embarrassing.

"She's angling for a screenplay assignment from David Geffen," I joked in a phone call with Suzanne Wickham who read it to me in a tremulous voice from an advance copy.

Their party cost me twelve grand — talk about trashy and embarrassing — which I surely could use right now.

But who's counting?

THE QUILLMEISTER'S QUAGMIRE—PART I

Seeking SANCTUARY, the WOMAN WRITER hurtles through the downstroke of a restless Night. SOUND of labored breathing under. A high-key black and white image fades up.

The WOMAN leans over a man supine in a hospital bed hooked to life-support paraphernalia.

Pull back through a one-way mirror snooping into their room. The WOMAN observes. The sound of breathing continues under. The lighting, chiaroscuro, continues as well . . .

She (sotto voce): What's the next line? I can't remember my line. There isn't enough time . . .

Pull back farther.
An old man's wizened hand touches the woman's arm.

He (hoarse whisper): How do you know?

The woman looks frightened; then bolts from the room into a Christmas blizzard straight outta *Dr. Zhivago*. As she runs toward lights in the distance COLOR BURNS THROUGH.

She hears the SOUND of an engine fading up through

white-light snow before she SEES the train, a ghostly presence swaddled in diaphanous puffs of steam.

The diaphayni conveniently part.

CLOSE-UP: A Sign — VULNERABLE STATION.

The uhhh-wwwwhhh of her breathing syncopates with the ttchhh-ttchhh of the train. It's a good groove and would be soothing if it weren't accelerating into panic.

Suddenly, hordes of people. She instinctively recoils.

Her Camera Eye pulls back widening for the larger view.

She is always widening for the larger view.

The throng is automatonish, threading in methodical patterns to and from large cylindrical containers on large cylindrical wheels on large cylindrical rails.

Uniformed Third World Men and Women proffer directions to the passing parade in civilized monotones: "This way . . ." The Prozac Posse. "This way, please. " Norepinephrine Nazis. The teevee people in the synergy-sodden cerebellum. "This way . . ." Brain-wavers. "This way, please."

The prosaic Protestant undertone of Mr. Rogers's "It's a Beautiful Day in My Neighborhood" muzaks in a mountainous vanilla wave from hidden speakers.

Fluorescent lights drain definition from her view.

Grinding her teeth with sufficient pressure to ignite her synapses she remembers why she's here and searches the crowd frantically for her daughter.

There! There she is!

Kate! Kate! She wants to yell but the brain-wavers have wired her mouth shut. She grinds some more. Tears well in her eyes and nose and she struggles to breathe.

I will get her attention! *I will save her from* . . .

Her mouth pops open and she pulls in a large breath for bellowing purposes but she has ground her molars to sand and it whooshes in painful gusts onto her glottis.

Kate! Kate! she screams in her mind.

"Chechechechchch," is what comes out.

Kate turns for a moment, smiles easily, then moves on.

She didn't hear me!

The human waves sweep Kate farther and farther away.

I have to call her again! Or she'll be gone forever. I can't breathe . . . can't breathe . . . too tired . . . too . . . oooh noooo . . . aahhh *shit!* It's . . .

THE TOOTH DREAM!

The female disempowerment/castration dream.

The pull-my-teeth-and-make-me-suffocate-on-their dust/throw-in-the-loss-of-my-dear-and-only-daughter-for-good-measure/I-hate-this-dream *tooth dream.*

She knows within the dream that she is dreaming and she orders herself to consciousness.

"Chechechecchchchch," I hear myself wailing again and I awaken choking, gasping for the next breath and the teevee's on and the schmuck is changing his shoes and donning his sweater.

"It's a beautiful day in my neighborhood a beautiful day in my neighborhood . . ." he sings.

Click. MUTE.

His lips move but he's silent. My kinda guy.

"Can you say Mr. Rogers's neighborhood is getting borderline?"

I bound from the hotel bed, which is too soft and leaves hard little knots in my back that I have to knead out every morning by wriggling on the floor.

I'm developing hotel carpet burn.

I pop a corner off one of Fanny's fabulous Fiorinals.

Fanny, who's half-English-Jewish/half-Pakistani and gets what she calls "mee-graines," has insisted I take some of her precious script to New York.

"For the headaches you're going to get," she said.

I break into a good hysterical cry for seconds short of three minutes. Work out ferociously with weights for another forty-five. Stretch. Shower.

Sit at the edge of the bed and inhale/exhale.

It's almost like coming. Close enough.

As good as it gets.

I hear the soft whoosh of a message envelope sliding under the door. Another indecipherable fax from Dick DeBlois and

Ruth Pregulman, the real estate agent he's found to sell
Sanctuary in order to satisfy the IRS.

Better than phone calls because Ruth addresses me in a
tone grade-school teachers reserve for hyperactive children.

And The Dick addresses me in a way I haven't heard since
Tanya died.

I can't tell if this morning's missive says $600,000 or
$680,000, which is considerably lower than the $850,000 I
turned down from the L.A. Kings' Luc Robiteil two years ago.

I'd like verrry much *not* to have to sell Sanctuary to
brighten E. McGuffin's day. I'd like to find another way to
cheer her up. If only to aggravate Dick DeBlois.

I'm counting on lunch with Joni for that.

I drop Visine in my eyes and pull on The Suit.

POWER ON

"Why are we talking about this now. I hate talking about
this before . . ." Joni says under her breath even though we are
the only two people in the Jockey Club. Dining on corn chow-
der and martinis in the hotel before we traipse over to NBC
for my guest-shot on *Donahue*.

Me and the support group: Air, Julie, Joni, Victor, Air's
mother and sister-in-law.

I have debuted at Number Three on the *New York Times*
best-seller list, the only one that counts to the publishing
industry, which phones a secret number early every Thursday
morning to learn which books will appear ten days hence.

If *Donahue*'s a smash I'll shoot to One this Thursday.

I've broached the concept of accelerated royalties.

"Inspire me . . ."

Joni thinks for a minute.

"I could let you have $150,000."

"That'd be fine," I say even though it's a hundred thousand
short of what I need. "Could you do that right away?"

"Tomorrow morning."

"How is Roger Friedman here?" Joni whispers in the green
room after Victor and Air's mother and sister-in-law are

seated in the audience. I've just sauntered in from makeup and I survey the face on my face in the mirror.

I'll have to spend a good twenty minutes tonight tearing away at my skin with this dissolver and that astringent to remove it.

Phil's stopping by to say hello, then lead me to the set.

I check my watch. Eight minutes to showtime.

I made phone friends with Roger when we cut and pasted an *YNELITTA* excerpt for *Fame* magazine, which folded shortly after it hit the stands.

"I thought you invited him . . ."

"Please . . ."

Roger is the only one diving into the cold cuts, etc., provided by the show. The door opens. Phil Donahue with the producer Ed Glavin, with whom I had a preparatory chat for at least an hour yesterday.

Kept me up half the night with all his instructions.

About four in the morning I gave up and shuffled into the parlor of the two-bed/three-bath Central Park Ritz-Carlton suite in which Random House had installed me and Air.

The place was ours in the late-P.M./early-A.M. but for the past week from ten in the morning till seven at night it belonged to the reporters and photographers and T.V. crews who sliced and diced my soundbites into palatable snacks for the InfernoTainment Soft Machine.

An hour of downtime around two, which I generally filled by visiting Norman, the bartender in the Jockey Club.

I've lapsed into a constant state of nervous boredom and I haven't been outdoors enough to suck in sufficient oxygen to replenish my depleted corpuscles.

Air had stashed a copy of *YNELITTA* in an armoire with some ancient leather-bound books. I retrieved it and started to read but I'd reworked it so many hundreds of times it held no surprises.

I checked the other volumes and found a thin T. S. Eliot. *The Love Song of J. Alfred Prufrock*.

Tough Shit Eliot, my father always called him, quoting entire passages over dinner.

Let us go then, you and I . . .
Took it to bed and fell into nightmare-sleep immediately.
Lettuce Gotham, Phil and I . . .

I've seen Phil dining with Marlo at Mortons but he's always been sitting down so I'm not prepared for how tall he is. Taller than he looks on teevee.

Larry King, too, whose radio show I'd done last week.

"This is the first book Larry's read himself in ten years," the producer said as she ushered me to the control booth.

He'd given me a plug that morning in *USA Today*. Norman pointed it out that afternoon when I stopped by for some between-interview sustenance, time off from the burning issue of Goldie's dirty hair.

"I knew Lenny Bruce," Larry winked and gave me permission to smoke. If he hadn't I'd have felt compelled to ask him if they did drugs together. As it was, throughout the show I found myself interior-riffing possible headlines one might read upon his demise:

Larry-King-Not-Live? Larry King Dead?

Tiny gray hairs cling to Phil's lapels and I brush at them reflexively. He doesn't like it.

"I had my hair cut for you, too," I say, backing off.

"C'mon. I'm leading you to the set," he says brusquely and turns on his heel.

I follow him and Air follows me. He moves like the wind, turns around a corner, racing to the lights.

I glance back at Air who gives me the thumbs-up sign.

"The next Mr. Phillips," I stage-whisper and she laughs as I turn the corner. I bump heavily into Phil, waiting.

I wonder if he heard me. I hope so.

Ed Glavin's warned me that Phil will pick on me for the first ten minutes, set up the controversy.

I still can't get used to the way these boys punch every sentence it seems so unnatural so while he rails on I pan the front row of the audience.

I notice a young woman in brown, plain face pocked with rage.

Phil repeats The Geff's accusation that I've not produced an important movie since the late seventies and I think, The Geff's not produced an important movie, period.

I can't stay still another second.

"May I say something?"

"Yes . . ."

"I think that says as much about the ensuing era as it does about me . . ."

And yadda yadda yadda. Yadda Yadda.

YaddaYadda. Yadda.

Phil asks if I've ever shot drugs.

"C'mon Phil, you know how Jewish girls feel about penetration of any kind," I smirk like I'm talking to a friend and the audience explodes.

Phil chuckles.

Ed Glavin races off the set he's laughing so hard.

There's $100,000, Joni.

"Let's go through the Academy Awards," Phil continues after a smattering of applause. Tonight is Oscar Night.

We're all planning to watch at the hotel.

I sneak a peek at my enemy in the front row.

Her eyes adore me.

I think I liked her better before.

The caller's voice is so overwrought and his Hispanic accent so heavy I can barely understand but the gist is he's upset I'm not in The Program. Working Those Twelve Steps.

Phil jumps in.

"But she's not using cocaine! Why don't we just celebrate that!"

Cut to commercial and I take some deep breaths.

The only Twelve Steps Program I'm interested in is FFA.

Hi I'm Julia and I'm a financial fuck-up.

Hiiii Julia . . .

The woman on the line sounds like she's reading from

prepared text. In an accusatory tone she says that she thinks I wrote my book to become a celebrity.

I try to respond honestly, tell her that appearing on shows like this is part of a vast PR machine and I'd really rather be home watching teevee with my daughter.

She argues with me, reiterates her point: I only puked my guts out the past three years for the public recognition.

I tell her it's a free country and it's her First Amendment right to believe what she will even if she's wrong. Grrrr . . .

The forty-eight-minute hour is over before I begin.

Lights dim and there's a rush of people to the stage.

"You stay here, answer a few questions. I'll see you in the green room," Phil says tearing at his tie, beating a hasty retreat.

"Those are very cute shoes, that's a wonderful suit, great haircut," a woman says. "Very masculine . . ."

Plain Brown Woman from the front row approaches.

"I saw you on Sonya yesterday," she says. "I loved the jacket you were wearing. But you seemed so nervous."

"I wasn't nervous. I was fending off an attack!"

I'd worn Le Gaultier over a black sleeveless catsuit.

Good thing too. I was *sweating* when our chat was over.

Sonya hadn't finished the book and referred to me as mean-spirited, a word The Geff had also invoked.

I thought: How is it these mean people bandy that word about so freely?

"Boy, you are some mother*fucker*!" I smiled as a soundman removed the mike from my lapel.

She cracked up so raucously I shuddered.

The highlight of my visit to CNN had been Myron Kandel, their daytime business reporter. He was sporting an interesting two-tone look: heavy tan makeup, save from his pale nose to his paler chin.

"I watch you all the time," I said to him outside the elevator. "For all the good it does . . ."

Air was carrying an *YNELITTA* and we chatted about it for a minute.

"You know Angie Dickinson? I just looove Angie Dickinson," he said and then the elevator was there and we said good-bye.

I handed him the book just as the doors closed.

Kent Holland, that New York Random House PR boy, called later to inform me Sonya phoned after our interview to tell him how much she enjoyed meeting me and that maybe we should have dinner.

"Love to," I said, dripping irony, "but I have other plans . . ."

"She said if not tonight maybe next time you're in town . . ."

"Does she know how long that's gonna be?"

I was, in fact, having dinner with Joni, Julie, Air and Fran Leibowitz.

I'd been curious about Fran because Julie had been regaling me with her most particularly bons mots for two years. I assumed she was equally curious about me because the one thing I knew about she who repeated others' lines to you was that she repeated your lines to others.

Thus was gossip invented.

Fran wanted the dinner a secret, presumably to accommodate her friendship with The Geff.

"Then why are we going to Elio's?" I asked and Julie laughed. Elio's was a high-profile hot spot on the Upper East Side owned by the wife of Joe Fox, a legendary editor at Random House, the only boy on the floor who hadn't interrupted my meetings with Joni and Julie during an editorial/vetting ordeal the previous summer.

Not nearly as serendipitous a sojourn as this one.

We'd spent three days in Joni's corner office arguing over my denouement on *Close Encounters* whilst Joni's curious staff ebbed and flowed in a pale-faced pear-shaped publishing riptide.

David Rosenthal. David Rosenthal.

Soundtracked by the relentless ringing of phones as Joni was bidding in an auction that had soared into the double-digit millions.

Jason Epstein. Jason Epstein. Jason Epstein.

"Is he jealous of something?" I queried crankily and Joni and Julie laughed knowingly. Guess so.

Alberto Vitale, CEO, Joni's boss, floated down from a higher floor. Beautifully pinstriped and noticeably short he exuded authority, sooo man with the power. Like Mr. Wald. Marty Scorsese. He was extremely charming but it was clear his visit wasn't about me.

He whisked Joni into the hall and they conferenced in excited whispers whilst I rolled my eyes heavenward and Julie suppressed a giggle.

When she returned Joni told me that Alberto had said, "If I'd known she was that good-looking I'd have insisted we put her on the cover."

I rolled my eyes again to let Joni know I knew she was lying and we continued our *Close Encounters* fight.

Maybe Joni thought the hushed jabber dribbling zeroes would inspire me but it made me cross instead and I indulged in dialogue I'd learned in my previous career from writers during movie pitch meetings. When I was imparting what I imagined were brilliant notes and they were just dreading the work.

You have some idea what the next line might be? one of them spat nastily as he departed *my* corner office.

"What's the next line?" I snarled and Joni and Julie laughed ha-ha isn't she funny.

"Feed her," Joni instructed Julie and we went to Elio's.

I wore Le Gaultier over a black bicycle suit and a deep tan. White spikes on my head and white socks with black and white spats on my feet.

Girding my loins.

We ran into Joan and John Dunne seated against the wall near our front table.

I asked after Quintana. They asked after Kate.

"We like each other's children more than we like each other," I told Julie as we sipped our first drinks and grazed the menu.

"Isn't that Freddy DeMann trying to get your attention?"

Julie smirked with a tiny head-jerk and there he was at the bar waving big waves.

Freddy's principal gig was managing Madonna, which was surely more work than any single boy could handle.

"Half the crew from M-word's tour are staying at the hotel."

Joni was perceptive enough to put me up in Suite 1704 at the Ritz-Carlton but even the panoramic view of Central Park didn't cheer me. Probably because it was so many trees and I was preoccupied with the attempted suicide by a favorite sycamore at Sanctuary.

It had fallen across the driveway and severed power lines the first night I'd arrived in the Rotten Apple.

Kate, baby-sitting the place for the first time, called Air who called Forthill Construction. Specifically Scott.

"It's cleared away. Power's restored," Scott had said in a disingenuously calm tone when I called. "No small task, Jools. It was a lot of fucking tree."

"Any idea why it fell?"

"We're all mystified. It was green and living."

"That's depressing."

"Yeah I know. Jews plant trees." Every time Forthill suggested clearing away this pine or that oak to ease my tenuous power situation I'd reminded them that Jews didn't kill trees, they planted them. "Look we have a drought and it's easily 110 degrees in the shade . . ."

"Earthquake weather," I'd blurted. "But the tree was alive!"

"Yeah well shit happens in heat waves . . ."

Freddy walked over, nattily dressed and sad-eyed as ever. We kissed air and I reintroduced him to Julie whom he'd met before in Los Angeles at Mortons. He eyed us lasciviously, much as he did me and Mary Lambert (from whom I'd adopted the habit of calling Madonna M-word) when we were dining one night.

Personally, I thought of M-word as The The.

Freddy's dinner date (The The's lawyer) arrived and he sauntered off to their table.

"Dreaming his three-way dreams," I snorted.

We ordered another drink and ignored him for hours until

he and The Lawyer and Julie and I were the only people left
in the restaurant.

When Julie asked for the check the waiter informed us The
Gentlemen Over There had taken care of it.

"He's waiting for you," Julie said.

"Don't say that. I'll feel guilty."

"I don't even know him and I feel guilty."

I linked arms with Freddy whilst Julie and The The's
Lawyer chatted a discreet distance behind us as we strolled
along Fifth Avenue to the Ritz-Carlton.

The spats were new and my heels commenced painful blis-
tering around Sixty-ninth Street.

"Thanks for the tickets! Whatta show," I said.

Brooke and Corey and Stuart and I had checked out
Blonde Ambition compliments of F. DeMann a couple of
weeks before in L.A.

"Is this girl a star or what?!" Stuart had stage-whispered
excitedly as The The strutted down the lighted staircase in her
pointy-breasted corset and *her* Gaultier to Express Herself
almost on key.

"So how's the tour?"

"Aw not fun," Freddy'd said.

"Why?"

"She's depressed."

"Sorry to hear that."

"I hear that cynical tone. Why that cynical tone?"

"Ah c'mon, Freddy, you know why She's depressed . . ."

"Yeah I know. No struggle. It's always more fun on the
way up."

"See you on page 803," Julie sotto-voced cruelly as we bid
farewell in the lobby.

I kicked her in the shins, took my leave and went upstairs
to meet VS and Barry for a nightcap.

I had just enough time to glue ten bandages over my torn
feet before they arrived.

"I dunno, Jools," VS said sadly over some VSOP. "I
don't think I wanna go to any memorials anymore. I don't

even know any of the people there. They're all the friends of the friends of the friends of *my* friends. Who died already."

"Hey everybody dies," I countered helplessly and pulled my jacket around me to fend off the air-conditioned chill . . .

I kept Le Gaultier wrapped around me for my first drink at dinner with Fran Leibowitz when *The New York Times Book Review* came up.

"Y'know," I said casually, "he and I worked at United Artists at the same time. I think he actually did some readers' reports for me when I was at Mirisch . . ."

Fran blushed with anger.

"That's a complete conflict of interest!" she exploded. "You should be writing a letter of complaint to them!"

"That's really what I wanna do just about now. Write anything!" I exploded back and everybody laughed.

I punched my linguine with a fork for emphasis and sauce flew off the plate onto a white stripe on the front of the jacket.

"Didja notice how many times she mentioned that she was Number Five?" Air said later, wrapping Le Gaultier in a plastic bag for the valet. "You're already Three. Please. Try and take a little pleasure."

"Yo tengo un tax problema!" I joked but I shivered too.

Am I bold? No I'm cold. And my Gaultier is old . . .

We're still high from the show, nibbling at hors d'oeuvres from room service, getting ready for the Academy Awards when Kate calls.

She sounds excited.

"Mom! I got into the University of Michigan!"

Her first choice.

Just then everybody in the room explodes.

I stick my finger in my free ear so I can hear her but they're all gesticulating wildly for my attention.

"Just a minute, Kate . . . *What!!??*"

"Billy Crystal's first line . . ." Roger says.

How is he still here?

"He said, 'Sorry I'm late but I was having lunch with Julia Phillips. We were talking about all of you . . .'"

"You have The Awards on?" I ask Kate.

"On MUTE."

I repeat Billy Crystal's line.

"That's so cool," she says dreamily and I feel guilty.

My moment has undercut her moment.

"Almost as cool as getting into the University of Michigan," I apologize helplessly.

Yeah right Mooommmm.

I've pegged five of the seven major awards.

At $10,000 per, I've earned the rest of my $150,000 . . .

Thursday morning, 6:30 A.M., Joni calls Air with the news.

Air waits until eight-thirty to wiggle my toe awake.

"You're Number One," she whispers then bursts into tears. "I feel vindicated." She sobs.

Oh this is about you?

THOSE BOYS/THOSE GIRLS
THE ASSISTANT

Mommy was a teacher of French in an extension course he took and caught the eye of Papa who knew a Rolling Stone.

Which is how It scored some primo West Coast interviews when It left State College in the midst of sophomore year.

It loooves The Business. Hates Its boss.

And why not?

It makes appointments for The Boss.

It breaks appointments for The Boss.

It makes reservations for The Boss.

It breaks reservations for The Boss.

It makes arrangements for The Boss.

It breaks arrangements for The Boss.

It makes excuses for The Boss.

I could make or break you! It thinks when It's abused by The Boss.

And It will, just as soon as It divines the secret:

How to Be The Boss's Boss . . .

YNELITTA's to be Number One on my forty-seventh birthday.

I go through the motions, call all the same people I called last week to tell them Number Three. Everyone's deriving far more pleasure out of this Sherman's March to the top than I am but they didn't have to write it.

Or vet it. Never mind live it.

Of the three, vetting was the most difficult and that's saying something.

"At least I have the pleasure of knocking *Iron John* out of the box," I grouse and decide to throw an impromptu bash tonight on Random House's tab. *They* didn't give us a party.

We fiddle with the guest list over coffee, divide the calls, phone our families first.

David Shipley at *The New York Times* asks if he can bring someone.

Lynn Nesbit says she'll send her younger staff.

Julie's bringing the entire Grau family.

Ed Glavin tells me when I call that my *Donahue* tied with *Oprah* and is spiking similarly across the country.

YNELITTA will be spiking right along.

Connie Sayre and Robert Riger want to bring Peter Mayer, president of Viking/Penguin, who's already read the book compliments of Frankie.

Winging from L.A. to Gotham a few weeks back.

She's told him a million dollars for the paperback rights and we know he likes it. He sucked the whole thing down on the red-eye and called her from the airport to kvell.

I've reminded Joni, who'll be conducting the auction with Wanda Chappell any day now, that Peter Mayer is our pigeon.

Penguin, she keeps correcting.

When I call the Dunnes, Joan answers. I've heard that John is abed recovering from bypass surgery but I figure I should invite them. Although they have been a tad cold the last couple of times we've run into each other.

Are they upset with their sides?

"We were jus' talking about you," Joan says dryly and declines.

We've been demoted from a capacious top-floor Central Park two-bed/three-bath/large-parlor suite to a claustrophobic medium-floor/medium-Park-view one-bed/two-bath suite and a single across the hall. A reward for staying a day longer. Or for being Number One. Hard to tell.

I'm scheduled for a last-minute *CBS This Morning* taping with Harry Smith, who's just returned from Saudi Arabia/Desert Sturm.

The crew pours in at noon.

They have trouble getting past each other in the thin entryway and they have trouble laying their cable.

It's a spring day and the air conditioning has trouble staying abreast with the heat of that many bodies.

Claustrophobic, I open the windows.

Harry's taller than he seems on T.V. and cute as he is, rather flabbier in his midsection than a man of his age should be. This is the first day I haven't worked out and I feel off. I'm entirely too California for my own good.

Harry lies down on the floor of the living room, which flattens his stomach somewhat. He naps.

The makeup woman does my face in a cramped clammy bathroom and it's hard to keep shine from my forehead. The mascara feels humid and clumped but when I look in the mirror there I am: Ms. Whatever's Good for The Project.

The interview's a short so-so.

"How's this make you feel?" Harry asks disinterestedly.

"Vindicated," I say with a see-how-I'm-smiling smile.

The crew strikes the set and leaves.

"At least he didn't ask about Goldie's (dirty) locks or Warren's kidding-on-the-square vamp(ire)ing. Makes me almost sorry I wrote it . . ." Air looks horrified.

"I said *almost . . .*"

We count guests. Forty at least.

We confer with catering, survey our doll's house and kid ourselves it'll be fine.

"I wouldn't mind a walk," I say when the staff arrives with their portable bar and hors d'oeuvre table and Air agrees.

We power along Central Park South in the balmy lavender twilight. I'm sidetracked from the triumph by the karma of a triumph on my birthday. The last time something like this happened (I won the Academy Award for *The Sting* three days before I turned thirty) I paid dues for seventeen years. We jay-walk the Plaza's plaza and turn ninety degrees down Fifth Avenue.

We approach Doubleday's. I've been hearing about *YNELITTA* dominating the front windows of toney bookstores but I haven't seen it and not one of my friends has thought to take a Polaroid. I squint. Nary a shining stiletto in sight. Air and I look at each other alarmed. Deep breaths. We pop in and the manager, an aged preppie, smiles a snaggle-toothed smile of recognition.

"Where's my book?"

"We ran out. Twice. I even sold my own copy. Love it by the way. We're waiting for our next shipment." I thrust out my lower lip and he smiles again. "It's due in tomorrow. Want to come sign some?"

I've refused all such requests, as I can't seem to shake out of my grueling-endeavor mode. Air says it's because I'm determined to enjoy the success as little as possible and I've countered, You can take the girl out of the (funny-you-don't-look) Jewishness but you can't take the (funny-you-don't-look) Jewishness out of the girl.

"Sorry she can't. We're leaving tomorrow," Air says authoritatively and propels me from the store with a polite U-turn. I love when she does that! Air is getting better all the time. Guess that means she'll be leaving soon.

We wave good-bye and head south toward the new Bendel's. Air says that even if I can't bear to step inside, we must check out the window.

Like architecture is my favorite thing.

"Y'know what?" I turn to Air.

"What?"

"I wish my mother was alive for this."

"Uh-huh," Air says in an unh-unh inflection.

We walk some more.

I stop and Air stops with me.

Up ahead faint vibrations of urban unrest.

"Why am I kidding myself? Number One wouldn't be good enough! Right?"

We proceed to Bendel's, minimalistic and airy but also purple clothes under harsh red lights.

"I can't. I'll have a flashback," I say and Air guides me through streams of people to the curb.

"Look up. Look at the windows," Air says reverentially so I follow her eyes. Old cut glass, gorgeously detailed work nobody knows how to do anymore.

I am enveloped suddenly by a sense of loss.

The quintessential Democrat, snatching defeat from the jaws of victory.

"I'm dizzy," I say and turn to see a small ugly crowd of protesters gathering outside Saint Patrick's Cathedral. "Welcome to the jungle." We execute another silent U-turn. "Who says the eighties are over?" We adroitly sidestep Thorazine-deprived homeless along our pathetic little retreat to the safety of the hotel. "I'm confused. Do we pity them or fear them?"

To the bar for an End-of-the-World discussion with Norman.

"You're not going to believe this," Joni says.

Whilst awaiting the car that will whisk us along the first leg of the endless sojourn to Sanctuary, I've called to complain that Dick DeBlois still hasn't received my $150,000-less-commission check.

Joni's called ICM's literary department, specifically Esther Neuberg, whom I've never met. It's a drag that Lynn cut my deal then split for a partnership with Mort Janklow. *I've* followed her to Janklow/Nesbit, but *YNELITTA* has not.

"I said, 'Esther, didn't I tell you this check needed to be turned around in twenty-four hours?'" Joni continues, "and *she* said, 'Well, she upset a lot of my friends.'"

"Oh, my tax problem is about her and her friends?! Maybe she'd like to pass the commission on to Lynn . . ."

"Jools, it's taken care of. I'm just gonna cut them their ten percent and wire the remainder to you directly. You need to sell that fucking house!"

"That fucking deal went south this morning! Why do you think I'm harassing you? And by the way, *that* deal would barely have covered the mortgage-to-the-hilt and *not* settled the tax problem. *That* deal would've left me penniless *and* homeless."

"Jeez," Joni says under her breath, appreciating for the first time, probably, the depth of my financial miasma.

I glance up at Air, who's been hovering. She needs the money too. The phone in the bedroom rings and she rushes off to answer it.

"I wanna send Those Capitol Boys a memo RE: THE DEFICIT. Once you're in the hole it only gets deeper. And God forbid it should rain. Slippery when wet!"

Joni laughs ha-ha isn't she funny and jumps off.

I feel in fact that God, snickering, has thrown me into a ten-foot muddy lagoon and said, Okay dig out. I've given you really strong fingernails. Don't break any!

No wonder I don't respect Him in the morning.

"The car's here. Are we gonna be okay?"

"Joni says so."

When the bellman arrives he says some *YNELITTA* aficionados have been ejected from the lobby.

"So now they're lingering curbside?" Air asks, nervous.

"Probably."

"Oooh fans," I coo but I don't mean it. I do, however, apply some blusher and gloss in the hall mirror, ignoring Air's disparaging reflection behind me.

We ride the elevator down in silence.

Check out in silence. Hit the street in silence.

The bellman and the driver are a short distance away, loading our luggage.

"Julia?"

We turn.

A beautiful girl stands a few steps up the street.

"Yes . . ."

"I've just come from Russia," she says in a thick accent. "Three weeks ago. I read your book right away because I want to be an actress. Happy Birthday by the way! Don't you have a birthday coming up?"

I nod and smile. This doesn't suck.

"I'm Aries too. March twenty-eighth. Julia, I know this is hard to believe but it was like you were telling my story."

"Thank you," I say warmly, wondering if maybe I *should* respect Him in the morning. Times being what they are and all. "From the bottom of my heart . . ."

I extend my hand but she steps back, alarmed.

I feel a large presence at my elbow and catch my first peripheral glimpse of a tall captain-of-industry type looming beside me. He grabs my arm, holds it tightly.

"I saw you on teevee," he slurs, spewing nasty garlic/alcohol breath at me. "Bought your book, see?"

He's holding *YNELITTA* in his other meaty hand.

I have asked Anne Rice if there's a reward for writing and she's said: You're in a city far from home. You've finished all the interviews and you're taking a breather on the street. A stranger's walking toward you and he's carrying your book . . .

Mr. My-Reward looks angry.

I jerk my arm: What are *you* so pissed off at!

He tightens his grip.

It hurts.

She'd have ripped her hands off to escape.

Peg Garrity said.

I freeze.

Air and the doorman push him away.

We jump in the car.

"I'm going home and I'm not coming out for a year," I kid, frightened, as the driver pulls into traffic, no small feat on Fifty-ninth Street.

Air sighs deeply.

I dial Kate's line and get through right away, first try, just like that, because for a couple of weeks I'm a seven on The 1–10 Celebrity Scale and a seven always gets through right away. First try.

Just like that.

"I had the tooth dream," my daughter wails and I comfort her with clucking noises but I think, I wonder if you'll ever graze through my book? Good ol' *YNELITTA*.

The one I wrote for you and then you didn't read.

Night befalls The City as we crawl to the Queensborough Bridge.

To Kennedy Airport, which resembles the Port Authority Bus Terminal more and more each year.

There we'll wait in what is laughingly referred to as the First Class Lounge to board a delayed flight.

Hope it doesn't crash whilst winging to Sanctuary.

"If I'm so New York how come I feel so out-of-town?" Air says wistfully.

"If I'm so Number One how come I feel so Number Two?"

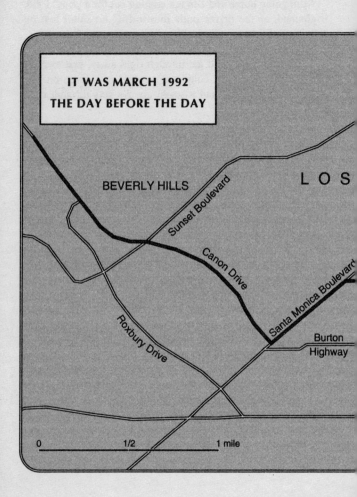

IT WAS MARCH 1992
THE DAY BEFORE THE DAY

BEVERLY HILLS

Sunset Boulevard

Canon Drive

L O S

Santa Monica Boulevard

Roxbury Drive

Burton
Highway

0   1/2   1 mile

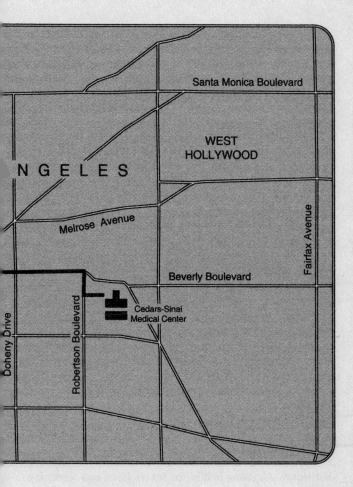

Click.

Cher.

I've spent an inordinate amount of time abed for the past month. Me and my cat Ramona who guards me and fights for space on the heating pad set permanently at HIGH. First there was the Christmas Lumbar Incident and a visit to one then another specialist. They prescribed expensive arcane script a brace and rest.

In between were rain and mudslides and deadlines and perigrinations from the omnipresent E., Ms. Taxperson.

Finally Tony Alter, star orthopedist, ordered two epidural blocks. Laura Audell, the Princess of Pain Management at Cedars Medical Center, furrowed her brow when she studied my CAT scan and said she didn't hold out much hope. The second, which she administered yesterday, seems to have intensified the disintegration of my already deteriorating discs.

Plus I've been sneezing the past three days for no particular reason, which certainly exacerbates the situation. Perhaps I've developed a sensitivity to Sanctuary. The doctors call such non-specific episodes environmental allergies, which always makes me laugh.

They've got that right.

Click. Cher. Click. Cher.

I've finally succumbed to a serious case of television.

Conscious that is but unable to read to think to do anything but *watch*. Alighting briefly for sex violence and screaming skulls but mostly grazing through the human zoo:

Fat flat-lit trolls with pale pockmarked skin weaving dark tales of incest and murder in trashy trailer-park tones. Corseted in too tight chairs situated on cheap afternoon sets.

Harassed and harangued by hostile hosts hurling cheap shots but never the right questions.

Roseanne without the surgery OR the chuckles.

And me shouting advice from my bed of pain in sentences that always start, Yo gir'frien', lissen-up!

A hundred stations and something shitty For Sale on each and every one.

"We're not performing brain surgery here," people in FernoTainment love to reassure each other over Big-Macher expense-account lunches but they know that's a lie. I've been at this for a relatively short span and the teevee has interfaced with my neurotransmitters. Supercharged my serotonin. Cyberspaced my synapses.

I'm strung out.

Christ, even freebase took a couple of months of dedicated use to develop a Jones.

I'm at that vortex of addiction where I've become deeply attached to the black-POP/white-FLASH *between* channels and I'm working up a good case of carpal tunnel syndrome thumbing the REMOTE. I think I liked freebase better but it's been so long, retrieving the information would be a hassle. I can't believe people still smoke it after all the cautionary dish about Richard Pryor and Grizzly Adams and me.

Or worse, given the current state of *my* affairs, retrieval would prove a too-too titillating excursion.

I choose to remember not.

And cough and wheeze and click click click.

And ow. And OW. And OW-OW-OOOOWWWWW.

Yo gir'frien'. Lissen-UP!

I am the masses my parents warned me against.

My parents. Adolph and Tanya. So young so sweet so free. Demanding innocents who required more explanation of life than God and money. Idealistic atheists who condescended to filthy lucre and people driven by mad love for mountains of the stuff. I might as well have been brought up by wolves for all the relevance their snobberies pretensions and aspirations have to the real world.

Exhibit A: I was a single-digit age (so long then, so short now) when Tanya taped a cartoon she'd clipped from *The* (old) *New Yorker* to the refrigerator. The Father, foreground, huge, imposing, angrily waving a report card: 4 As, one B+. Yelling at his son, background, a small boy in a beanie quaking in his boots.

Caption: "B+ isn't good enough for a Zimmerman!"

Mom, kidding on the square.

No wonder she/we had/have back/tax problemas.

I drag my leg to the bathroom for an excruciating pee and a bracing braceless hot shower.

And what should my mantra be today, Mr. Rogers?

Can *you* say Quasimodo?

Noooo, Mr. Rogers. But I can say Sanctuary.

Oh I'm sorry, that's not the right answer. You'll have to come this way. This way please.

I swallow some more script. How many today?

One? two? three? etc.?

It is time to work.

Go fuck yourself. I don' wanna.

Go fuck yourself. I WON'T!

GO FUCK YOURSELF! okay-i-will . . .

I tighten my brace for the endless five-step trek to The Creature's room, an eight-foot square nestled between my bedroom bathroom and kitchen. Sanctuary's You'veGotSome Nerve Center. It used to be a breakfast nook, but situated as it is in the midst of my favorite places to be, The Creature's comfort took precedence.

If I can bring myself to turn the power ON, as I do now, and let it um, hum, sooner or later I drift toward it.

Sometimes it's a fourteen-sentence day, which is not much. Sometimes it's seven pages, which is a lot. Three and a quarter pages is what you wanna do. Three and a quarter pages per day is productive. Whatever the fuck that means.

Outside of the dining room table and chairs, which I've removed, I have left all aspects of the breakfast nook intact. On one wall a baker's rack, still accoutred with planters and a large brass tub filled with dried flowers and books, mainly of the coffee-table variety.

Dad's André Gide collection sits on the top left shelf.

When he remarried a decade ago, Dad got compulsive about clearing his condominium for his bride's arrival. He sent me cartons and cartons of books, among them Gide's *Journals* and a disintegrating copy of his novel *The Counterfeiters*. In the same shipment Dad included a manila envelope filled with my short stories from high school and college and beyond. Reminding me that notwithstanding some tasty movie-producing credits, an Academy Award for *The Sting* and my tax problem, I was a writer.

My personal favorite, "The Persistence of *e*," evolved out of my perturbation with logarithms. I hit the wall on logarithms in a calculus class, 3:50 P.M. just days before Christmas break. Weeks after They told us JFK was murdered by a composite photoentity titled Lee Harvey Oswald.

"The course of history can be changed with the rise or removal of a single man," Peter Viereck had emphasized repeatedly in his overcrowded Modern European History lectures that fall. Sue White, who sat next to me, would draw a goosestepping boot in the corner of her notepaper and "Here Comes Hitler" every time. "Hister," I'd correct because I was daytripping through Nostradamus's *Quatrains*.

That covers it, I understood that long November weekend.

But calculus!? Logarithms!? With rules that subverted the English language, like: The derivative of *e* to the *x* equals *e* to the *x*? Waitasecond. Derivative means drawn from therefore *less*, right?! *Less* is . . . the same?

I wrote "*e*" to perturb Dad, a scientist, a mathematician, a man of reason who was proud of the story instead and tried vainly to impart the essence of *e* to the *x* in simple elegant fashion one last time.

"But what will I ever *do* with logarithms?" I protested, puffing my Marlboro, hitching my skirt, late for a date.

"Well, they show up in seismic charts, growth curves . . ."

"Oh yeah, I'll require a firm grasp of those issues when

I'm president!" I kidded and got a reluctant laugh. "E to the x equals eee-eee-eee, Daaadeee."

Dad.

Who has the unsettling predilection for addressing me by the names of his wives — first Tanya, now June — in a hoarse asthmatic whisper, compliments of vocal cords scarred by chemotherapy.

He's on a daily diet of prednisone and like all smart people he meddles with his milligrams per day. If he eats enough to breathe, he develops infections. If he reduces the dose, he has to fight for air. Chechechechchch. Makes him older and frailer than his active brain can tolerate. When the medical miasma overwhelms him, he checks into intensive care and sucks on a respirator for a week or so.

Adolph's concept of R&R. Très fin de millennium.

On another shelf, an ancient boxed set of Shakespeare. The comedies the histories the tragedies the whole catastrophe. Behind a bowl which props them up, a hastily rendered kitsch portrait of me by Brad, who is a brilliant painter still struggling for movie stardom. I'm dressed black, salt-and-pepper spike-haired, square-jawed, thin-lipped, arms crossed over a chest he's kindly endowed with cleavage, staring unswervingly through oversized gray-blue orbs.

DUDE . . . THERE ARE NO RULES! he's inscribed in large block letters on the green-and-blue-striped wallpaper in the background.

Aaah honaayyy. Sometimes you ask too much . . .

Hung on the adjoining wall a blue-on-blue litho of Don Quixote on his nag. Sword aloft, pointing certainly: No not this way . . . *that* way! A present for my first-and-last ex-wedding. From Tanya, what a surprise.

On another wall a multihued Norman Rockwell. *Saturday People*. A lot of them were famous/a lot of them are dead. A present from a goodold/badolddays dealer who owed *me* money.

Tucked discreetly in another corner, the catbox. Does anyone but me find it ironic that I create in such close proximity to, well, where Ramona creates?

Different shit, same old day?

Ramona didn't used to expunge with extreme etcetera inside Sanctuary until the rains and the floods, but I don't want to think about that now.

Blupp.

Blupp Blupp.

BluppbluppBluppblupp.

My fingers cruise The Creature's keyboard in perfect syncopation with a white-hot salsa backbeat piercing my left leg from ass to toe. I ignore it but that's because the Soma's kicking in.

Safety Safety Safety

Scroll Scroll Scroll

I read.

Work in Progress/Notes — ShowBiz IS Real Life

CRACKERS, a talking dog (possibly black lab), is a movie star. He's ten years old, which is verrry old. Paunchy and jaded and worried that any moment he'll be required to shoot the pilot of *Three Quacks for Mister Mack*. Or worse, sign a long-term contract for Alpo commercials costarring Ed McMahon.

He resides in a suite at a mansion mortgaged by his mentor/manager/nemesis, THE MOGUL KLAUS FENNIG (né Menom Shvartzerfergerberger) and Klaus's fourth wife, SHARI. Young and gorgeous and more shrewd than smart, whose twin-sister CHERI lives less opulently but more independently near-enough-by.

Those Girls everybody calls them.

Those Girls looove to eat Ecstasy and be eaten by Crackers, uninhibited courtesy of Quaaludes they have increasing difficulty scoring for him. They pretend they don't know he's addicted because Crackers gives the best head in Hollywood. He's the last safe sex in town.

But sometimes. Lately. Crackers feels so depressed when it's over he excuses himself and trundles back to his suite. Pops a Prozac in his mouth and a black-and-white cassette of Billy Wilder's *Sunset Boulevard* in his VCR and howls mournfully for hours.

Open on a set piece: Christmas Eve Dinner.

First Year. Last Decade. Second Millennium.

Gorbachev — seasonally vulnerable — resigns from the
U.S.S.Are-Nothing on T.V. screen to T.V. screen throughout the
night and the following day.

Do I need ghosts?

NO.

Spirits?

NO.

Thirteen Steps of Sacrifice?

YES.

Virtual Reality?

E-X-P-L-A-I-N.

Is Crackers a virtual effect gone haywire?

M-M-M-M . . .

Is The-World-as-We-Know-It Crackers's virtual reality?

M-A-Y-B-E-E-E . . .

I chortle painfully and glom onto my reflection in the mirror behind The Creature. I'm pallid and furrow-browed and
the incipient dewlapage assaulting my jawline seems especially pronounced. With the white bangs I bear a disturbing
resemblance to Tanya, who also suffered slipped discs. L-4
and L-5 specifically. Like me.

Swinging in my swivel chair, I catch strobing images from
the bulletin board nearby where I've posted my most inspira-
tional piece of unsolicited mail . . .

DEAR JEW-LEE-AH

YOU ARE A MACHO CUNT, A SELF-CENTERED PIECE OF SHIT*

NOT A FAN

*BUT TALENTED

. . . and attempt a deep inhale; I cough instead and the
brace cuts sharply into the six inches above and below my
waist. My left leg dances the Lambada from hell and my eyes
and nose sprout involuntary tears.

"All pros work more than one thing at a time," Lynn counseled when I complained about my cacaphonous P-L-O-T, so I transfer to an assignment on the Academy Awards I've accepted from the Los Angeles Times Syndicate, I'm that poor. OSCAR KNIGHT.

But tha'th not writing, tha'th typing, as Truman Capote once lithped on Jack Paar's B&W *Tonight* show, referring to Jack Kerouac. And there I was agreeing and disagreeing, caught in the intersection of Tanya's literary prejudices and m-m-my generation.

My Vulnerable Season's running neck and neck with Gorbachev's.

And it's getting longer each year.

I close my eyes.

I remember . . .

HOW I SPENT MY BULNERABLE SEASON
BY JULIO PHILLIPPE, 1992

Time's Man of the Year was Ted Turner, The InfernoMation Superhighwayman who made the world safe for Jane Fonda. Jane Fonda safe for the world? Whatever.

So we celebrated at Sanctuary.

Todd and Brooke and Corey. Me.

Fanny and Fanny's friend Pauly, a tall and slender exotically beautiful mixed-race specimen like herself, the brother she never had. Half-Scot/half-black and the first grown man I ever saw sporting striped tights under polka-dot boxer shorts. When I asked him how it was to grow up in Glasgow he smiled and said, "Verrry ruff, lass, verrry ruff!" Pauly, who'd commenced his culinary career at Helena's in The Eighties, was a chef in Aspen, just down for the week.

Zoe, who grew up in East Boston and knew from the time she was six she needed to get as far away as possible from her subdivided joint-custody family. Zoe looked like the

hypothetical offspring of Paul Newman and Rita Hayworth
and should have enjoyed a six-figure-a-year career in commercials at least, but she was not ambitious and bided her
time producing videos for the sub-MTV generation.

Dalee, for David Lee, a wild-and-crazy black hairdresser
who designed dazzling short cuts; his Diana Ross posturing
aside, he was one of the ten sweetest people I'd ever met and
he always got my jokes. Anyway, he laughed when they were
over.

And Lee, whom I met through Dalee and with whom I
shared an infintely more intimate relationship. Last year for
six weeks before *YNELITTA*'s hardcover release Lee and I hit
the tanning salon every other day together in preparation for
Julia's Visit to the Soft Machine. Lying in that compressed
ultraviolent chamber keeping The Big One on hold was the
closest I ever got to religion. Lee's hobbies for the past two
years had been giving up alcohol and cigarettes and growing
his wavy blond hair to the top of his ass.

We turned on the T.V. and as the ball in Times Square
began its descent, we gathered around the dining room table
with a bottle of Jagermeister and our glasses.

I poured shots for everyone but Lee.

"To Anita Hill!" Fanny toasted the moment before midnight and we clinked our glasses ceremoniously and drank.

Another round.

"To Jack Kevorkian!" I toasted the moment after and we
laughed and clinked and drank again.

"Who's Jack Kevorkian?!" Corey exclaimed. "Who's Anita
Hill?!"

"There is no fucking hope!" Brooke joked and winked at
me conspiratorially.

Brooke wouldn't have known Anita Hill from Anita Bryant if
he hadn't dropped by for a visit whilst I was T.V.-witnessing
her daytime testimony. He watched with me, riveted, until we
bailed on Clarence Thomas's "high-tech lynching" prime-time
appearance.

"He did it. He's *reeeallll* sorry!" Brooke laughed as we barreled up Deep Canyon Road toward the Glen Center for some impromptu sushi and sake bombers with Todd.

"Yeah, but I suspect the only thing America hates and fears more than an uppity black man is an uppity black *woman*!" I spat angrily as we sat down outside Sushi Ko, where we could smoke and drink whilst awaiting Todd's arrival. With one antismoking ordinance after another passing one city council after another I imagined that pretty soon my martinis and coffee would be accompanied by pieces of Nicorette gum parked in my cheek, hardly the most gratifying parentheses to dining out.

Todd and Brooke and I were just settling into our first drinks when the clump clump clump of major motorcycle boots caused us to look up sharply. Alec Baldwin, black-leatherjacketed and bluejeaned, beamed a blue-eyed Black Irish smile in my direction.

"I read your book. You're very funny . . ."

I'd heard that from a number of men. Funny.

Women cued into the pain. Moving, they often said.

"I like your work too," I smiled and he nodded assent and sat down heavily at the next table. He was joined almost immediately by Kim Basinger and another couple. Kim sat with her back to me and when she and Alec kissed hello, he whispered something. She whipped around.

"Are you Julia Phillips?"

"I am."

She extended her hand. "I'm Kim Basinger," she smiled and we shook on it.

"You certainly are!" She was more beautiful in person than onscreen, if such a thing were possible. Which cost her dearly later on, when she drew eight cranky women jurors and one sullen woman judge on the *Boxing Helena* lawsuit and they found her guilty guilty guilty.

Sometimes the only people I disliked and distrusted more than men were women.

"I just loved your book . . ."

"Thanks . . ."

I introduced Todd and Brooke. She introduced the other couple, her sister and brother-in-law, and we returned to our separate parties.

I had always liked Kim Basinger for the brave words she'd uttered nervously on behalf of Spike Lee's *Do the Right Thing* two Oscarcasts back, which I watched with Julie Grau during our week of recutting *YNELITTA*. Although The Kim was decked out like a decoration on a birthday cake, so it was hard to take her seriously.

"Think Prince lent her that dress?" Julie smirked.

"Probably had to let it out," I smirked back.

Too intimidated by the possibility of violence in the theater where it was playing, I'd have never seen *Do Right* — arguably the best picture that year — if Universal hadn't sent videocassettes to Academy members.

Times being what they were and all.

I actually bought Public Enemy's CD for "Fight the Power," its relentless soundtrack/theme song. Chuck D. Flavor Flav. With the oversized sunglasses and the oversized clock hanging around his neck and the overwrought delivery.

Those were some angry oy gevalte meshuggener shvartzers!

Chunga chung chung chung chung.
Chunga chung chung chung chung.
"Fight the power! Fight the power!"
"Fight the power! Fight the power!"

"Jesus, Jools, I don't know how you can stand that shit!" Fanny complained. Fanny was a rock 'n' roller between record deals and I couldn't blame her for being frustrated, but it was New Year's so Brooke and Corey and I danced to the ranting whilst Fanny and Pauly cruised up to the pool/deck for a look-see. Pauly came racing down almost immediately, his face as pale as it could be given its basic burnt-sienna hue.

"Ooooh, I goot a verrry bod vibe oop therrrre, lass," he shivered but I poohed-poohed him: Notwithstanding its water-dribbling waterfall and generations of rats living large and multiplying fruitfully in the shack where the equipment was housed, the deck was part of Sanctuary under permanent surveillance and protection by the house-spirit, Virgilia-the-Good. VTG.

Later, he picked up the Oscar stashed between rooms on the floor, just to look, and the thing fell apart in his hands. A shiny alloy dust drifted from its base and I told everyone to stay away, it looked toxic. Packed the pieces in a Maxfield's shopping bag and went back to the party.

Air took the wretched refuse to the Academy for repair. They told her it was too degraded and they'd replace it with a new one. Cost: three hundred dollars. I could barely afford it, but I figured I'd better. If my cash-flow prospects didn't brighten shortly, I'd probably have to consider selling it.

I'd watched a piece on *Hard Copy* about the rising prices the little devil was fetching at auction with unseemly attention. Never mind how unseemly it was that I was turning on tuning in and dropping out to *Hard Copy* in the first place.

I should've listened to Pauly's bad vibe more attentively but I was so thrilled that Kate was taking a break from freshman year at the University of Michigan for a couple of Vulnerable Season weeks with me and that I hadn't celebrated Christmas with root canal I didn't notice the lower back aches, the intermittent leg-numbness, the spinal crookedness until it was too late.

A week after Kate's return, though, I awakened with back pain traversing such a broad territory of muscle nerve and incidental tissue it was ecumenical in proportion. I hauled myself from bed and hobbled down Sanctuary's cracked and pocked driveway for the *Sunday Times*es — New York/L.A. — heaven forfend I should be deprived of enough information to render myself incapacitated by dusk.

By the time I lugged myself into the kitchen to brew coffee, walking was a job and I was doing triple overtime.

At the other side of the house, Kate argued softly long-distance with the boyfriend in New York, who left truculent messages on her machine and never seemed satisfied with the level of her affection.

I hadn't met him, but had classified him in the Entirely Too Demanding category. If he continued to make Kate feel lousy at his present rate I suspected I would *never* meet him, but she was easygoing, laid-back, and cut people far more slack than they deserved. Me included. Me most of all. Hell, she polished her slack-cutting skills on me. He might pick at her for years before she dumped him.

The thought ambushed my heart and pierced my back. I gasped. Jeez, that was loud for a gasp.

"Mom . . . *Mom* . . . what's wrong!?" Kate called out sharply and I oh-nothinged her. She hung up the phone and padded down the hall. By the time she reached the kitchen, I was grimacing wildly. Tears puddled in my eyes.

I decided I must sit down. Whoa. This pain was alive, thrashing about inside me. Pursuing its liberty and happiness, so to speak. I think I'll name it Alpha, like a hurricane. Make that Alfie. I lay down groaning.

"Uuuugggghhhhhh!" I explained. Kate towered above me and her eyes were solemn and concerned but the muscles around her mouth hip-hopped to some inner rapper and then she couldn't help it, she exploded into The Girlish Giggles.

"I used to do that, usually upon being informed of somebody's untimely demise." Kate fought for control of her face.

"Are you serious?!" she hee-heed.

"Nah, I just thought this display would be the most fabulous homecoming I could dream up for the child with everything."

"Mom, I know you make a living from one-liners but I wish you wouldn't practice them on me." Alfie accelerated and I writhed with her wind-chill factor.

"I'm not kidding. This pain is from outer space!"

"Well then call the doctor."

"It's Sunday . . ."

It would be leave word with his service then he'd call back and I'd have to pick up the phone, which I never did anymore.

I let the machine with the message from the previous number do it.

"Mom, if you don't call I'm gonna lose all respect for you." Kate was quoting me from our recent mother-daughter welcome-home fight. The one in which I told her I worried that she didn't know how to take care of her health, i.e., when to call the doctor.

"Gimme a hand here . . . " We pushed-pulled until I was upright, with just the hint of S-shaped spinal curvature. I dialed Al Sellers, who once confided I was the sort of patient for whom he'd become a doctor. Whaddya mean? I asked and he said, Because we all believed you were gonna die and we saved you.

Oh, I thought ungratefully, It was about you?

Sure why not?

Al, who made house calls, had a vested interest in my good health. Al was one of the few people I considered a friend who was older than me. Al, actually, was probably one of the few people in Los Angeles older than me. The rest of them moved to San Diego. Al had survived bypass surgery and two marriages. His children were grown. When he retired, would there be anyone who was a responsible adult who still cared about me?

I didn't count Dad, who cared too much.

Dad was not a responsible adult.

Al called back within minutes and I described my symptoms. He prescribed an anti-inflammatory, a muscle relaxant and a gastrointestinal soother. That oughtta set my insurance company reeling.

"Get into bed and put a smallish pillow under your knees. Heating pad if you want. *Don't* work out!" He knew to be emphatic on that point. He knew the exercise kept the fragile mechanism called Me together.

The exercise and the smoking more precisely. Together.

The endorphins and the nicotine.

The Yin and the Yang.

The pink and the blue, so to say.

• • •

After Kate departed for second semester, The Pain cut as
sharply into my time with The Creature as my vertebrae; a
problem, as I was in great need of new money, which wasn't
forthcoming sans new pages. I asked Sellers to set me up with
Tony Alter but got an appointment with an associate in the
office, Jack Moshein, instead. Moshein had the white hair
deep tan and unctuous manner of an agent from the variety
department at William Morris. He asked me to perform mini-
mal toe-touches, ordinarily a piece of cake for workoutaholic
me. I couldn't.

He ordered X rays, showed me the disc pressing on my sciatic nerve. The nerve was on fire. It was thin and white and
looked exactly like an exploded root in a dying tooth but it
went from my lumbar to my toes, which is a lot of territory to
be on fire.

"Oh, the poor little nerve," I squeaked, alarmed.

"Let's try these exercises first," Moshein said disinterestedly and handed me a printed red foldout. "I'll see you again
in two weeks."

Grinding my teeth on the drive home, I decided I must
pressure Sellers again. I called him just before cell-phone
fadeout in AlmostColorado Canyon and insisted on seeing
Tony Alter.

Yes, even in the morning!

Tony Alter suggested traction in the hospital. I told him
that wasn't an option as *YNELITTA*'s paperback edition was
on the brink of release and I was required to do publicity. He
snorted condescendingly and fitted me for a brace.

"Wear it whenever you're not lying down and stop lifting
weights," he instructed in that edged-out authoritarian doctor
tone that always made me want to disobey.

"I have to do some sort of exercise," I declared, panicked.

"All right, stationary bike no tension," he allowed reluctantly, observing my tapping foot with obvious displeasure.
"Y'know you don't have to move fast to be smart," he said

sagely, but I didn't believe him and wondered instead if I should be moving on to a third specialist.

I was late for a date with Air and Peter Mainstain, my moderately-upward-mobility business manager. Last summer, after The Dick, DeBlois, savaged Air over nothing one day, I searched for someone new. The Mainstain, who was smartly swathed in cashmere and spun entertaining vignettes about his Hasidic Jewish immigrant parents, seemed the obvious choice.

"I have some bucks now," I told The Mainstain. "Think twenty grand would keep E. McGuffin at bay?"

"Five'll probably do it," he smiled confidently.

He and one Stafford Matthews III, my tax attorney, met E., a middle-aged Caucasian woman they conference-called excitedly, and proposed I refinance Sanctuary — again — and split $100,000 with the IRS. Half a year later, I was still awaiting her response, running out of money. Every once in a while I'd ask The Mainstain or The III if we shouldn't be nudging her and they'd slough me off.

"He's gonna be a bit late," Air informed me when I got home. "Lemme go over some interview requests." She grazed a list whilst I wriggled and tugged at the brace. "This is one you should definitely do. Bernie Weinraub, the new ShowBiz guy for *The New York Times*."

"Oh, like they were so great the last time," I groused, but my body language betrayed my interest. I'd followed Bernie's byline for two decades. From far east to far west as he wended his way from Vietnam to Washington to Hollywood. From war to war to war, as it were.

"I've spoken to him a couple of times. He's a real nervous halalia, but he says he's a fan."

"That's what they all say."

"Ah c'mon, Jools, it's *The New York Times*. Julie Grau says she's never heard of a writer getting a piece with them for both hard- and softcover."

"Fine. Fine. Just so we do it at the Polo Lounge."

She booked My Luncheon with Bernie a week hence. "Pictures too," she cautioned as The Mainstain rang the gate-bell and I wondered if I could fake serenity for two braceless hours with sufficient aplomb to fool the camera.

The three of us hunched over the dining room table.

"The news is not good," The Mainstain began gravely. "Your nut is up to $15,000 a month and you're gonna have to pare down your expenses."

"Like I'm out having a grand old time."

"Nobody's accusing you but we have to cut somewhere!" He shot Air a meaningful look I pretended I noticed-not.

"You can't afford me," Air said, her voice expressionless. "I'll do New York with you for the PR. If you make it at all. But you have to let me go."

I inhaled deeply, looked her in the eye and fired Air.

Boom. Like that.

I'd fired Jackie boom-like-that the summer before the summer before. For a year I'd been warning her I had to trim my nut and neither one of us could really call to mind any other high school seniors still tended by a nanny, but that didn't make our parting any less traumatic. Stuck in New York on *YNELITTA*-legal, running out of money, I called her in London where she was tending her demented Mum to convey the terrible news. We both cried.

The day after, strenuously vetting with Julie Grau and Lesley Oelsner (Random House advocatess) I surrendered to stress and opted for a nervous breakdown on page 795.

"I did it! I confess! I'm the only one who ever got laid, did drugs, and listened to rock 'n' roll!" I screamed. "I have an affidavit! Signed in blood! Waitasecond lemme find it!" And I shunted hundreds of pages of my blood sweat etc. off the table with a Stanley Kowalski arm-sweep.

Joni sent me home the day after the day after.

It was Kate's first stint as The Keeper of The Flame and when I returned home the lights were out, the cupboard was bare of Evian and cigarettes and a mound of nosehair-twirling catshit lay prominently in the front hall.

"Kate!" I'd bellowed, exasperated. "From now on it's gotta be *Risky Business*! Do whatever you want while I'm gone but when I return everything's perfect . . ." Why am I invoking The Geff's movie to illustrate a life lesson? I worried. Because it's easy?

". . . except a hairline fracture on The Egg," Kate smiled wisely.

After booming Jackie like that, I reduced the gardener's and poolman's Sanctuarial obligations and summoned Angel Plumbing and Forthill Construction only in the most dire circumstances.

Scaling the financial cliff.

UP! Toward Zero.

Later, much later, after the departure of The Mainstain and Air, I played with the words to placate The Panic and gave myself an astrological thrill:

fire air earth water water everywhere . . .

Rain pelting loudly onto the skylight in the bathroom woke me and I knew there was a huge storm raging outside. I hoped that tree-roots hadn't grown through the ninety-degree-left-turn pipe that Angel Plumbing installed for runoff a decade ago. The cost of that job was more than I had in Checking.

Ignoring the knife serrating the back of my knee I got up, desperate to check the patio outside. The Pain's sharp steel surged down, subdividing around my outer calf and across my ankle, wrapping snakelike under the ball of my foot. I hurt in parts of my body I had yet to acknowledge but I limped outside.

Angel's drain brimmed sporadically with muddy waters but there was no overflow yet.

Maybe the rain will stop, I prayed, knowing such needy requests are almost always ignored.

I was in crisis mode by high noon.

For hours three of Angel's biggest boys fought an effluent tsunami overcoming the steps from the pool and the deck and the little rivers cascading down my densely ivied hill. Twice they dug three feet of mud from the patio but they couldn't begin to keep up with the persistent tide.

The garden and front yard were under two feet of brackish bronze water. It looked mutated.

"This is bigger than snaking the line, Jools," Ed said breathlessly into a cup of steaming industrial-strength coffee. Ed was the calm guy Angel sent to cope with type-A me and I'd never seen him thrown by anything. Beyond his fogged-up glasses I saw his rheumy brown eyes were overwhelmed and I was frightened for the first time.

By the afternoon a Forthill Construction team headed by Scott and clothed in spiffy yellow raingear accessorized with navy-blue high-topped rubber boots had surveyed the territory and tracked down the culprit.

Not God not Nature but a developer above me who had insufficiently sandbagged his illegally flattened terrain.

The jerry-built dyke had crumbled from the force of the storm — fallen as swiftly as the Maginot Line — and his boo-boo was pouring onto me.

Goddammit, who knows better than I the breakdown of the infrastructure!? I inveighed interiorly.

Why do *I* require this lesson?

"We're gonna call a city inspector," Mike Cross, the beautiful blue-eyed white-haired mason said, his heavy Irish accent curling around the consonants, and I felt the knife turn in the back of my knee.

"Why?"

"I have a plan for how to stop this," he gestured at the mud and waterfalls under which my stairs and hill and patio used to reside. "But we need it approved. *Plus . . .*"

"Plus," Scott said, "we wanna get a structural engineer out here to ascertain how *safe* the pool and deck are . . ."

Not safe?

Sanctuary?

What are they talking about, Mr. Rogers????

That afternoon during a break, we T.V.-witnessed the spectacle of a fifteen-year-old boy on a bicycle swept away in the flash-flooding Los Angeles River. Heroic rescue attempts. To no avail. Millions of viewers watched his small head speed past the camera, dip under the roiling sea of sludge, reappear and disappear forever.

Till the next Catastrophe, Live and Ringside.

We conferenced around my dining room table. Those Forthill Boys, the engineer, and a city inspector encased in orange rubber gear and black boots, a high-key psychedelic contrast with Scott's yellow-and-blue crew.

Is that dawn's early light or residual retinal flash?

I was in my brace, which helped the back and leg marginally, but felt like a corset. How did women wear these things all day long? No wonder they were always having the vapors and passing out and being the weaker sex.

They weren't getting enough oxygen!

"So here's the deal . . ." the structural engineer started. He was very tweedy, rather more nattily dressed than the rest of us, a strange choice considering he'd been scrounging around my deck and hills, so soaked they were dripping even in the sun, which had made a brief afternoon appearance.

"Tell me the deal," I smiled, because I found it best to start with a smile. Learned that from Nancy Collins.

"The flagstone's been pried loose, the hill and waterfall are unstable and more rain is forecast. We'd like you to get out of the house. We'll board up the back, stick a large sump pump in the pool —"

"And I'll approve the work Forthill has proposed," the inspector interjected in curt bureaucratese.

"Well if you're doing all this why do I have to evacuate?"

"We're real concerned about the flagstone around the pool."

"And there's no guarantee the Forthill dam will work . . ."

"So you're telling me that if I finally get to sleep and there's a heavy rain and a power failure so the pump can't keep up with the flood, it could wrench loose large chunks of flagstone which might careen down the hill through the doors to my bedroom and decapitate me?"

"In so many words . . ." the inspector and engineer cho-
rused/overlapped.

You . . . fuck . . . my . . . ?

"I was kidding."

"We're not," Scott said.

"Then I guess I better start packing and making some
plans," I said in a chirpy voice to overcome anxiety. I knew
they were overreacting to the Live at Five Swept-Away Cyclist
but then so was I.

Marshall McLuhan was wrong I thought as I packed and
wondered where to go. Television is *not* a cool medium. It is
hot hot hot and do I even have a credit card up and running?

"Don't be ridiculous you're not going to a hotel you're staying
at my place and when Kate comes in this weekend, she can
stay there, too. I'm going away . . ." Lance said in the same
insistent tone my daughter had used to inform me she was
flying west to keep me company through the ordeal of poverty-
stricken physical displacement. "I'll pick you up, we'll drop
the cat at the kennel, that's it . . ."

Lance. He of the wavy chestnut hair and ivory teeth and
azure-bluesky eyes. He who grew up happily in a wealthy
California ménage and was really named Lance. He who once
worked for CAA but had since opened his own personal management company.

"This is not my movie," he told Mike Ovitz shortly after he
read YNELITTA in galleys.

Lance lived in a bachelor-pad condo in Century City. Two
bedrooms, two baths, a kitchen with a breakfast nook and a tri-
angulated gas-fed-fireplaced living room overlooking the courtyard.

Kate approved.

"It's like hotel-living from the old days. Suite at the Sherry
Netherland, suite at the Ritz-Carlton, suite at the Kahala
Hilton," she opined wistfully. It was Kate's dream that any day
I'd score enough filthy lucre for us to indulge in a spontaneous
hejira to Hawaii.

"Yeah, but no room service."

We drove up Avenue of the Stars for a couple of empty high-rise/office-enclave blocks to the Century City Hamburger Hamlet and for the first time I was done and antsy before she was. Since she was four dinners with Kate had been punctuated by the steady ulcer-producing beat of where's-the-waiter-where's-the-waiter/where's-the-food-where's-the-food/where's-the-check-where's-the-check? until I complained about my Zantac intake.

That night we slept together in Lance's bed and the next morning she returned to school. My back was exponentially worse than premudslide, but Kate's visit had cheered me sufficiently to face the mess at Sanctuary. Although I wasn't sure I was up to coping with it.

When I arrived Scott and his men were unboarding the french doors along the patio.

"Hey," I said, glad to be home.

POWER OFF

"Oh fuuuuck," I wailed and Scott promised he'd stay until the God of Water and Power said, Let there be light . . .

"Oh fuuuuck!" I whine because no matter how hard I push I feel my POWER waning from ON to OFF and I have to finish this "Oscar Knight" fluff before noon.

Then suddenly all three phone lines spark into service.

Ooohhhh Noooo. But instead:

"Hi it's Julia and yadda yadda yadda. Yadda yadda. Yadda. . . ."

"Jools. It's Joni and Julie. We waited as late as we could. The paperback's debuting at One! Pick up the phone!"

"Huh-huh-huh," I gasp into the receiver.

"Did you hear?" Joni sparkles, so blood-and-money-ly. "You're Number One, Sunday, March fifteenth!"

"Beware the Ides of March," I blubber. "Beware The Peter Mayer," I add and they laugh uncomfortably.

A year ago, Peter had indeed outbid everyone else in an

exciting auction the week after *YNELITTA* hit Number One in hardcover. I was in San Francisco for a day of promo, and Air held more fingers up from studio to studio as the figure escalated whilst I deflected hostile queries re: Goldie's dirty hair. By the end of the day, *YNELITTA* had beaten the record previously held by *Barbarians at the Gate* for a nonfiction book, and I belonged to Viking/Penguin.

That evening we dined with Cynthia Robbins, who had interviewed me for the *San Francisco Chronicle*, and her socialite friend Jo Schumer, who made her money the old-fashioned way by outliving her filthy-rich husband. Infinitely more driven and ambitious than me in my most extreme woman-producer incarnation.

She wanted Victor's name and number, figuring no doubt that cutting her hair like mine would make her head like mine. And Cynthia had become a tad obsessed, like if she stuck to me she'd absorb The Secret by osmosis.

Whatever the fuck that was . . .

Leonida Karpik, the head of PR for Viking/Penguin, couldn't seem to grasp that publicity for the release of the paperback was going to be seriously constrained by my leaden lower lumbar.

Finally, I called Peter for some relief. Instead he excoriated me loudly for at least ten nonstop minutes, which made me wonder if he were performing for others in the room.

"Well, I guess you told me," I said tiredly when I could get a word in and he went off again. Finally, referring to the downtrodden Leonida, he shrieked:

"You're not very nice to the 'little people'!"

"I *am* the little people!" I exploded and hung up crying.

"No one's talked to me like that since my mother died," I joked weakly to Frankie on the phone a while later. I had complained to her for weeks about his unhelpful manner in the matter of my disc.

"Well, what can you do," she said. "He had the same problem and he used to have it shot up with novocaine so he could go skiing."

"How come Peter Mayer gets to be just another manic tough-guy? If I behaved similarly, I would be —"

"Committed to an institution . . . ?"

"Maybe this debut will make Peter a little nicer," I say now to Joni and Julie. "Mmmm, fat chance . . ."

Joni is saved from overexposure to empathy by call-waiting.

Victor. He sounds worse than I feel and that's saying something.

"Where are you? You sound funny/peculiar . . ."

"I'm in the hospital. I was admitted over three weeks ago . . . full-blown AIDS-induced pneumonia . . ."

Denial works. And then it doesn't.

"Circling the drain . . . as the doctors say to each other. Scrubbing off."

"Knocking on the doors of the Afterworld . . ." We crack up and Victor breaks into protracted coughing whilst I gasp with each sciatic samba step.

"Why'd you take so long to call?"

"I was working up to it . . ."

"So what happened?" Pain too much pain. Gimme details details instead of feelings feelings.

"Oh I went out partying Saturday night and Sunday I woke up gasping for air. I went into psycho-mode . . ."

"Whaddya mean?"

"Well I sort of *knew* I was dying and I had all this, y'know, *stuff* around the house. I crawled around the apartment on my hands and knees for five hours collecting leftovers and paraphernalia . . ."

"I used to crawl the carpet on a quest for chunks of freebase but they looked a lot like English muffin, which they'd force-feed me when I was awake. I can't tell you how many crumbs I turned on to in my life . . ."

I think that covers it.

"I mean, God forbid if I died my Italian Catholic family should find any of it!" Victor laughs. "So finally it's all disposed of, and I reeeeallly can't breathe . . .

"I dial 911 with my tongue and the paramedics arrive in ten minutes. They stick my insurance card between my teeth and race to New York University Hospital . . .

"I'm admitted immediately and as they're finally putting the oxygen mask over my face and I'm blacking out I think, 'Hey I'm forty-eight, I've hit all the clubs with Jools, I could go anytime now.' Jools, I gotta hang. Call me, okay?"

"I love you, VS," I say but he's already disconnected.

Click. Cher.

I dial Kate at school to impart the *YNELITTA*-good news/VS-bad news and to my chagrin she bursts into long mournful sobs. I there-there her until she calms down.

We say ILoveYouGood-bye.

I am impressed with the directness of her grief and heave my shoulders to see if anything happens. Maybe some Patsy Cline? IIIII fallll to peeeecessss. Dooodooodoooo.

Nothing.

Might I be too anguished to cry? Too medded-out?

More to the point, if some overweight schoolmarm from western Pennsylvania copped thirty-five hundred dollars on *Jeopardy!*, might I sob for an hour?

Click Cher.

I pop a Motrin and a Zantac, flop on the bed, crank the heating pad and plop Long John Silver onto it. I have taken to naming my leg like most boys I know name their willies.

I dial Air, roll my eyes through her impossibly long instruction-filled recorded greeting.

"Nowhere to go but down," I tell her machine and she picks up.

"I know," she says. "They called me first . . ." Oh right, I forgot. This is about you.

"And there's a fax from Peter Mayer, but it'll piss you off . . ."

"I wanna hear it!"

"'Dear Julia: Number One twice is not a bad thing —'"

"In other words it's a bad thing. This is sounding very B+ isn't good enough for a Zimmerman."

"He goes on to congratulate his sales staff for two paragraphs. Trust me, you don't wanna hear."

"It'll just make my leg freak out even more."

"I know the one: something very sharp stabbing the back of your knee, right?" Air understands viscerally. Many years ago she cracked her back breaking in a horse whilst whacked on Quaaludes. She's ambulatory compliments of a ten-inch stainless-steel rod implanted in her spine.

No wonder she elected to become stone cold sober.

ClickCher.

John Kennedy was plagued by his loused-up lumbar, his snafued spine, his broken back for two decades, it occurs to me as I print out "Oscar Knight."

Five minutes to twelve, right on schedule.

I save I fax I crank up the heating pad.

Tear off the despised brace and my leg implodes.

Jeez, Victor's afraid he'll die any minute and I'm afraid I won't.

Another Soma.

I lie down.

Tell me the truth, JFK.

Were you at all relieved at your moment of gist?

No more cortisone. No more pain pain pain pain?

I crash into fitful molar-meltdown sleep.

I dream of brief euthanasic sex with Jack Kevorkian.

He pulls my teeth one by one until I can't stand anymore.

So I get rid of him.

Send him away.

One.

Two.

ClickCherClickCherClickCher.

CLICK!

cher.

THOSE GIRLS
THE NURSE

Mama was a Tonkin tootsie and Papa was A. Rollin Stone.

A Huey pilot. AWOL.

INCOMING eradicated her family the day before the day before.

She walked barefoot for a hundred miles of Monsoon Madness, slogging through the Mekong Miasma.

Seeking Sanctuary.

A nurse who was born in Nebraska and came of age in Southeast Asia brought her — and a persistent heroin addiction — back to the States. Adopted her.

Small town derided and harassed them. Stepmonster never beat her Jones, so she beat her boat child.

One day the product was too fine and she choked on her vomit. Died in her surrogate progeny's arms.

I wanna be just like Mom, The Girl decided on the spot.

She headed west.

Toward the weather which was for once in her life dry.

She made a fine upscale caregiver. Bought a condo in Century City with the money They paid for her soul.

My secrets are stashed at a nurse's station on the eighth floor at Cedars, she tells Those Other Girls in Santa Monica singles bars. Saturday Night.

And they laugh like she's kidding, ha-ha.

Don't they know her first-and-last joke was being born?

"*Good Morning America* won't do a satellite hookup for twelve grand, I'm not a 9.4 on the Celebrity Scale!" I josh long-distance to David Debin, who's bailed on Hollywood for Woodstock again. David is one third of the Debin-Phillips-Devore triumvirate.

Gary Devore, who's still in town and whom I occasionally call GOD (I pretend his middle name is Otto) is the other side of the isosceles triangle and even though they're guys and sometimes we don't speak for months they're my soulmates.

Cranky writers like me.

Big bad middle-aged babies. Like me.

Funny and Jewish but not necessarily Jewish-funny. Like me.

We've been friends — good friends — for decades.

I've hung in through at least five ex-wives.

Debin and I crack up and then I start to cry.

"Debs," I whimper, "I can't walk . . ."

"This is not good, Jools."

"I gotta call Al Sellers. I'll callya back, okay?"

I lobby Sellers heavily for an outpatient shot of Demerol. He puts me on hold, conferences with Tony Alter, comes back on the line.

"You belong in the hospital. We're getting you a room on the orthopedic floor at Cedars. I'll meet you there. Should I send an ambulance?"

"No, I'll get there under my own steam," I sigh. Denial works until it doesn't. I give up.

"Within the next hour . . ."

"Within the next two . . ."

I make half a dozen calls: Hi it's Julia. I'm celebrating my debut at Number One by checking into Cedars.

I call Debin.

"I'm flying out," he says. "I'll be there within two days. Who's taking you to the hospital?"

"Those strong young boys."

"Good casting. I'm calling Gary."

Brooke and Todd speed me to the hospital, writhing like one of the baby rabbits Ramona likes to kill during springtime. In 329WOE, how on the nose.

"You look so small," Brooke mutters worriedly on the drive to Emergency parking on George Burns Drive.

"Uh-uh-uh," says Todd, the man of few words. Uh-uh-uh is very expressive for Todd.

Al Sellers is waiting with a shot which doesn't kill the pain and doesn't get me high. The experts try traction for about an hour, probably one of the longest hours I've ever endured.

Sellers stands on one side of my body-in-motion and Gary Devore, materializing from nowhere, on the other.

They tsk-tsk and rub my head — my hair which I hate! Presumably to soothe me.

I'm so preoccupied with staying perpetual, racing The Pain, I don't protest.

"The leg is atrophying, isn't it?!" I say to Sellers in a moment of vanity-inspired clarity.

"A bit."

I weep.

Sellers cancels the traction and puts me on an every-three-hour regimen of Demerol and Soma.

A nurse brings me a disposable heating pad with little canals of water coursing through the clear plastic. It provides relief, but it also reminds me of my recently decimated deck and hill, so I indulge in a solitary sobfest. By late afternoon it's engraved a crosshatched tattoo on my calf that won't disappear for months.

Tony Alter visits me early evening, twitches a bit from the heavy perfume emanating from floral arrangements that have been arriving all afternoon. Joni Evans. Peter Mayer. Peter Mainstain. Peter Nagai, third-string haircutter after VS and Dalee. Forthill.

Julia's Flower Farm.

"Surgery, right?" I whine.

"Surgery," he says. "But we need the leg to settle down first. How about Friday morning?" Three days hence.

"Friday the thirteenth? Not with the luck I've been having . . ."

"Well, the insurance company . . ."

"Fuck them . . . with *my* premiums . . ." $1040/month. Numerikarmically connected somehow to my IRS-irritation.

"Then Saturday the fourteenth it is," he agrees.

Just as he departs with his characteristic very-more-important-than-me bustle, Air arrives with my suitcase of clothes, toiletries, periodicals.

I shuffle through magazines whilst she hangs up two Dolce & Gabbana catsuits (one black one red) and my red-piped black Sergeant Pepper military jacket, my Don'tAsk/ Don'tTell drag, purchased on sale from Charles Gallay in more prosperous times. A century ago. *Vanity Fair, New York*. Condé Nasty bullshit bullshit. *People*, with a full-page ad for *YNELITTA*. They've flopped the picture and the copy's a tad melodramatic.

"This is bodice-ripping prose," I pout. "Think Anne Rice wrote it?" Air laughs. "Where's my *New Yorker*? My *Scientific American*?"

"Here. In the side pocket. With your blow-dryer."

"Oh yeah, I'll be doing a lot of shampooing . . ."

"Y'never know."

She tosses me the copies I've instructed her would be in the vicinity of my bed. One features an article on Seasonal Affective Disorder, from which I'm sure I suffer; the other a second-in-a-series piece on Africanized Bees. Kate's allergic to bee stings. I'm torn between attending to myself and caring for her and have therefore divided my limited perusal-time equally (a page for KP/a page for JP), the way Tanya used to measure Bing cherries from the can for Matthew and me, each by each, so neither of us felt shorted on dessert.

From what I can gather, the only successful combatant for SAD is a lightboard that costs at least thirty grand, which excludes me from the ranks of the recently cured. Besides, one has to sit in front of it for hours and I can't be still for minutes.

And the bees (who unlike our Euro-American species work twenty-four hours a day and abscond if they don't like the color of the sky) just keep interbreeding and expanding their territory northward. A few have been sighted in Canada. Who knows when the temperature will be too cold for them?

"I'm sorry I won't be able to be here for you," Air says sadly and brushes away brimming tears. She's taken a production gig with an indie prod, must leave tonight for one of the Carolinas, location-scouting.

"Oh this is about you?" I say aloud and to my surprise we crack up, then break into two-part-harmony laughtears.

"Well the last time it was. About me, I mean . . ."

"Next to last time."

"Penultimate time."

I'm the second chick.

No *I'm* the second chick.

"It was about you and me and Neil and Jody . . ."

We smile.

Neil is a top ten Beverly Hills plastic surgeon and Jody's his wife and they are probably the only heterosexual couple in my circle who still know how to have a good time.

I met them when Debin turned forty and Neil tucked his eyes. The four of us spent that New Year's in a limo with a couple of bottles of Cristal '79 and had a memorable evening. Shortly after that, Debin made his first escape to Woodstock, but Neil and Jody and I stayed in touch and broke bread occasionally at Mortons. We bonded several years ago, weeks before the crash of '87, on the downstroke of a hot September day when my trainer almost broke Brooke's face with a ten-pound weight.

I had presented him three sessions with her for his birthday and she was putting Brooke through his second circuit on the patio. Air and I were in the color-coding corner returning phone calls.

She put me on with MikeLevy MikeLevy and split for the kitchen to replenish our Evian supply, came bounding back instantly, white-faced with alarm.

"Hang up. You have to come with me now!" I followed her to the kitchen and emitted the same horrified gasp I did upon opening the door to Kate's room after a busy weekend or when I passed a mirror too closely with my glasses on.

Brooke lay on the counter shivering uncontrollably and the trainer was leaning over him. She lifted the towel she held to his face long enough for me to see a nasty gash along his right cheek. His face was pallid and his eyes were vacant and he was gushing blood.

"What happened?!" I shot the trainer a cold glance and she focused on her Nikes.

"A weight fell . . ." she muttered.

I raced for the phone and dialed Sellers, who told me that to stanch the crimson tide we must continue pressure on the wound.

"I'll meet you at Cedars Emergency if you want," he said, "but this sounds like a job for a plastic surgeon. Aren't you and Neil good friends?"

"Lemme try that," I said.

"Call me back if you need me."

I instructed Air to get another towel, continue bearing down on Brooke's battered bone structure. Checked the time. Six o'clock. I dialed Neil at home and Jody picked up. I ran down the situation breathlessly.

"*Neil's* jogging somewhere with *his* trainer," she laughed. "Hold on. Lemme beep him."

"La la la la la la la . . ." I hummed to pass eternal seconds.

"What?!" Air queried anxiously.

"She's finding Neil." Jody came back on the line.

"Okay, honey, wrap him up and bring him to Neil's office. We'll meetcha there."

"Thankyou thankyou thankyou."

"Don't be silly."

We packed Brooke into 329WOE and I blasted down the hill and through the flats into Doctor Heaven on Bedford Drive, noisily berating the trainer who sat glazed and mute in the backseat with Air.

Neil and Jody were waiting.

Neil escorted Brooke to one of his *three* operating theaters, Air comforted the traumatized trainer in the waiting room and Jody and I repaired to Neil's office.

"Honey, you gotta joint with you?" Jody grinned conspiratorially and shut the door.

Jody and I had been decrying the limited availability of

decent organic bud for the past year. Not to mention its escalating price. One by one the growers in Humboldt County
were being driven from the business by their neighbors.

Our particular guy was now in his sixties, high-strung and
vacationing between runs — which were causing him escalating stress and paranoia — with increasing frequency.

"Guess who's buying the land?" he'd grinned the last time
I saw him.

"Who?"

"Hasidic Jews. Hah!"

"That'll serve Those Darn Republicans right!" I said and
wondered if The Mainstain's parents had gobbled up a parcel.

I had pulled on Don'tAsk/Don'tTell, which was certainly
from the right era for such a leftover; I scrounged through
pocket after pocket, finally found a roach that judging from
the color of the lipstick and the smell of the cologne was at
least three years old. It took some time to get it lit. I passed it
to Jody who took a long grateful toke.

"Long time no see, what's up?" I said.

"Well my father is terminal, I'm adopting a baby and I just
had liposuction." Jody took another puff and smiled.

"Where?" I asked, homing in on the least taxing issue, so
to speak.

"Oh, you know, saddlebags . . ."

Neil, like many in his profession, practiced assiduously —
compulsively, one might say — on his wife. An occupational
hazard, I supposed. They had met, actually, when Jody sought
his services to repair a botched eye job performed by a less-
skillful, less-pricey practitioner.

It took her a year of purposeful pursuit to snare him.

"Did it hurt?"

"Big-time. It's like being beaten up from the inside, and
you know how low my threshold is. I've been on Neil's case
about this for years but he wanted to track his patients and
some studies before he did it on me.

"So this year, for my birthday . . ."

"It's a hell of a world," I said, referring to our casual

attitude toward altering our physiognomy, not to mention what we considered appropriate gifts from a SignificantAutre.

"Hey," Jody said defensively, "I'm a whole size smaller!"

"Wow!"

America the Superficial judged the book (it didn't read) by its cover. Me, as patriotic as the next guy, included.

THOSE BOYS/THOSE GIRLS
THE PERSONAL TRAINER

Mommy played lacrosse and Papa was a Rolling Stone.

It spent a decade on the pro circuit.

And fucked all Those Boys.

All Those Girls.

It had no attention span and got bored.

Placed third last year and decided to hang up Its Nikes/Adidas/Converses/Reeboks.

Moved to California where It knew a lot of people.

Makes house calls.

Every once in a while when It hits the wall on body-sculpting Those Girls and Boys, just to be as nasty as It wants to be It says, "Maybe liposuction?"

And leaves for a secret rendezvous.

One morning shortly after Brooke's thin facial scar turned from red to white, Jody woke up and spotted two tiny triangles of unwanted flesh at the bottom of her buns in her recently installed three-way mirror. She called Neil, begged him to blow out an impending rhinoplasty, then headed his O.R. for some impromptu liposuction. If I were interrogated nonstop by the Prozac Posse, I'd have to concede that Jody is a junkie for the occasional surgical adventure. An occupational hazard, I supposed.

The triangles didn't show on Jody prone, so Neil decided to try something new. He dosed her with Valium, shot the triangles with Novocaine, and had his nurse hold Jody (bare-assed and incredibly relaxed) upright.

Down on his knees he went with his trusty fat-vacuum. Cut cut, zip zip, stitch stitch and off to the Bistro Gardens for lunch.

Neil was pretty excited with himself because nobody performed surgery, even as gross a procedure as liposuction, on a patient who wasn't hors de combat.

Jody was equally pleased because she didn't have to look in her new mirror and be annoyed.

"Maybe you're onto something, Neil."

"I'd love to try it out on someone else," he said, "but who? It would have to be the same kind of layout, as it were."

And then they locked eyes over their nouvelle salades and exclaimed together, "Julia's points!" It was true. The points showed up more when I was sitting, even when I kept myself at an unhealthy low weight and I'd complained to Neil about them ad infinauseam.

They called me from the carphone after lunch to report on their groundbreaking foray. As it happened, there was a Santa Ana brewing and I was on the patio catching rays.

"We're on our way . . ."

I rushed indoors to pull on a high-cut bathing suit I wouldn't *think* of wearing to the beach.

We convened in the driveway. From a tape playing in the idling Blazer Serafina, their adopted daughter, sang "tomow-wow tomowwow" in a high peepy voice I recognized from Kate's childhood.

Neil pulled a pen from his pocket and squatting, started to draw on my hips. He talked to himself whilst Jody recounted her latest day-trip on the Miracle Mile of Makeover.

"I *did* get a bit faint but if I can take it you can take it, Jools, 'cause I'm a woos when it comes to pain and you're—"

"Such an expert!"

"So when should we do this?" Neil straightened up from his body-painting and smiled.

"Neil, I can't afford it. Taxes. Cash dearthage . . ."

Christ he should know. Neil was one of the names on my lengthening Personal Debt List.

The one I dismissed every month in favor of the IRS.

"That's okay. It's research. I'll front it to you."

"What about after the release of the English version of the hardcover?" I suggested. "Nothing like a little *more* pain as a reward for all the pain."

"Nonsense, honey," Jody said authoritatively. "In the long run, you'll forget the pain and it *will* be a reward!"

"That's what they said about childbirth!"

We cracked up.

"Tomowwow tomowwow tomowwow's another day . . ."

Pre/Post-Op Confabs. Tests. Pictures.

First, Gerry snapped Polaroids. She was one of five nurses who would throw themselves in the path of a berserk DeLorean to save Neil. He repaid their loyalty with whatever cosmetic adjustments they desired.

"He did my stomach for Christmas last year," Gerry confided. "You're the perfect candidate," she said encouragingly. "Just these two little spots . . ."

I grabbed them, and we focused on Les Points for a quiet moment. "Yo, suck this!" I exclaimed, and laughed as she fired off a commemorative shot.

Then a short interchange with Neil focusing on postoperative care:

"If I'm going to suffer, let me be as high as an elephant's eye." As an ex–drug abuser I felt I had a right to make such a request.

"Dilaudid, I should think."

"Dilaudid."

Whoop-de-doo. Something to anticipate besides cardiac arrest.

Last, the required-by-law meeting with the anaesthesiologist, Kevin, a pear-shaped polyester priss from Pasadena who insisted on walking me through his part of the procedure step by arduous step. He spoke slowly and condescendingly, apparently unable (unwilling?) to differentiate between me and the Arabian princesses who generally padded down Neil's quiet corridors, since they were among the few who could still afford his services.

And The Stars, whose names Neil *never* divulged but I saw them at his parties.

I knew it was Kevin's job to tell me all the ways I might accidentally expire in Neil's O.R. because Air had warned me.

Air had started this all in the first place. Well in the second place. After Jody. She was preoccupied with breast implants from the moment she knew Neil and I were friends; we saw him together to discuss personal tune-ups. Neil and I discussed crownal, eyes (upper and lower), nose, boobs, and liposuction on the points, which was the only procedure I really coveted.

Blessedly short of coin I passed on everything.

Air had squirreled away a little something, an inheritance from an ancient granny she detested, and went ahead with the augmentation. She'd had arcane, sometimes startling health problems ever since but she never regretted it.

Finally Kevin laid a Dalmane, a Valium and a scopolamine patch on me, along with a xeroxed pre/post-op instruction sheet. The Dalmane was for sleep, the Valium for serenity and the patch to counteract the noxious effect anaesthetic had on the human organism.

Aspirating on her vomitus is what torpedoed Sunny Von Bulow into coma. Should I remind Kate to pull the plug if the patch proved ineffective?

"I fight downs," I told him. "It takes a lot to put me out —"

"I'll be the judge of that —"

"Hey just trying to be helpful . . ."

I hated this prick, especially since our little chat had forced me to reflect on the downside of point-removal: my premature demise. Sooner or later all human endeavor led to the mortality quandary.

I drove home in tears.

• • •

"I don't approve but I'm prepared to be supportive!" Kate exclaimed. She of the narrow waist and hips, the cellulite-less thighs, the pert protuberant bosom. Donnez-moi un fucking break. We were indulging in our night-before-I-might-die mother-daughter discussion in the kitchen.

"That sounds a lot like what you said about the book."

"No, *that* was: I'm very proud of you, I'm one-hundred-percent supportive, I wish you hadn't done it!"

Kate was considering a prelaw college curriculum. A good choice. Then she could be argumentative for a living, how U.S. of American, circa nineteen ninetynothing.

"This is not the way to send me off to a general anaesthetic, *plus* these points drive me wild, I hate them, I've hated them for three decades, which was once the average person's total life expectancy!"

"What's your point here, Jools?" Kate smiled.

"No, *where's* your point here, Jools. *More* to the *point!*"

"Oh well, I suppose having something removed is better than having something put in," Kate observed solemnly.

"Referring, of course, to surgery of the *plastic*, not *heart*, kind," I said and we laughed together softly.

Later on, she trundled into my room. "I can't sleep, Mom . . ."

"Presurgery anxiety . . ."

I'd already applied the scopolamine patch behind my clean right ear and taken my own Xanax, eschewing Kevin's stash. After a brief interior debate with my better self I offered her a choice, along with a précis of possible side effects. She considered them seriously for a second, pulled a just-say-no face.

"Liposuction is a piece of cake, right?" she said.

"Piece o' cake."

She yawned, embraced me in a big hug and headed for her room. I jumped out of bed, suddenly restless.

Fifteen agitated minutes later, in an impulsive better-living-through-chemistry moment I popped the Dalmane.

I slept and dreamt of catsuits.

• • •

Fussing with my angel robe whilst he drew along my points, I strategized with Neil. Thump thump pound pound. Was that my heart, or were they now piping rap music into the O.R.? One posed this sort of question to oneself in Hollywood.

"So we'll put you *out* out and turn you on your stomach, and I'll do this weird top part on your buttocks, then we'll turn you over and wake you. You'll sit up, so I can isolate them—"

"I should straddle the bed, so they really stick out, don't you think?" If I was doing this, I wanted it ALL GONE. I'd heard a few horror stories about doctors who weren't lipo-literate leaving curls and crevices and lumps. Apparently, there was a necessary waving back and forth of the vacuum, but Neil was an artist and I trusted him.

I just wished I didn't have to be *out* out at all.

What a shame, I ruminated as Kevin inserted an IV drip, if I died on the table for something so silly.

I awoke abruptly in a nasty mood. The angel robe fluttered at my sides. I turned over, sat up and straddled the slab. It was a very crowded room: me, Neil, Kevin, Eloise, Neil's right-arm nurse. A second nurse hovered in the background. I experienced a hot flash and removed the robe. Nobody winked an eye, but they exchanged glances.

Neil moved fast.

A slice the size of a knick and insertion of a chrome instrument that looked very like the curling iron I used on backswept VS haircuts of The Seventies.

I peeked over Neil's shoulder at the receptacle on the floor behind him catching my fat, which was in fact a viscous gray-white goo, and I wondered if one's internal toxicity could be determined by the color of one's fat. I was about to ask, but Neil commanded sharply, "Be still!"

Kevin rubbed my head comfortingly. Was he kidding?

Didn't he know *nobody* touched my head!?

"Keep your hands off my hair!" I heard myself yelling, but he continued stroking. Men! I grabbed his hand, pushed it away.

"Be still! Don't move!" Neil hissed. I looked down at my soon-to-be-previous right point. The one with the curling iron jutting from it.

"Neil," I coached, "there's some more over here."

I'm alive I'm alive . . . and I'm detached! I've always *wanted* to live here. Yo Neil, suck this!

I indicated the spot with my index finger but I also appeared to be reaching for Neil's curling iron. Was I really about to engage in a mud-wrestling match with Neil over control of this process? I sensed Kevin peripherally, magic-fingers at the ready, which escalated my wildness a notch.

Okay, Neil, let's discuss our creative differences.

"Don't even think about it, Kevin!" I shouted. "Tell him to go away!" I demanded. Eloise signaled Kevin with her eyes and he left. The other nurse wisely followed suit. Neil moved like the wind. He couldn't wait to get rid of me.

"You could add another one over here," Eloise suggested, indicating the knick on my right hip flexor, and Neil stitched obediently. He looked over me at her: May I go now? She nodded and wheeled me into recovery. "Try not to move around for a while," she smiled, strapping steristrips over Neil's needlepoint. "I'm sending Ariel in to keep you still."

I sat up.

"Planning on going somewhere?" Air said in the calm voice she used when she was nervous.

"Why am I so defiant?" I asked myself.

"Jools, you're high." Uh-oh. The Answer to the Question. Had I spoken out loud? I lay down.

Thump thump pound pound.

My throbbing hips syncopated to the beat of my heart.

"I wanna go home," I whined to Air.

"Soon. Very soon . . ."

I carried on vociferously until I was allowed to dress. Eloise wrapped an industrial strength girdle around me, fastened the snap-out crotch. It reminded me of torture-structures

Tanya wore in the fifties. She wouldn't have had to if exercise had been de rigueur, or if liposuction had been an acceptable practice. "Keep this on until he sees you in five days. Except for showers . . ."

Kevin insisted on escorting us right to the car. Rolling my eyes I swatted at the air around me, brushing him away.

"He's just doing his job," Air whispered.

"If he touches my head I'm going ballistic," I whispered back and Air smirked.

"Oh and where are you now?"

I'd chosen to wear a pale pink Madeleine Gallay peplum jacket over a serviceable black Ghost pleated shmatte (something, per instructions, easy to put on and take off) and bled through the bandages on the drive home.

"A test for Beverly Crest Cleaners," I said as Air parked in the tight little garage, "or we'll dye it persimmon."

I jumped from the car and pranced up the steps as if I were just returning from a medium-fierce afternoon game of tennis.

I downed two Dilaudid and an antibiotic with a shot of Jagermeister at the kitchen sink. Kate and Air urged me to bed but I marched instead to my full-length mirror and tore off my dress to examine The Results.

I saw right away that the points were gone.

Save for a small wobble on the left.

I focused on it for a moment.

"What about *this*?" I objected to Air.

"What?"

"*This*! This . . . furfel . . ." Air's brow flickered.

Aha! She saw it too!

"What . . . furfel?" she said in the neutral monotone she affected to lie and tossed me a pair of loose pajamas.

I pulled them on and flopped into bed. Ouch!

"You think I'll miss my dollops now that they're gone?"

Was that a real question or was that the Dilaudid talking?

Air burst out laughing.

"Are you ca-raaaazy? Not for one minute!" she said positively, her voice absent its preceding prevarication.

The phone rang and the machine picked up.

"Well I hear you were just impossible — excuse me, unique, what a surprise — it's Jody, honey, pick up pick up . . ." I reached the phone before Air.

"Impossible?"

"I said unique, too. I hear it took a record amount of drugs to put you under and you woke up immediately in a savage state—"

"Kevin ignored my instructions re: my capacity. And then he had the nerve to pat me on the head!"

"Do you know you made him cry?" Jody laughed.

"I made *him* cry. He was horrible."

"Kevin is one of the sweetest people on this earth. . . ."

"Kevin is an asshole and we can't talk about him anymore. He makes my hips hurt."

"Stay off your feet, honey. I'll call you tomorrow. . . ."

"What did she say?" Air wanted to know.

"She said I should lie still. Jeez, that's the first time a woman's ever said that to me . . ."

I shifted around, releasing a swift barrage of tiny arrows that pierced my hips from deep inside. Whoa. Big pain. How did women stand this from knee to ass?

And when — exactly — did I get to be as high as an elephant's eye?

"What about this furfel?" I queried crossly, compliments of five days of painkillers, and Neil rubbed the area forcefully. Out, damn spot! It was hard and substantially more black and blue than the rest of my hips, which were verrry black and blue. It definitely was NOT there pre-liposuction. On the other hand — or hip, as it were — neither were the despised points.

I had some nerve complaining.

"Massage it and stay in the girdle . . ." Neil decided. "I can't really tell if it's a curl for six months. Of course, I'll fix it, zit zit, if it is."

"A girdle?!"

"I never knew anyone who wore spandex as regularly as

you." It was true. Tights. Boots. Major jacket. I'm there, pick
me . . .

"Duuuude," I whined. "You know how I like perfect."

"Not any more than me," Neil commiserated and ripped
off the steristrips. The knicks were sunset orange–lavender
dings. Nothing. I wasn't wrong to dream of catsuits.

"Whooooaaaa . . . bay-beee . . ."

Neil smiled. "Damn right," he said, and we hugged good-
bye, now that we weren't doctor/patient anymore, but friends
again. A good thing, too, because in the wrong light I was
sure I saw dewlaps forming under my chin.

Several weeks after Neil's experiment, when the bruises
faded, I charged too much against a Visa card some New
Hampshire bank had *foisted* upon me to purchase the Dolce &
Gabbana catsuits now hanging in the closet in my lonely hospital room.

I'd never have *considered* them before liposuction.

I wear them all the time, even at my healthy weight,
although with all the shots my hips have exploded into one
giant furfel.

Funny how I obsessed on my mortality on the elective
surgery, I think and sink uncomfortably into the arms of
Morpheus. If the excision of L-5 doesn't excise The Pain I'd
just as soon die on the table . . .

The English nurse charged with deploying me to surgery is a
nasty piece of work and my leg flips out from our extrava-
gantly unpleasant interaction. I insist on another escort to the
operating theater and ultimately I'm wheeled down by a light-
eyed mulatto male nurse who keeps acting like we know each
other.

He reminds me he's Earl, the dude who set up my torture-
traction a couple of days ago when I was first admitted.

"So much for what effect Demerol has on short-term memory," I kid and he nods empathetically.

"Had L-5 removed two years ago today," he smiles. "You'll

be much better in a couple of hours, you'll see . . ." He persuades the anaesthesiologist to dose me immediately as I pin a post-it with Dad's New York number on Tony Alter's scrubs. Dad has volunteered to come west but I'd just have to worry about him worrying about me, so I've told him I have sufficient support. Ditto Kate.

"Don't forget to call my Daddy," is the last thing I remember.

I awaken in recovery and my leg doesn't hurt. There are parts of it that I don't feel, but numb is good for now. I confer with Laura Audell, the Princess of Pain Management, on the matter of which heavy drug should fill my PCA.

"May I be breathing in a detached sort of way?"

She prescribes Dilaudid. The doctors' drug of choice. The one with which they down themselves when they need to kick back.

Mara's waiting for me in the hall when I'm rolled up to my room. And Debin's on his way. I figure the young friends have seen me through the emergency and my contemporaries are for aftercare.

I'm conscious enough to notice a catheter's been inserted and insist noisily that they call my doctor at home to get permission to disconnect it. I speak to him briefly and convincingly.

"You know the disc was exploded?" he says, sounding impressed. With himself? With me? "We had to scrape it off muscle and bone and cartilage . . ." With himself. I tell him crossly to cease and delete his explication de disc by reminding him I was once a filmmaker.

I'm very visual, I have complained already when he grossed me out explaining that discs look and feel like crabmeat.

"You'll never be able to pull yourself up," the nurse snorts condescendingly but she removes the catheter.

"Wanna bet? Hey I work out with weights."

I drag myself sideways then up by pulling mightily on the bedrails.

"No wonder you have back problems," she scoffs and splits with a signed *YNELITTA* under her arm.

I've brought a few newly minted paperbacks for my incarceration. I'm not in a position to lay cash tips on anybody and just the other day the entire staff exalted in the fact that I was a question on *Jeopardy!*

For two hundred dollars; not too much not too little.

"So here I am, holed up at Cedars Sinai post–back surgery, which is as good a way as any to commemorate the prospect of watching myself drift down and off the list like a drop of water sliding inevitably to the bottom of a hill . . ."

I crankily dispense some Dilaudid from my PCA. My Ides of March visitor tosses me her copy of the *New York Times* Bestseller List and I permit myself a small sly grin.

Yo suck this! *YNELITTA* LIVES!

Christine Cuddy slumps in the chair next to my bed.

"Can you believe it? Penguin Books wanted to do satellite hookups of you in your hospital bed . . ."

"Wild with discal discomfort and whacked on Demerol. Oh yeeaaahhh, *that* would've sold *millions* of copies . . ."

Michael, my first-and-last-ex-husband, comes to visit. We embark on a soulful journey up and down and around and around the North and South Towers, me trailing my PCA. We discuss our rise, fall, demise, daughter. I feel we're finally making peace with each other. Another patient on the floor runs after me to sign a copy of my book, which someone's brought her as a present, and Michael, who used to flinch at moments like this, smiles approvingly.

"That's so cool," he drawls and walks me back to my room. He kisses me on both cheeks, like a favored niece.

"Good-bye."

"Good-bye."

GOOD BYE.

Good-bye yourself.

The Dilaudid induces exhilarated phantasms — Is that Top

Quark I see before me? Alternating with wicked nightmares underscored by constant sadness. Somebody's sobbing all night.

Who *is* that? Me?

My neighbor, hidden behind a consistently closed door, has been weeping for two days running sans surcease. When a nurse drops by to track my vitals I ask her about it.

"Oh, it's a terrible story," she says brightly, relishing her moment. "Beautiful girl, nineteen years old, a model . . . she has bone cancer . . .

"They had to amputate her hands and feet."

I gasp, chastened: The nerve of me to feel a moment of anguish and the nurse nods, Indeed! and thrusts a pen in my hand to sign her *YNELITTA* before she continues her rounds.

Debin arrives and I'm compelled to repeat the story immediately.

"Jesus . . . God . . ." he mutters.

"Jesus and God had nothing to do with it! Filthy humanity did it! I wonder if she grew up near a nuclear power plant . . .

"Or went to a grade school with peeling lead-based paint . . .

"Or slept in a room with asbestos trickling through the ceiling."

Gary Devore materializes simultaneously with the delivery of an auspicious-looking refrigerated package from Lynn. When she'd asked during our high-octane prehospital phone call what she could do to make me feel better, I'd wisely gasped, "Send caviar!" and she laughed.

"Lynn," I sobbed. "I figured it out. You don't wanna have too little money because then all you think about is money. And you don't wanna have too much pain because then all you think about is pain."

Too much pain too little money too few pages.

No wonder I'd become so limited.

"I have to go," I whimpered. "Too much paaaain."

"*Life* is paaaain," Lynn said.

"You have a Jewish grandparent, I know it! Next year I want too much money and too little pain."

Lynn chortled mordantly.

"This is so cute!" I exclaim. "I love how literal Lynn can be sometimes."

Gary and I tear at the package.

"Whoa, God. This is major!" I exclaim. "Let's take the long walk to the nurse's station . . ."

It's my first day off the PCA and I'm entirely too excited. When we return to my room a half hour later laden with armsful of crackers and some plastic cutlery, Gary pries open the two-ounce tin and I regale him with the grim fairy tale of the amputated hands and feet of the woman — check that, *girl* — next door.

"Jesus! God . . ."

"Jesus, God, had nothing to do with it! And yadda yadda yadda. Yadda yadda. Yaddayadda. Yadda."

We finish the fish eggs in fifteen minutes.

3:00 P.M.

Debin and I await Tony Alter's arrival restlessly. He's shown up before seven every morning but not today. He bustles in, finally, with *YNELITTA* tucked ostentatiously under his arm. He checks the dressing and pronounces it fine, signs my release form, writes some script for erythromycin and Vicodin ES, and tells me he'll see me at his office in ten days. He turns to leave.

"Oh by the way, I took this on a plane last week to visit my daughters," he says, indicating my book, "and I have two words for you: Grow up!"

We fill my prescriptions at Rox-San Pharmacy, head up AlmostColorado Canyon. It is late afternoon and getting dark. The maid's beat-up car is parked in the driveway. Uh-oh.

It takes us a moment to absorb that the electric gate is inoperable. We ease out of the car, pry open the gate and edge up the steps.

A shiny black stray cat who's been sussing out the premises since New Year's Day crosses our path. He turns for a moment, hisses and blows out his fur. His eyes sparkle opalescent green and amber in the setting sun. He flies up a hill of ivy and disappears into foliage. He fills my heart with dread.

A dark beast slouching toward . . . Sanctuary?

We approach the front door apprehensively and peek inside. No lights. Ohhh nooo . . .

"Amalia? What's going on?"

"Eet was like theese when I got heere."

She hands me a yellow shut-off notice.

"Waitasecond, I'm not *that* poor," I say to Debin. DWP, food, phone, health and car insurance. Credit cards. I don't know how I manage it but I get those bills paid. If there's anything left it goes to the mortgage and the IRS. "I better call Tardia," I say, referring to my bookkeeper at the new management firm. The perfect name for The Someone cutting my late-payment checks.

"Look, there's a number here. I'll deal with this," Debin says and he dials on one line whilst I dial another.

Call-waiting. Fanny and Zoe, ready to visit. I do a short précis, tentative title, *I've Got (No) Power!* Helpless, Fanny asks if they can pick up anything on their way over.

"I wanna coffee malt!" I sob unreasonably and switch back to yelling at Tardia. Call-waiting.

Gary Devore on his way.

Debin sweet-talks DWP and Tardia, who hasn't received a bill in months, reconfirms their computer's input of her firm's address. Apparently DWP has been sending my tab to The Dick, DeBlois, who decided that six months after I fired him, he was no longer required to forward my bills.

Water and power are restored in forty-nine minutes.

But who's counting?

Fanny and Zoe and Gary and Debin redesign and rearrange the area on and around my bed. With a flourish, they move the phone, the wastebasket, and simplify the bedding whilst I prop myself uncomfortably in a chair in the color-coding corner. I sip my coffee malt like a child, soundtracking their efforts with a ferocious sucking noise not dissimilar from nails on a blackboard.

"So The Dick got the *pink* late notice and the *red* shut-off notice, right?" I fume when they've finished and I've climbed into bed. "And I gave him thirty-five hundred dollars in kiss-off money for goodwill! When I could ill afford it!" I had planned to devote myself solely to recuperation upon returning from the hospital, but The Dick's nastiness spins me in another direction. "I hate my life!" I wail. I jump out of bed and try to pace. "*Ow!*" I yelp.

"You've got to calm down!" Fanny and Zoe shout.

"Get into bed!" Debin bellows. Debin generally whines at a half-decibel above a half-whisper.

I obey but I feel myself palpitating into hysteria.

"The water and power shut-off feels like a symbol!"

"I know, I know . . ." Gary soothes.

"We understand," Those Girls croon.

"No you don't understand! No! You don't know! You don't know what it's like! To be a hit! Academy Award. Number One twice. And I can't pay my taxes and I've got less than three thousand dollars to my name. I've succeeded again and again. Over and over. Right into the toilet!

"And this fucking back!"

I burst into noisy tears, but I don't have the energy to sustain them. The racking pulls at my stitches.

Well there it is. My Shakespearean soliloquy.

I snurfle and reach for a tissue.

Ow. Ow ow owowowowow . . .

Those girls study their hands.

Gary coughs.

Debin surveys the room.

Are they as appalled by this unseemly display of self-pity as I am?

Silence. Silence. Silence.

Is this white noise?

My ears begin to ring with it.

"Yeah," Debin finally half-whispers, "but do you have your hands and feet?"

"Are you sitting down?" Pierce O'Donnell flirts over a crackling early-morning phone connection and I have to laugh.

It hurts.

I'd connected with Pierce last year. Just as the hardcover *YNELITTA* drifted off the Bestseller List.

We met for drinks at the Polo Lounge.

Pierce was Hawaiian-princess large — tall and heavy — and oozed confidence. With a boyish face and a shock of sandy hair. Blue eyes hidden behind glasses and large white teeth when he smiled, which was often.

Now here's a guy with balls! I thought.

Here's someone to send after Big Bad Bert Fields.

Pierce called from Martha's Vineyard a few days later to inform me he'd been chatting up Arthur Liman, Power Lawyer to The Power Brokers.

"He says David Geffen would rather throw money at you than be embroiled in a lawsuit," Pierce chuckled.

"You're underestimating his anger," I said.

"We'll see," he replied and I saw those chompers. I knew he thought me self-aggrandizing, and I wanted to correct him: I know I'm not that important, but he's that petty. I didn't.

Litigation felt so negative, though.

And foreign, oddly. I'd only ever defended in court, not complained, and I suspected the deck (even in civil cases) was stacked in favor of the defendant.

"You don't really wanna do this, do you," Pierce said after his assistant researched some similar cases and discovered the odds based on precedent were only 50-50.

"I do but I don't. And I hate our prospects."

"Yeah, me too."

After we hung up I was struck by how similar Pierce's voice was to Rush Limbaugh's. Which was funny/ha-ha *and* funny/peculiar, considering his civil-libertarian stance.

It turned out they *were* alike, though.

A bully is a bully is a bully . . .

"Dude, I just got home yesterday. From major surgery. I'm *lying* down! Where are you?"

"I'm on a runway at Kennedy Airport waiting for MGM Air to de-ice their wings. How are you?"

I perform the most entertaining DWP-meets-The-Dick routine I can muster, given the hour.

"Jeez . . ."

"Go after him, Pierce, okay?"

"I've got something better. I saw Alberto Vitale yesterday. . . ." Pierce feels so glum about not suing The Geff for me that he's gone to Alberto for accelerated paperback royalties. Gratis.

"Y'know I've been so wild, I forgot to tell you how short he is . . ."

I'd considered instructing Pierce to make his entrance on his knees.

"Oh I was plenty shorter by the time he saw me," Pierce chuckles. "He kept me waiting thirty minutes . . ."

"Here's the deal. They're gonna release your first two paperback payments. With a small deduction for lost interest of course. It'll come to about $125,000."

"Wooowww. That's the best news I've heard since Nixon resigned. Thankyou thankyou thankyou . . ."

"My pressure," Pierce joshes.

Hardeeharhar-and-a-hodeehoho.

Damn right the first two payments.

Probably didn't hurt that I debuted at One with back surgery.

They looove to help you out when you're a cripple. Grrrrr. . . .

Quit complaining Jools it's an early Spring.

Kate'll be home for summer vacation soon.

Six weeks, tops.

Hey. You've got your hands and feet.

Dear Julia Phillips

I am President of the Junior Class at Saint Andrews.

I read your book. You're my role model. Could you
sign the enclosed three by five card so I can hang it on
my wall?

I'm your role model?
Then we're in big fucking trouble!
I laugh and tack the letter to the bulletin board.
Next to macho-cunt/self-centered-piece-of-shit.
I'm your role model?!
I pace The Creature's room in tiny distressed circles.
Ouch!

Craning my neck, I suss out The Orthopedic Star's incision in
the full-length mirror, emit the required horrified gasp and
pull my shorts up quickly. Denial will have to work for a
while. At least until that looong exceptionally ugly bright-red
scar fades into dim memory.

I walk to the kitchen for a large bottle of E-coli-flushing
Evian and open a bag of chips as Todd will be here soon and
Todd, like all dancers, loves the occasional junk-food binge.
What better occasion for such a treat than Oscar Knight?

"Don't freak out for the first month after you get home,"
one of the Cedars' nurses had advised on release day. "You're
gonna get tired suddenly. Just don't push too hard and lie
down."

Tired is not a word I've ever heard sprouting from my lips.
Nor is the concept of not-pushing-too-hard. Or lying down,
for that matter. Nevertheless, halfway through The Creature's
room I'm so exhausted I have to take five on the floor. I know
I'm just a traveler through standard postoperative terrain, but
the journey's depressing me, particularly since the recently
scored accelerated royalties are dwindling faster than I can
remind myself:

Yo tengo un tax problema!

We settle in for the long night as Billy Crystal is wheeled in à
la Hannibal Lecter.

Todd, the man of few words, has been the only one of my close circle who's been discreet enough not to wonder aloud if I'm going to rate an opening line again this year.

"I hear he's got the flu. 103 temperature," Todd confides. "Tried to cancel this afternoon . . ."

I don't know his sources but Todd is a wellspring of heard-along-the-circuit information.

"Sick like that is a lot like drugs. He'll either be terrible or he'll be great!" I exclaim, looking forward to the show, considerably less entertaining now that Fred Hayman was fashion consultant and had replaced the celebrities' spectacularly bad taste with subtle-siennaed *safe* taste, i.e., Uber Armani.

Billy launches into his one-man production number.

"From Julia Phillips to Stephen King," he sings almost on key.

Todd and I gasp delightedly and slap palms lightly.

I fall backward onto the spread from the effort.

Kate calls. "Mom, did you see? Did you hear?!" she breathes excitedly as her sorority sisters chorus huzzahs in the background.

Mara calls. "He really loves you . . ."

Zoe: "This year will you please write him a thank-you note?"

Brooke, laughing: "Damn right, a second mention! This isn't like last year, Jools. Now your book with your picture on the cover is stacked right next to the counter where they buy their M&Ms."

The Silence of the Lambs, one of half-a-hundred movies I've received on tape this Academy season, sweeps the Oscars.

"So what do you think it says about America?" I scowl into the sink as we clean up the kitchen and Todd pretends he doesn't hear because he knows the answer.

It is the day before the day before Passover when I receive a notice from E. McGuffin. Which makes me wonder if she noticed *YNELITTA* as she checked out her groceries-for-one. Or maybe Billy Crystal's production number jogged her memory.

She's gonna take the house, the car, the kid if she doesn't hear from us in thirty days. At least The Mainstain and The III have been notified as well.

I suppose this missive is E.'s way of turning down our refi/fifty-fifty proposal, tendered nearly a year ago.

When I finally connect with my erstwhile representatives after the long weekend, The III tells me, "I bought you eight months!"

"But I wanted to solve it!"

The Mainstain doesn't return my calls, which infuriates and debilitates me simultaneously.

I must be getting better.

Finally they confab with E. who says after some delay, Okay she'll accept the original proposal.

"But by now I'm not such a good prospect for refinancing, am I?!" I challenge them in their ensuing conference call.

"That's not my department," The III says stiffly.

"Don't worry, we'll find somebody," The Mainstain purrs.

"First-class round trip. MGM Grand. In one day out the next. Wanna come?" I've acceded to a teevee appearance too soon after surgery courtesy of E.-induced I'm-no-longer-Number-One-I'm-Number-Two! panic and I'm breaking all my rules: a panel, air travel, *Geraldo*.

I've kidded myself it'll be okay because I've telephonically bonded with the producer of the show.

She's sent me Geraldo's recent epigraph, *Exposing Myself*, which she assumes akin to *YNELITTA*. I guess she doesn't have much time to read, I try to think charitably during a cursory perusal.

It is the only book I've ever considered burning.

"I'm gonna be in New York anyway to visit the clan. I'll meetcha there."

Air is always going to New York to visit the clan, which at pushing-forty seems to me a tad extreme in the family-values department, but I was brought up by wolves so what do I know?

I wouldn't mind seeing VS and Dad, come to think of it.

Air scores us some tasty cut-rate digs at the Plaza and we dine with Dad and June before the show.

Dad is wheezing and cranky. And older. Much older.

He seems to be shrinking.

"Not the best move to visit with him pretaping," I whisper to Air, upset, on the way over. "I think maybe I should cancel dinner with Victor . . ."

The producer has guaranteed one or two solo segments, then I can-or-cannot join the panel, depending on my mood.

The panel consists of Cindy Adams (gossip columnist), Jean Hagen (fifties movie star), Paul Rosenfield (ex-publicist/author), and a woman in cheaply conceived incognito who claims to be a $2500-a-night Hollywood hooker.

I don't think so.

I introduce myself to Paul Rosenfield, author of *The Club Rules*. Paul was scheduled to have lunch with Norman Garey (a dear friend and my seventies/eighties lawyer) the day Norman committed suicide instead and I'd always wanted to meet him.

A short year later, after the colossal failure of his book, Paul committed suicide himself. "Geraldo made him do it!" I kidded Air when I imparted the depressing news.

"A simple daytime look?" the makeup girl queries, just as The Legend in His Own Mind pops an enormous head in the door. His too tight tiny little body follows. He's in iridescent orange makeup and his eyes vague into the middle distance.

He fixes me with a fixed smile and hurries on.

"Sure," I say, nonplussed by the appearance of RoboHost.

By the time I check myself in a monitor and notice I look as sick as I feel, it is minutes to taping. I have just enough time to ask another makeup artist, one of those older boys (aka a pro) to paint a mouth with some hint of color on my thin lips.

"How many people have read Julia's book?" Geraldo asks the audience, which looks to be populated from the projects and one lone black woman near the back raises her hand.

My heart sinks.

Geraldo is totally unprepared and our ensuing interview slides downhill from there. When it's over I'm ready to bail, but Air tells me backstage whilst they set up the panel's seats that Miss Cindy has been harrumphing and sighing loudly throughout my camera-time and I probably ought to hang around to protect myself.

Near the end of the taping Geraldo opens the floor to questions. The black woman in back stands up painfully and he pushes a mike in her weathered face.

"Julia, I read your book in hardcover last year," she begins and I'm ready to be told Go Find Jesus. "And I thought it was just brilliant," she continues, "but there was an awful lot of sex in it . . ."

Too much sex? I always worried too little.

Unless one counted movies as sex.

I am so astonished by her praise I fumble through an inadequately flippant It-Was-The-Seventies response.

"Jeez, he used to be really something! Remember him on ABC? What happened?" Air says wistfully on the drive to Kennedy Airport.

"He was *fired* by ABC at the pinnacle of his success! I guess some people never get over a heavy fall," I reply, thinking of my own ups and downs and all the energy it took to recover from them.

I lean back into an almost comfortable position.

"I'm so grateful to be Number Two and not Geraldo."

That Sunday my back is sufficiently unswelled for a late brunch of eggs Benedict and Bloody Marys with Todd at the Polo Lounge. What will I do when the Sultan of Brunei, its current owner, closes the Beverly Hills Hotel for two years of renovation?

Rip, the maître d', brings Tone Loc and his brother Chris and mother Betty over for introductions.

"Haaayyy," Tone intones in his Froggie-the-Gremlin growl and I wonder if this rapper-of-the-moment knows he sounds exactly like a popular character from early television.

Plunk your magic twanger, Froggie, eh-eh-eh . . .

Ahmet Ertegun, cofounder of Atlantic Records, sounded like Froggie, too. I met him one late-seventies night at Mr. Chow's. He was seated at the round booth up front opposite Mick Jagger and he made me so anxious my hand flew from my side and touched The Mick's hair.

Desperate to escape, The Mick bolted from his chair and crashed into the art deco beveled-mirror screens in front. Humiliated, I tried to apologize, but it was definitively an I'm-sorry-that's-incorrect-you'll-have-to-come-this-way-this-way-please moment . . .

Chris, who is seriously lighter skinned, better dressed and altogether less intimidating than Tone, grins conspiratorially. He's just finished reading *YNELITTA*.

Tone doesn't look like he ever reads.

I explain I'm gearing up for my daughter's return from college.

"Why?" Betty giggles.

"I miss her. I went into a deep state of mourning when she left." Betty giggles again.

"Oh in my house when they turn eighteen I kick 'em out!" she chuckles emphatically. "And then I do this! Ya ya ya . . ." She dances a little jig and we crack up.

They leave.

"I'd kick Tone out too," Todd observes with a small snarl.

"I surely don't think I'd wanna be doin' noooo wiiild thing with him."

"Some man of the people you are . . ."

THOSE BOYS
THE BODYGUARD

Father Frank first flogged him when he was four.

Fellated him at five.

Fucked him for his fifteenth.

He scoped the scene at St. Sebastian's.

Sucked down a six-pack.

Scored a Saturday night special.

Blew the bastard's brains from Boise to Birmingham.

Fuck thee Father who art not anymore.

Browbeat bus fare from his brother and bolted. Drifted west.

Another dreg with disciplinary deficiencies of the Dysfunctional Diaspora.

Joined a gym. Grunted and groaned at Gold's.

Self-administered steroids. His daily bread.

Mastered a .357 Magnum. Trespassed.

Stoically steers The Stars and their secrets on Earth through streams of screamers.

Strokes their scrotums in sterling fashion.

Isn't he a little bit of Heaven? They say.

"I need my days off to paint," Ruby says sternly when I call to negotiate a forbidden house call.

Flipping channels. Making phone calls.

I'm taking a break from a fourth start on my virtual real-ity/talking dog ShowBiz-*is*-Real-Life novel, set against the backdrop of the death of Los Angeles.

Duh.

Work in Progress, W.I.P, because I can't come up with a title, which worries me. I don't know why I bother anyway, since Joni's hated the first hundred pages and dispensed a dis-appointingly low-five-figure option-check to keep me afloat.

"What's it about?" she keeps asking.

"She's worried too many puns and anagrams," Julie's reported.

I've been fiddling with cataclysmic finale — say an earth-quake and ensuing multicultural urban unrest — but I'm stuck, so I've returned to my Christmas dinner set piece, color-coding the guests with blue and pink Post-its alternating around a coffee table conveniently located three feet from The Creature.

Yellow for the sexually confused?

YES.

The whole table would be yellow!

YES.

I've been agonizing over seating all day.

When did this become my party? It's so easy to interface The Real with The more-or-less Real.

Probably easier in L.A. than anywhere else.

Thing is, though, L.A.'s been purveying its dysfunctionally induced image of itself (movies music T.V. videos) for fifty years and it is how we all see ourselves. The disintegration of Ronald Reagan's Evil Empire was probably more profoundly driven by *Dynasty* than Star Wars.

Will the disintegration of capitalism be equally affected by *Dynasty*'s angst-ridden offspring: *90210* and *Melrose Place*?

And what kind of Empire was it?

Evil maybe?

When I start pontificating like this I know it's time for a manicure. I track my hands on a keyboard all day so it helps for the nails to be groomed and painted, especially if the words suck.

"You have to come to the shop. It'll be good for you," Ruby persists. "Research . . ."

"Maybe you're right," I say. "Get out of this bunker mentality, take a little expedition, see how the other half lives."

This, notwithstanding that I reside at what real estate mavens call a prestigious address.

I wonder from which half I might be The Other.

"So you'll come."

"Yeah, I guess. It'll depend on the weather."

We laugh and make an appointment for next week.

I turn the page of Week-at-a-Glance and circle 11:30 A.M. Thursday, May 7.

I flip channels some more; they are all announcing the soon-to-be-live telecast from Simi Valley of the jury's verdict on a case that's come to belong to an individual alleged to be Rodney King.

N-O-O-O-T-T-T-T!?

If I'm shocked-but-not-surprised/enraged, imagine how They . . .

Those Others . . .

The phone starts immediately.

If someone in the Top Twenty doesn't call me, I call him/her/it.

Within an hour everyone is accounted for, save Dalee.

I permit myself an image of him wandering bewildered through the flames wailing, What waaas the deal, again?

Am I a black woman? A white man? Oh yeah. Right.

I am an African/American *man*, god*damn*.

I suppress all feeling by working out vigorously to *The Adventures of Stevie Vee*, a recent acquisition, the result of a major search by Todd. We heard "Dirty Cash" almost two years ago. In some after-hours/borderline-neighborhood/bar-or-other. Seductive breakdown, great lyrics, great chorus, great rap. It is not until he finds the last CD in Los Angeles in a funky store in a funky part of town that we discover they ripped themselves off for another song on the album. A hit, but not as good: "Jealousy."

A beeeyyyond eighties gesture.

"Dirty Cash" runs eight minutes. I play it ten times, sound-track for the coming-to-you-*live* beating of a white boy caught in the wrong intersection at the wrong time of day.

Oy gevalt meshuggener shvartzers.

This is what happens when you oppress people! I think superiorly and then I remind myself that as far as those boys at Florence and Normandie are concerned — those boys rear-ranging Reginald Denny's brain — *I am* the oppressor.

Where's LAPD?

Hiding. Like me.

"Money's the fiend!!!! Do you know what I mean??!!!"

I do I do I do not sleep.

"Dad, I could be in Colorado," I reassure my father.

Dad is overreacting to what he sees on teevee a continent

away. I pause briefly for the thought that the last time I saw this kind of action it was caused by the death of another man named King.

Unless you count Junior as a surname.

Surely Nixon did. Reagan did. Bush did.

They did it for all of us.

That's what the rage is about.

And the fear.

For the last thirty years — hell, for the entire history of America — white people have been anywhere from racist to benignly neglectful when people of color are concerned.

I wonder how Ross Perot related to the matter and wonder further what the H. is for. Does anyone but me think he looks like Daryl Gates if he had been pummeled repeatedly from above?

Squoonched, as it were?

Say by Officer Lawrence Powell?

A Fight-of-the-Century kind of deal, promoted by Don! the one black King who doesn't make the White Male Establishment uncomfortable, he is so peculiarly — albeit electrically — like Them.

Am I too retro-knee-jerk-liberal-reactive when I worry that H. Ross Perot, an incredibly rich incredibly short boy with jug ears *and* a Southern accent, *really* wants us to elect him . . .

. . . KING? aka H.R.H.H?!

April is the cruelest month, breeding riots out of the dead ground, as Tough Shit Eliot never said.

I feel removed, despondent, alienated.

Situated on my bed, despairing over live feed from the Eve of Destruction. Ringside at The End, in my bunker on the hill, hooowww L.A.

Me and Dad are watching the same pictures on CNN.

I have forsaken the local newscasts hours ago. The reporters' sanctimonious editorializing has pissed me off.

I bet they don't have a tax problem.

"And look at that!" one of them had barked this morning. In the background, a small emaciated pregnant Hispanic

Woman wheeled off a cart of groceries. Her two children, also small and emaciated, clung to her skirt. "Why that woman must have a week of groceries there!" he exploded, righteous outrage imbuing his cheeks with a high red blush I'd seen on the masklike visages of habitués at underground clubs in borderline neighborhoods Friday night.

"Dude, that's probably the first time that woman's had a week of groceries in her life!" I shouted.

I have a new game, verrrrry nineties.

I call it *Talk Back to the News*, as in:

"Okay, the baby whose parents are teenage crack addicts (and happen to be brother and sister) has been born, not aborted, per your wishes. You wanna take care of it?"

Or:

"Where's my peace dividend? There's more war than ever, and besides, among us, we have at least a quarter of a million nuclear warheads. Average half-life, say, a hundred thousand years.

"Given Man's record so far, and I do emphasize man, don't you think there'll be at least one boo-boo?"

Or:

"Wow, look at Sarajevo. Beirut looked like that once."

AND:

"*Why* is it Bosnia-Hercegovina on CNN, but Bosnia and Herzegovina in *The New York Times*???!!"

The Question That Asks and Says It All.

"You're fired," I talked back to the news.

"This Republican reign of terror!" Dad spits in his harsh chemo/fin-de-millennium whisper and I wonder briefly how it must feel to be as old as my father and see it all turn to *this!*

And how does it feel to be as old as I am and wake up to *Blade Runner*, live, coming from another part of MY postindustrial town? The movie was set in Los Angeles, 2019.

I guess the future happened sooner than we thought.

Time flies when things suck.

And whoever said L.A. was a city in the first place? Nineteen suburbs in search of a city was what we — who

were all dying to live Here — called it when I lived in New
York. Young, poor, happily hitched, fairly sixties.

Right before m-m-m-My Generation . . . was squelched.

And turned away from the Larger World to tend our own
gardens. Often in L.A.

"Do you think we might be on the brink of insurrection?"
Dad (who worked on The Bomb but worries about the recent
trend toward inhibition of civil liberties and individual free-
doms) whispers apprehensively/hopefully.

"It'll depend on how the weather is." We relax. We laugh.

But: Santa Ana winds, 92 degrees in the shade, first stage
smog alerts, coming on to a full moon are all phenomena that
have a profound effect on human nature. Which is whacked to
begin with.

Anyway in California they do.

And as goes California so goes The World.

"It's over, Dad. It's The End . . ."

"Yeah, June, five hundred years, that's it."

"Dad, try fifty!"

"Nah, Jools, five hundred at least . . ."

"There isn't enough time!" I shout, exasperated.

"How do you know?" Dad counters and I shut up.

I channelsurf MUTEly and turn up Power 106, which has a
basic techno/industrial bent. It is the number-one radio station
with gangstas in L.A. The phone lines have been open since
The Verdict and callers are anywhere from blown-away/suici-
dal to blown-away/homicidal.

The deejays try to be responsible:

"Stop the Violence and Increase the Peace," one black star
after another pleads. About every three cuts.

By phone? Live? Pre-recorded?

I reach Michael in his car. Kate is planning to fly back
from school Friday, May 1. I don't think so.

"Today is today and tomorrow is tomorrow," Michael says,
a soothing counterpoint to the College Boys coming to me
Live from the [Ghetto in the] Year 2000, but Michael also says

"D.V." for "don' vorry" a lot. I think he's in denial, not to anticipate how far things will go, but I don't argue, reminding myself that Michael was born under the sign of the moon, which will be full any day now, and may be operating with altered — dare I say diminished — capacity.

Three hours later we talk again. He is standing on top of his hill a canyon away, binoculars plastered to his face, portable phone glued to his ear, checking out the ring of black smoke that is encircling The City of Angels. Michael seems shocked. I am shocked that he is shocked but working at home I probably catch more CNN than Ted Turner.

We agree that Kate should hang around school an extra day or so and conference-call to tell her to stay put.

"Are you guys okay?" she asks. Scared.

"Of course we're okay," we say. "As long as the fires go out."

Fire. Always a dirty word in Los Angeles.

More so after six years of drought and arson.

When she hangs up I can't resist jabbing Michael with a verbose tone poem titled "I Told You So."

Call-waiting. Todd.

He's been helping another friend move into a new office and they've been corncred off Wilshire, near Bullock's. Close. They've locked everything in the truck and are camping out at the barren office.

"Mean-looking guys tooling up Wilshire. Mean-looking crowd following on foot," Todd reports tensely. "Listen, when I can make a move do you mind . . . ?"

"Of course not."

I wouldn't wanna return home to Todd's unsafe neighborhood either, but who's to say what — or more specifically *where* — is safe anymore.

Hold on. Was this the deal?

"You know that place I finally found *Stevie Vee* at?"

"Yeah . . ."

"Torched. To the ground. Toast."

I play "Dirty Cash" several times after we hang up.

In memoriam, as it were.

Todd brings a bootleg *Truth or Dare* to keep our minds off the news, but we are junkies for the live FEED ME FEED ME and punch the remote like Nintendo instead of grooving with The The.

Todd fiddles restlessly with the *Scientific American* on the bed opened to "The Search for Strange Matter."

"I don't understand a word of it," I joke. Actually, depending on the intellectual terrain, I generally grasp around half. Of it. "Lemme tell you about the first *Scientific American* piece I ever absorbed and you'll understand why I subscribe.

"When I was a kid I got bored one day and grazed an article in one of my Dad's copies. It was about a stress experiment conducted at Harvard on rats."

Todd pulls a face and glances at the large-screen monitor. The picture tube is finally going after a decade of constant use and every once in a while there's a flurry of light and sound that seems to emanate from Deep Space.

"No lissen-*up*! This is very interesting . . .

"Rats are civilized creatures: monogamous, attentive to their young. No vandalism, no funky diddling, no cannibalism. Like the rules and regs *we* pretend to observe.

"Those Harvard boys compressed the rats into too small a living space. And guess what? Suddenly, mothers dropped their young whilst chatting. Then left them behind. Adolescent males roved in gangs, beating up older males and raping their mothers.

"Sometimes they feasted on the abandoned babies . . ."

"Uh-uh-uh," Todd says expressively and cranks the volume to drown me out.

"No conclusions could be drawn about any species other than rats, they said at the end of the paper!" I shout, pointing at the screen emphatically. "Hah!"

We focus on the fire-breathing FEEDME FEEDME and laugh.

"There is no fucking hope!" Todd jokes.

"How do you know?" I say because I think I should and we head to the kitchen to microwave popcorn and refill drinks.

Todd departs for home about ten, calls twenty minutes later to let me know he got there.

I do not sleep.

It doesn't matter what Michael and I say. Kate needs to assure herself that things are settling down and insists on returning home as scheduled. She and two girlfriends, similarly motivated, will trek bravely from the Midwest together. Teenage girls never travel in anything but packs if they have been adequately educated.

Times being what they are and all.

I try not to recall that when I first moved to California and smog was already an issue, the sun was still a clear ball of yellow in the brilliant blue sky.

I've been checking out sun and sky on a daily basis for a while and on a good day the sun is hazy, sorta white.

And the sky is, well, *silver*.

Do those particles affect the psyche as they do the lungs?

Sure, why not?

Midday. I work out to Rodney King, struggling through his statement: Can we . . . Can we . . . All get along? I think he's handsome, shy, damaged. He moves me, but George Bush would move me if he said the right words, which he doesn't.

Later, I listen to Arsenio Antichrist, deejay-ing for two hours on just about every major radio station in the city.

"Stop the vaah-ooo-lence and increasse the peaccce, baybee." Ordinarily, I eshew him on grounds similar to my Perot-prejudice but he moves me too.

I wouldn't mind resting.

The girls are delayed by half a day, which isn't much considering the circumstances.

"I never saw so much camouflage in my life!" Kate reports over Michael's carphone en route from LAX.

Get used to it, I think but don't say. And by the way, honey, did you register to vote? I mean, as long as it's open season on women, per the courts, soooo Rodney Kingish, don'tcha think you should?

Ah ease up, Jools. She's just finished finals.

And she's glad to be home. And she's safe . . .

The fires are burning out, the weather is cooling, the National Guard is arriving. Tomorrow for sure.

And just how *do* I feel about that?

How did the citizens of Beirut feel?

The citizens of Sarajevo?

I sleep.

I dream . . .

THE QUILLMEISTER'S QUAGMIRE—PART II

Seeking SANCTUARY, THE WRITER hurtles on the down-stroke of restless night, hitches a ride on a stray Santa Ana with the black stray.

"I've seen you around," she says to the cat.

YES.

"You have a name?"

T-U-P-A-C.

"You know where we're going, Tupac?"

F-F-A.

"Financial Fuck-ups Anonymous?"

YES.

"Hi I'm Julia and I'm a financial fuck-up?"

H-I-I-I J-U-L-I-A . . .

"How come you're in FFA?"

G-A-M-B-L-E-D I-N C-Y-B-E-R-S-P-A-C-E.

"Qu'est-ce que c'est?"

L-O-S-T T-H-E V-I-R-T-U-A-L F-A-R-M . . .

"Quoi . . . ?"

D-E-R-I-V-A-T-I-V-E-S.

"Uh-oh. Tupac's kaput . . ."

YES.

The Santa Ana sputters and they land on the lip of the con-
cave cement scar engraved in a hill that used to be Sanctuary's
pool. Dark figures lurk in the distance but she can make out
Flavor Flav in the foreground, his trademark oversized clock
hanging around his neck.

A white-faced black square.

1 2 3 etc. is what it says.

"Tupac, you know the next line?"

YES.

"What is it? I can't remember."

NO.

"C'mon, you can tell me. What's the big deal?"

GOOD-BYE.

Good-bye yourself.

"Here's the big deal," I explain to my Sunday afternoon
guests. "You hear the car, you throw the grape. If it goes
under the wheel at just the right moment, it makes a great
squa-wish . . ."

The curfew has been in effect since Wednesday and
everyone — even me, who hates going out — is antsy.

My visitors are:

Brad, the artist;

A brilliant gay interactive type, who calls himself WFAG;

Claire-the-Jock;

And Claire's dog, the chocolate Labrador who's so
impressed me I've made him the star of my novel, good ol'
Work in Progress.

I am one of the few not tangibly affected by recent events.
Pretty soon my area code will be 310, a new line of demarca-
tion. The phone company was supposed to make it happen
yesterday, but in view of the complete lack of rule of law,
they are delaying the changeover.

My guests have toured their soon-to-be-213-borderline-
neighborhoods, checking out the wreckage.

Some have carpooled to South Central with shovels.

Cleanup duty.

"And do you feel better, now?" I challenge.

"Marginally," WFAG says, making a mezzo-mezzo gesture.

"Borderline covers so much territory," I worry, "y'know, like cancer . . ."

"So when they let the buildings just burn?" Brad says, "there's nothing left but the girders. They look like steel skeletons. Spooky."

"I was freaked out — the liquor store on the corner was looted and burned — but y'know, it was . . . exciting!" Claire smiles, looking down looking guilty.

Something heavy, (funny-you-don't-look) Terminator-Twoish, chugs the hill. We hear its efforts miles away. Everyone stands and assumes their Orel Hershiser position (in my case, Nolan Ryan) grapes at the ready . . . and

Dammmmnnnn if a Hummer — wait *two*, no *three* — doesn't pass in front of us.

Military vehicles huffing through my canyon?

Plugging along from one trouble spot to another, their camouflage intermingling with my foliage?

Is this how it started in Beirut?

Sarajevo?

I arise early in order to precede my hejira to Ruby with an hour of aerobics for maximum coping ability.

How perfectly silly of me. There is almost no traffic, and the drivers of the few cars on the street focus straight ahead, motoring verrry fast from Here to There.

When the breakdown starts on Burton Way and Crescent Drive, I turn up the radio. I've been fooled so many times by this seductive introduction into that *other* cut but I get lucky and Girlfriend whispers:

"I wantch'your money . . ." by the time I'm at Burton and Alpine. And I sail along Easy Street whilst she intones:

". . . Just wantch'you to use me

"Take me and abuse me . . .

". . . Money talks money talks

"Dirty cash I wantcha, dirty cash, I needja . . ." she's railing by the time I pull up to ThirdWorld Valet behind the shop.

I make him wait, chair-dance briefly, feeling guilty.

Smiling, he bops to the beat in impatient little circles but what's really on his mind?

Does he wonder, too, if that song defines our relationship?

Okay.

All right.

The deal?

Well I'm pretty sure that if this absurd uptown venue becomes a fire-zone — if there's shooting — the bullets will miss *them* — the targets — and hit *me*, The Innocent Bystander. The Fires of L.A. are less than a week's memory — smoldering embers still — and nobody here would call me paranoid.

The woman, an Imelda Marcos-wannabe (from that period when she was no longer beautiful but not yet a parody) has minimally six perfect blue-white carats screwed through each ear lobe and the man is big and black.

With a big black gun.

In a black leather holster slouching off his right hip.

I have a bag just like it. Prada, I think.

His is not Prada.

Homeboy's highly developed biceps ripple provocatively against the short tight sleeves of his spiffy navy blue uniform. He hovers solicitously over DragonLady whilst she selects a color for her toenails.

I shift in my seat practicing dodging and weaving and feeling exceptionally white-middle-class-middle-aged, expel an involuntary oy-veh backnoise and three-sixty the room. Nobody but me seems perturbed by the presence of firearms, engrossed as they are in the bleaching and cutting and blowing of it all.

White on white and mirrors and the help in white, very that way.

No smoking.

I chomp anxiously on my Nicorette, which imparts a rush and gas simultaneously.

Why am I in a Beverly Hills salon which was trendy when it opened three decades ago and now caters to a clientele too rich and too old to care to be trendy?

And more to the point, why is That Boy — the big black dude in the uniform with the gun — here with me?

I feel so Other.

I call Jody to report on the private cop at the salon.

"Oh, a lot of people are doing that," she says matter-of-factly. "If they have the money. We've been bringing clothes and food downtown. I wish we were still rich so we could throw some cash at the situation, like Barbra Streisand . . ."

"I wish I owned a gun," I laugh.

"You don't."

"You're right, I don't," I say, thinking of all the times I might use it on myself, my daughter, my cat, the neighbor, the neighbor's daughter, the neighbor's cat. Or is it dog? I don't really know my neighbor. "Do you guys own a gun?" I ask, and of course they do and of course they don't keep it loaded and of course they really don't know how to use it . . .

And of course, since nobody ever answered the "Where's LAPD?" question, the working poor in Hollywood (the top 1 percent in annual income but they can't pay their bills either) are buying guns (their cars, after all, are the ones stolen).

And the idle rich are buying *guys* with guns.

"Yup, those are my relatives you see on the rooftops," Christine says wryly, referring to armed Korean men guarding their stores, their livelihood. Tonight's teevee images. Add-ons to the human zoo. I've called her because I've read in the *Times* that two women named Park were shot by rioters yesterday. One of them is Christine's aunt.

"Oh God, Christine . . ."

"That's my family being shot," she says in a wobbly voice.

"You know, I've gone to the dinners and worked the elections. Limousine-liberaled it. I'm so alienated right now. Pierce O'Donnell has been pushing me to spend $125 for breakfast with Hillary Clinton."

"Pierce is verrry FOB. Did you know they were room-mates at Georgetown?"

"Then why aren't we being invited for free? Comped?"

"Not in Hollywood . . ."

"I mean I'll vote for him, but with money the way it is, I just don't think so."

"Ah c'mon, she's the best man in the field."

Christine chuckles.

"Don't make me laugh. I don't feel like laughing right now."

"Me neither. Did you see the picture of *The New York Times* photographer the crowd beat up yesterday?"

"Noooo . . ."

"He was the same guy who photographed me at the Polo Lounge. When we had lunch with Doris Bacon . . . remember?"

"You're kidding."

"Nope, same guy. Weird, hunh?"

"More and more. Every day . . ."

"That's InfernoTainment."

I've been off the best-seller list three weeks when NBC reruns my year-old *Donahue* tour de force.

Directly preceding a Big Game.

That Thursday Leonida Karpik leaves a message:

I'm to pop back on at Number Eight, which feels comfort-able.

Kate and I celebrate at Our Place, Hamburger Hamlet.

A middle-aged faghag with her two boys catches my eye as they pass our table.

"I just finished your book," she says. "Story of my life. You sucked my dick . . ." They move on.

I sucked her dick?!@# I mouth in silent alarm to Kate.

"Why are people always saying that to me?" I complain.

"That's so cool, Mom." Kate smiles.

"Talk about damned with faint praise. See I knew I didn't like going out!"

"Ah Moooommmm, you just started again! Besides it beats 'infuriatingly charming'!" Kate smiles cockily; she's invoked our favorite credo, extracted from screed-masquerading-as-review penned by John Dunne for *The New York Review of Books*. JULIA PHILLIPS' NAKED LUNCH. Who stayed awake at night to come up with that???!!! Anne Rice???

Joni was so flummoxed she FedExed tearsheets.

Joni's timing, as usual, sucked.

The arrival of the seven-page Passion of Mr. Didion coincided with a high-strung but nonproductive premenstrual SAD interlude. Intermittently, for an insanely sleepless seventy-two hours I revised rebuttals:

Qu'est-ce-que c'est "infuriatingly charming" Johnnn?@#!

What you're N-O-O-O-T-T!? . . .

"I'm going home and I'm not coming out for a year," I say and Kate laughs uneasily because she's uncertain if I'm just kidding.

The club Maxx with a double x is in a borderline part of town.

Homeboy's overdeveloped biceps ripple smartly in his brown-on-tan nightcop uniform. His pants and holster are tight too, ooh-ooh, and he's blocking the entrance to PARKING LOT FULL.

I lean out the window proffering a ten: Here's the deal, we've circled the block three times and have nowhere to go but you.

He palms the ten easily and slips it in a pocket. He acts for a moment like he's embarrassed but we laugh together, co-conspirators in his little joke.

We wonder if we know each other from somewhere else.

Or is it that all white bitches in German cars look the same to him and all black biceps girdled in a uniform . . . ?

Double X is hot and cramped, its energy so intense the pitch is borderline-hysteria.

Everybody is an outlaw: That's-why-I'm-here-Duuuude! and they're verrry excited to be out.

The deejay does a first-class job keeping the room heavily boom-and-throb.

Todd and I thread through the bodies to the dance floor. There's no room to express ourselves so we head toward a patio beyond. My retina and the strobe lights interface and I stop in my tracks a foot between a couple of Omar's Men.

Humping and pumping.

The strobe is powerful, a residual-retinal-flash-from-The-Seventies and those boys flicker like an old-time movie.

In a heartbeat, I travel from 1972 when I cried over McGovern to 1980 when I sneered at Reagan.

And did you two beauties, who should have, vote?

Not likely.

Todd, who has never seen me move at anything less than a hyperventilative New York pace, nudges my elbow and I disengage from the recent past and shudder into the moment.

Is it the future yet?

And why does that make me wanna leave this desperate venue, power up my hill to . . . Sanctuary?

More sanctuary than *here* anyway.

I expel an oy-vey back-noise and we agree it is that second before it's time to leave when it's time to leave.

We hit the outside on the down-stroke of an angst-laden-positive-ion wind sweeping in from the Desert. Two boys, consciousness-altered on anything from Saturday-night-testosterone-buildup to heroin, are altercating on the sidewalk.

Innocent bystanders waiting for their cars fan out in fearful circles but Mr. Black Security Man, holster unsnapped so his gun is accessible, ends it with a swagger from the 'hood.

Yo! Tengo un problema??!!!

He turns to check if we've witnessed every second of his moment and we smile and applaud.

Definitely that homeboy from the salon.

Definitely glad he's here. I imagine we'll be bumping into each other from time to time in the next little while.

"So how d'you think the summer's gonna be?" he queries behind a grimace masquerading as a smile. Holding my door open. It's the new "have a nice day," that question.

I slide into my seat, lock my door, blast the engine.

"Money talks, money talks . . ." The Bitch reminds us from the radio and we glance tentatively at each other.

Aaahhhh ease up, Jools. Maybe he really wants to know.

I roll down the window to tell him from the bottom of my heart: One man one vote.

Mine equals Robert Dole's, yours Ross Perot's.

His cold eyes diss me, Bitch, I don't wanna hear about it unless I'm getting paid. I've got four ex-wives and six ex-children to feed.

"Well, it pretty much depends on the weather, don'tcha think?"

Yeah right. Rainbow Coalition this!

I drive away, hurt.

But catch him waving in my rearview:

Bye-bye, Miss-us Ten Dolla's . . .

. . . and wonder from which side I might be The Other.

"Dirty cash I wantcha dirty cash I needja . . ."

Compulsively on the lookout for an epistle from E., I empty the mailbox before screeching up the driveway.

Phew! Nothing.

Later, hastily sorting the innocuous stack of magazines and come-ons care of Occupant and/or Resident, I drop an envelope. Bent at the knees like Daddy's-good-little-girl, I retrieve it from the floor. An invitation to a Good Cause, one of Those Beneficent Events Hollywood loooves to sponsor and attend so It can show off Its Uber Armani.

Addressed to Don Henley.

Just days ago, I had nearly interfaced with Mine-Enemy-Grows-Older-Than-Me at Sushi Ko but Lance, who wore his glasses (as opposed to me, who had developed a taste for foggy focus) apprised seconds before: HenleyAlert! HenleyAlert! and steered me past his anger without incident.

The street is many many miles and miles from Sanctuary.

"*This* is too karmic even for me!" I snicker aloud and toy briefly with the notion of forwarding it.

Covered by some pithy Go-fuck-yourself/Okay-I-will.

I tack it unopened to the bulletin board instead.

Center stage. Equidistant from macho-cunt/self-centered-piece-of-shit and you-are-my-role-model.

Maybe it'll inspire me.

What goes around comes around.

The Don said.

IT WAS MARCH 1993
THE DAY BEFORE THE ⬍

HOLLYWOOD

Sunset Boulevard

WEST HOLLYWOOD

Fountain Avenue

Santa Monica Boulevard

L O S   A N G E L E S

Fairfax Avenue

0   1   2 mile

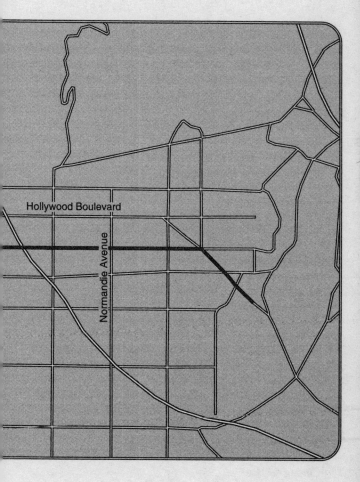

Hollywood Boulevard

Normandie Avenue

Tick!

Bbbrrrrrr-ttccchhh.

Tick. Bbbrrrrrr.

Ttccchhhh.

E. McGuffin punches her calculator.

Bbbrrrr-ttccchhh bbrrrr-ttccchhh . . .

E.'s moving finger writes.

Tick brrrhhh ttccchhh.

And having writ moves on.

Tick-a chung tick-a chung tickachungchungchung.

E. clears her throat. "Here's the deal . . . " she starts and I sidebar with myself:

Why are people always saying that?

Here's the deal, says TalkShow Host.

And renegotiates.

Here's the deal, says TalkShow President.

Then reneges.

Did I say *here's* the deal? TalkShow God disinforms disingenuously when I importune: *Where's my fucking deal*?!@# Oh I meant *there*. *There's* the deal, T. S. God repeats condescendingly, waves vaguely toward Infinity and returns to whatever more-important-than-me endeavor in which It was engaged when I interrupted.

Busy very-busy.

Taking calls.

Cutting deals.

With a few points open, just in case.

Here'sTheDealHere'sTheDeal, E. McGuffin drones in her mild middle-European accent and I perk up attentively, but . . .

"I vill inform Random House by fax I've lifted the lien on your royalties. And you *vill* pay me fifty percent promptly."

. . . the thing is, even though I had to harass Pierce O'Donnell for ten days to *call* Alberto Vitale (who referred him to Peter DeGiglio, an accountant whose job description is: screw the author) just to *discover* the lien . . .

"Allowing for off-the-tops . . ." Neal Hoffer interjects with a whine.

I've only commenced phone contact with The Hoff recently, after his partner The Mainstain burned out on my IRS Imbroglio, threw up his hands and passed me off to that taxing boy who should've been leading the charge in the first place.

Yesterday he'd asked, Are you a good actress?

And I said, Oh like crying? And begged him to pick me up.

The thing is, even though my portion of the take won't see me through more than a month-and-a-half . . .

"Commissions . . ." my 5-percent-of-gross business manager explains.

Make that half-a-month more . . .

E. nods that's fine with her. E. is short and pear-shaped. Could be my age but looks years older. E.'s wavy gray hair is pulled back with tasteful tortoiseshell combs. Tasty pearls in her ears and around her neck.

Earlier, I'd decided against pearls, God forbid E. of the pale blue eyes, aquiline nose and receding chin assume I have any estate left at all.

"D'ya mind not smoking?" The Hoff had whined as we eased down the driveway and I made a move to light up.

I smiled charmingly, broke off a Nicorette gum and thought, as I often did, If people in L.A. were as concerned about the use of cars and guns and words as they were about cigarettes Southern California would be a better place.

The Hoff drove his racing-green Mercedes sedan with a tentative on/off foot to the pedal. I phantom-accelerated, chomping my gum ferociously, to the bottom of the canyon.

Don't scoff at The Hoff.

Chomp chomp chomp . . .

I park my gum in my cheek and rotate puffy eyes from one to the other, two ravenous marsupials divvying up my score.

My hard-won etcetera.

But the thing is . . .

"How much do you expect from Random House?" E. queries patiently, like she's repeating the sentence.

"I dunno. Fifty, maybe seventy-five grand in royalties. Who knows what for the new pages . . ." I respond, dutifully returning my attention to the dueling marsupials.

The thing is . . .

"I vill *try* to get the fax out today, but it's old and on the fritz," E. says apologetically. Budget cuts. Proposition 13 by Howard Jarvis. The Ross Perot of my youth.

The thing is I can't get over the *E* of it all.

The derivative-of-*e*-to-the-*x*-equals-*e*-to-the-*x* of it all.

The Look-Ma-the-IRS-collector's-named-E.! of it all.

And every time I face off with her in this tiny space that calls itself a conference room I flash on what a funny letter *E* is. Like some numbers — 49, for example — as in:

E. to Me: You owed us 89,427 dollars and 49 cents in
    1989. With interest and penalties — which have
    been frozen, temporarily — your bill comes to
    about mmmm . . . $165,000 . . .
Me to E.: And 49 cents . . .

Since my hits average one a decade E. might have to wait a spell for the next chunk of new money.

I have in mind a workout tape for people who drink and smoke. Or a CD-ROM game for girls called EatingGossip.

The thing is my situation is so grave I have to fight the tee-hee-hees.

The I-swear-Officer-A-B-C-D-E-E-E. Of it all.

"What I don't understand," I started — badly — an hour ago, "is why you didn't accept my original offer. I could've gotten a second mortgage, split it with you, worked out a payment schedule. We'd be on our way to resolving this."

E. shuffled through my file and I studied The Hoff squeezed uncomfortably into his corner of the table occupying the entire room. Which was itself the size of a table. I stifled a smirk.

"Ve are nutt in ze biss'ness uff ne-gotiating," E. huffed.

Chomp chomp.

What's the next line? I can't remember my line.

Vell den, vvvat em I doink herrrre!

Chomp.

"Well then, what am I doing here?" I said and whipped off my blue-tinted hexagonal spectacles.

E. gasped.

Yesss!!!

I've been up all night crying in a deep personal way that will probably obviate the need for sit-ups for a fortnight. When I arose from my 5:30 to 7:30 A.M. nap, my eyes were clamped shut and I had to pry them open but I didn't perform the usual ice and Preparation H suppository miracle. The one Kate says is an Old Wives' Tale but always works for me.

"How'd I get to be the outlaw here?" I continued. "I'm a relatively law-abiding middle-aged Jewish-American person who has paid huge sums to the government . . ."

Back in The Seventies when the big money was rolling in and the big government was tithing top personal income at 70 percent and the big checks payable to the IRS were seven figures.

I had read that The Government grossed taxes on a million dollars over the course of an average American's lifetime. By my forth decade I'd paid for one two three etc. lifetimes.

The way I saw it I'd overreached my quota.

The way I saw it I should be exempt until my federal ID number expired because I did.

E. frowned. What have you done for me lately? was the question on her mind.

"This situation makes me wanna kill myself and leave a

note that says: I can no longer bear the persistence of E."

E. clucked, alarmed. I nearly added, "I said '*wanna*'!"

But when I remembered who she was and what she was and where I was and how I was I thought why? and kept my own counsel.

"I've even gotten it into my head that you saw my book at the checkout counter when you picked up your groceries one night, recognized the name, picked it up, read it and hated me!"

E. smiled gently and I stuck my glasses on so she didn't have to see my soul anymore.

Life is moments. This was one.

"Let's do this deal," The Hoff broke in with a helpful whine.

To Do: To accomplish. To fuck. To kill . . .

Kate departed dramatically for spring break in Cancun with Those Boys and Girls last night. Early evening I took her and Jackie (who now nannies Natasha, Kate's half-sister compliments of my first-and-last-ex-husband and his third wife Juliana) for a seems-like-old-times farewell dinner at Hamburger Hamlet.

"Where's the waitress?" Kate nudged after an intense forty-five minutes.

The tired old black woman who'd served our food desultorily *had* scooped up my MasterCard a while ago. Kate was right. She seemed to be gone an unreasonably long time.

Finally, diffident, Tired-Old-BW shuffled over.

"Don't get mad, Mrs. Phillips, but I've lost your card," she drawled.

Don't get mad?

Mrs. Phillips.

Don't. Get. Mad. But I've lost. Your card?!@#

My last and only credit in the world.

Four hundred dollars maybe.

I remember when it was four hundred thousand.

Then forty large.

Then four with three zeros.

Forty small?

Where's my card? Where's my card? I got hysterical.

If I hadn't been a seminame drawing negative attention to myself it would've gotten good to me.

Ahh it got good to me anyway so I went ballistic.

I stayed ballistic through kisses with Kate and Jackie curbside and called Todd, overwrought, from the car.

The man of few words found some choice ones, got heavy with the Hamlet and they found the card.

He drove it at top speed to my house and was relieved to find me wailing in the driveway but still intact.

"Uh-huh-uh," Todd said when I kissed the card first and him second and we bounced up the stairs.

"So are ya gonna wear The Suit?" Todd joked, referring to wardrobe for The McGuffin.

"Nahhh too prosperous."

"You shouldn't have worn it to a funeral."

"I never saw so much good hair in a room in L.A. . . ."

"On so many good-looking people . . ."

"A testament to his coolness," I said, wishing I'd known him better when he was alive — flashing for a moment on The Other Jools sobbing in an adjacent pew.

I shuddered and reflected on how UnHappy New Year had been . . .

HOW I SPENT MY BULNERABLE SEASON—
THE SEQUEL BY JULIO PHILLIPPE, 1993

The Advocate's Man of the Year was David Geffen.

We're here. We're queer. And so are some of you.

January dawn, dressed gray, insinuated itself into my consciousness and moist all over from a marathon mud-wrestle with Morpheus, I was still auditioning for the part of Philosopher King.

As in:

I'm the Vampire Lestat! It's my turn.

Oh yeah, fuck you, I'M immortal more or less!

No, *me. I'm* the second chick!

No, me.

Okay, why not? Try sucking THIS for a while you think it's so easy.

Aahhh why're we fighting? Let's give it to Him . . .

Who?

Him. Over there. The Man with The Power . . .

Every night I writhed in bed worrying about money and every day I arose worrying about money, which didn't promote much healthy alpha beta delta sleep.

Toss. Money. Turn. Money. Sweat.

Moneymoneymoney.

Money had replaced *death* as my mantra . . .

All the phones rang and I feared a brief POWER OFF.

Water and Power early-morning-relaying.

I had a dilettantish acquaintance with relaying and grids and networks and rolling brownouts courtesy of research I'd conducted with The Spielberg, preparing *Close Encounters of the Third Kind*, which I'd maintain to my last breath it was his purest effort.

Including *E.T.*, which always made me cry.

We spent two days with a charismatic blue-collar-who-rose-through-the-ranks-Con-Ed-troubleshooter who bore a strong resemblance to Peter Boyle. He put us in the right direction conceiving Roy Neary, played by Richard (she's-committing-suicide-with-this-book) Dreyfuss but the network yadda-yadda inspired a giant left turn.

We designed a two-day scene that took four.

Shot it. Cut it.

Could've financed a decent Head Start program for what we wasted. Could've settled my tax problem for sure . . .

"Jools, it's Fanny," she sobbed into the answering machine. "Pick up!"

7:09 red readout roared from the digital clock behind my bed.

"I'm here . . ."

"I've just had the most devastating news. Pauly's dead."

She started to sob again.

"I guess *he* gets to play the Vampire Lestat," I said before I thought and Fanny cracked up.

"Thank you for making me lawhhff," she said.

"Should I find us some pizza? Death always makes me hungry, especially since I've given up fucking."

"Latuhh," she said. "I have to go over there, sort some stuff out, but latuhhh would be good."

"Sure fine, I'm at your beck and call."

"Thanks, Jools. They're gonna haff to do an autopsy. What could it have been?"

"O.D.?"

"Not his style."

"How old was he?"

"Thuuuhhrty."

"Then it's probably a heart attack. Or an aneurysm . . ."

"So you'll bring pizzahhh latuhh?"

"In less than thirty minutes." We hung up.

I checked red readout. 7:11. The lucky numbers.

Seven and one and one equaled nine.

The number of completion.

Pauly's completion.

Well this is certainly not my style! I laughed to myself on the drive down Sunset. Jools east of Fairfax?

Alone? Latuhhh? I hate this concept!

Times being what they are and all.

The spaces in front of the building were taken so I U-turned and parked some hundreds of yards north on the other side, safely stashed under a street lamp.

When I decamped a boy walking his dog recognized me and insisted on carrying my packages to the door.

"Do you know you're the hero of West Hollywood?" he vamped and Fanny buzzed me in.

• • •

"You want someone to walk you down?" Fanny suggested some hours latuhhh when others came to call and I got antsy.

"Nah, It's only 10:15." But I wrapped my keys between the fingers of my right fist like I learned in grade school. P.S. 92. Brooklyn. The Fifties.

I ambled into the night air and the second I stepped off the curb I spotted two dark-skinned sidewalk denizens. One on the corner and one across the street. Easing ominously in my direction. A post-riots ambush! Shocked but not surprised I moved at an aerobic clip toward 329WOE.

They picked up their pace. Not quickly enough though.

Hah! Fooled you with the gray hair.

I unlocked my door, slid in, locked it.

Started up the engine but they kept coming.

One mounted the trunk, the other the hood.

I turned on my lights and jerked away from the curb and that boy on the trunk fell off. That boy on the hood, however, held on tightly and crawled toward me. The closer he got the more I noticed his eyes were demented.

He smiled crazily, revealing straight white teeth, and licked the windshield.

Angling to sever his tongue I set the wipers on HIGH.

I lurched the car back-and-forth violently but he hung on. We stared each other down through the windshield and I must have had as much murder in my eyes as in my heart because he backed off.

Not enough for me so I lurched again, but I couldn't wrench him off the hood and now *he* had murder in *his* eyes.

We'd escalated to 7.9 on The Racial Scale.

Well at least we have *something* in common!

Another car pulled up and sensing danger danger danger flicked brights and honked horn and in the confusion I edged into traffic.

Meshuggener Shvartzer slid off my hood like the last drop of water gravitating to the bottom of a hill.

With a grandiose bow and arm-gesture he indicated:

You're free . . .

I peeled out, furious.

"Where'd he get those teeth?!" I yelled and dialed Fanny. Throughout, 911 hadn't occurred to me.

"Of all people for this to happen to," Fanny said disconsolately. "I guess you'll never come out in this town again."

"That's a pretty fair bet," I laughed. Yo, suck *this*!

I'm alive I'm alive. And I'm *detached*!

I've always *wanted* to live here.

"Good thing you didn't hit the bahstahr'd," Fanny said. "If you killed him you'd've been chahhrged with muhhrder. He was probably just fucking with you."

"The whole time I was in a rage: Is this what I can't pay my taxes for?!"

"We gotta get outta here, Jools, The City of Angels is dying a bit more every day . . ."

"I think Lost-in-Angeles died already but nobody told it."

I waited for a clever riposte but only static emanated from the receiver so I replaced it gently in its cradle.

No, Fanny, every day the angels are dying a bit more in the city. Like Pauly.

I brushed an angry tear from my left cheek, pressed my right foot *hard* on the accelerator and flew up the canyon.

Seeking Sanctuary . . .

"I gotta have a smoke," I huff and The Hoff doesn't disagree. Fighting funky fumes rising from the funky street, we loiter near the elevator inside the cement parking structure. Below DWP repairs a main they probably broke in the first place. I toss my gum into a garbage receptacle and fumble for a cigarette.

"You earned it, kid," The Hoff says sweetly, smiles fondly and fires me up with my lighter. "I can't wait to tell Peter Mainstain."

"Grrrr . . ."

"He bet me we'd never get the lien lifted."

"I shoulda gone for sixty/forty."

"You'd have ended up right where you are."

"That's true." Puff puff. Wonder what they bet?

Probably more than my current net worth.

"At least you're doing what you wanna do," The Hoff whines, edging onto lower Wilshire Boulevard, an obstacle course of deconstruction and reconstruction. "I really wanted to play professional ball but my parents urged me to be safe. So now I'm an accountant . . ."

"I'm not sure I'm even doing what I *wanna* do, I'm doing what I *have* to do." I certainly don't miss the debilitating Left-Words and Return-Calls concomitant with the soul-battering endeavor of putting and keeping movies together. Interacting with The Uptight Man, trying to put him at ease.

Talk about not good for one's self-esteem.

"I coulda been a contenduh," The Hoff whispers wistfully.

"Me too." We chuckle together.

We don't exchange another word.

When he drops me off I pick up the mail, which includes a large envelope from Viking/Penguin. Letters to The Author. I dump it on the table in the color-coding corner and dial Pierce. He congratulates me and promises he'll deal with DeGiglio toute de suite.

I fling open the bedroom doors, light up my first gratifying smoke of the day and settle in to reading fan mail/hate mail. I'm in the midst of the eleventh negative in a row when Pierce calls back.

"There's $108,000 in your royalty account and DeGiglio insists he must hold back a considerable sum to cover returns . . ."

"It's two years after the book's release. What returns?" Pierce sighs.

"Look I pried loose fifty grand."

"Shit!" Pierce sighs louder.

"He wanted to give you only thirty."

"Like it's his to give."

I fiddle with a postcard postmarked Chicago, Illinois.

Dear Julia Phillips, it starts, I'm a sixty-one-year-old Plain Jane. I've worked for the same mean boss for twenty years.

And been diagnosed with lung cancer. I read your book. I got a raise and my cancer is in remission. Thank you for putting some clean air around my head.

"Have Neal Hoffer call DeGiglio with wire-transfer instructions. I gotta get going, I'm late for this meeting already." Busy very-busy. Taking calls. Cutting deals.

With a few points open.

Just in case.

"Like he doesn't know already! I *always* need the money yesterday!" I'm becoming addicted to the adrenaline-rush provided by: Will the check reach the account in time?

Pace pace. Puff puff. Ooh ooh. "Anything else?"

"You could say thank you," Pierce says dryly.

"Damn it, Jools, Be Nice to the Lawyers!" I chide myself when we hang up and I head to The Creature's room to tack Raise/Remission on the bulletin board.

"Be nice to the lawyers," Jerry Chaleff had advised with a twinkle in his bespectacled eyes and a smile in the midst of his salt-and-pepper beard during our first-and-last meeting some years back.

Jerry Chaleff was one of L.A.'s top-ten criminal lawyers and had the slender build, sleek look and cheerful mien befitting a man who cut deals on his clients' behalf with the devil, aka The Prosecutor, with whom he dined daily and knew on a first-name basis.

I'll be able to settle Jerry Chaleff's bill with my imminent infusion. Not to mention something for Christine.

Finally.

$50,000 less 10 % for ICM.

Ticka-chung.

Less 5 percent for The Hoff.

Ticka-chung.

Less at least twenty grand to E.

Ticka-chung ticka-chung.

Less two months' late payments.

Ticka-chung ticka-chung ticka-chung.

Less next month's payments.

Ticka-chung ticka-chung tickachungchungchung.
Less less less.
Make that half his bill . . .

THOSE BOYS/THOSE GIRLS
THE PROCURER

Papa said, Mommy is a tramp and tramped on.
    Mommy said, A rolling stone gathers momentum and did.
    Ended up in foster care.
    Down at the bottom.
    Yearned for life at the top.
    Developed strange charm.
    Used imagination.
    Avoided confrontation.
    Finessed recrimination.
    It had heaps of aspiration.
    If too little inspiration.
    It has the right words.
    If they're desired.
    It has the right connections.
    As required.
    And of course It has the right attire.
    Auctions Clients' Secrets to the highest tabloid buyer.
    It has the right.
    It is For Hire.

I will narrowly avoid foreclosure on Sanctuary, which E. and I have agreed to put on the market immediately. And DWP deprivation. Not to mention Food. If there IS a God, he'll defeat Clinton's budget and sell my house — check that, my *home* — by the end of the quarter.

The new real estate agent — a friend of Lance's — has knocked the asking price down $100,000, reminding me there are nothing but For Sale signs up and down the canyon.

"I've noticed some are being peddled directly by the banks," I remarked and he smiled ruefully.

"It'll be tough, but I'm willing to give it my best shot," he said in an ambitious yuppie treble. "We need to do A Broker's Open ASAP."

He took notes as we traveled the turf together. On approaching my domain he got flustered at the clutter. I opened the door to the closet and he gasped audibly.

He suggested kindly I straighten the place up.

ASAP.

So I'm standing helplessly in The Cabinet of Dr. Caligari, unable to focus and I pause at a Moschino sailor blouse, circa 1990, whose purchase Air strongly opposed. Too butch, she pronounced, and we had a good laugh since the George Sand look was always stylish and Air wore pants all the time. She was right though. I never wear it.

I keep telling myself I haven't found the right bottom to create an ensemble yet.

Mara, who's in the recycled clothing business, says I should give it to her. Later for that. I flick away nontears and run my hand across my head because this is going to be some job and I need all my strength.

And a little help from a few good friends.

I put out the calls.

Air and Mara who have gone through it before. Todd. And Claire the Jock, a more recent friend.

A perfect mix for my closet party.

Like Club Louie used to be.

Before the back surgery.

Before the riots.

And waaay before the tax problema.

In preparation for their arrival I agitate through clearing the floor and a chest of drawers. Nattering nervously to myself about the talking dog, my perfect boyfriend. Crackers. An acronym, I've decided, for Cosmic Regenerative Alpha-wave Creation of Knowledge Ergo Rewarding Solutions. Or is it Searches. Segues?

I haven't a clue where to take this trifle but I spent some serious quality time fucking myself on its conception so I have a vested interest in pursuing it.

A clear violation of The Writer's #1 Rule:

Love Nothing.

The gang makes short shrift of my equivocation. A steady stream of those girls and boys flows through my office — my seventies cave, wherein I never lurk anymore — to scout leftovers before I contribute to South Central L.A.

Bye bye Gianni . . .

So long Jean Paul . . .

Bienvenuto Gee-orgy-o . . .

I hum "Skeletons in my closet," and we laugh.

"I read something somewhere that reminded me of you," Claire grins, tossing early Anna Sui into the South Central pile.

"What?"

"Asking a writer how their work's going is like asking a terminal patient, 'How do you feel?'"

Claire is capable the way Air is capable.

And she's not as close a friend, to be called upon for this sort of labor.

"It's my birthday this weekend. Wanna come to a party?" she grins when it's over, hustling her chocolate Lab into her white Cherokee, tossing Harriet Selwyn linen structures I've forced on her into the backseat. I hesitate. "Bring whomever." She grins and tells me the address.

Frankie and I dine at The Monkey Bar, a trendy new restaurant financed by trendy Old Stars, located some convenient blocks from Claire's and run by a core group from Mortons. Doug. Darryl. Jerry. I like to think they've moved because they missed me. Haven't seen them much since my banishment. Except en masse at Pauly's funeral.

Pauly was sous-chef here and the food isn't as good since we buried him.

FLASHBACK: Zoe's birthday.

I was very late, sweaty and irritable from circling the blocks surrounding The Monkey Bar's Beverly Boulevard address. Nobody had bothered to tell me it was off Beverly and unmarked. I found it only because I called and insisted Doug stand on the corner and guide me to the entrance.

Richard Perry and Stan Dragoti were with Sally Kellerman at the adjacent booth.

"I'm not a vampire. I make vampire *movies*!" The Stan scowled, referring to *YNELITTA*'s Mortons-she-said-she-said denouement, and pulled away when I pretended to kiss his cheek.

"I don't mind the vampire reference," The Perry smiled toothsomely, "I take it as a backhand compliment."

"Those boys don't have a sense of humor," I groused to Pauly, alighting briefly in the kitchen en route to an anxiety-pee.

"Chechechch-phtooey!" Pauly mimed spitting on the Vampires' rock shrimp order . . .

Pauly's spirit took the edge off the restaurant's aggressively heterosexual atmosphere (drugs and alcohol and cash cash cash) which brushes in belligerent bursts around the shoulders and between the legs of the seven-foot women swathed in spandex, The Monkeys who linger in the packed bar nursing kamikazes.

"I still think you should've gone with the other ladies to have your picture taken," Frankie argues.

"The Academy of Arts and Sciences Salutes the Year of the Woman?! Less than 400 awards?!?! Out of 4,000!?@#!!!

"Frankly Frankie, I don't *give* a damn."

Conversation-over. Learned that from The Geff.

Frankie opens her mouth, reconsiders.

Todd joins us for a drink.

I light up a Marlboro happily. Drink drink puff puff.

"It's gonna be a good party," he smiles. "Different crowd," he adds, mentioning some names that are familiar.

"How's that different?" we laugh at him.

"Oh it'll be fifty-fifty straight/gay, but the other way . . ."

"Gym teachers and models, how new. But hey it's early on a Friday night and Club Louie isn't good anymore."

"Why is that?" Frankie laughs.

"Because the mix is hard to maintain and the eighties — the greed/AIDS/leveraged-buyout/megamerger decade — came and went faster than speed in Hollywood."

One holdover from the eighties was that there were fewer women than ever with big jobs.

Frankie and I had discussed that at dinner.

Women. Men.

"Can you believe Anita Hill and Hillary Clinton have become lightning rods for the discontent of the Uptight Man? Not to mention the Uptight *Woo-man!*" I said and glanced past Frankie's shoulder to spot Nick Wechsler, alternative manager-producer extraordinaire.

Seated at a corner-two with a glowering boy who looked like he should be Nick's homely older brother.

Nick had produced his-first/my-last movie with me and I considered him some of my better work.

Nick hied to the table to say hello.

Alighted for a brief twitchy moment.

"Who're ya with?" Frankie asked.

"Don Henley. He's one of the backers."

Nick snickered and so did I.

"He doesn't have a sense of humor."

"I know." Nick suppressed a cackle.

"He better not see you laughing with me . . ."

"Good-bye."

"Good-bye yourself."

Nick kissed us and rejoined The Don.

"What was that?" Frankie wanted to know.

"It's too boring trust me."

"Men."

"Men."

"Women."

"Yeah that too . . ."

• • •

We entrust our cars to the restaurant's valet and walk to Claire's.

"We'd better discuss something interesting," I fret. "I'm very edgy on the street since my Conflagration with The Other outside Fanny's."

"David Koresh?" Frankie suggests.

"Grrrr . . ."

"Jools was the only one watching when David Koresh had thirty-five uninterrupted minutes on CNN," Todd says.

"I got so mad I called the switchboard. I hadn't recovered from the World Trade Center bombing Friday, and I'm chilling to the Sunday news and suddenly there's unedited feed: inadequate ATF agents blown away, ex-*live*, and this nut-job on an open line and David French is too stoopid to cut him off —"

"Please, the only reporting coming from NearWaco is what the press said to each other that day," Frankie says.

We laugh.

"It's finally degenerated into stories about themselves. Donnez-moi un fucking break!"

"Kim Basinger . . ." Todd mutters. Me and Frankie smile.

"Man, if I could hold every Star to their handshake," Frankie complains, referring to the $8.7 million *Boxing Helena* judgment against The Kim. We snort knowingly.

"See how fast Guy de McElwaine disengaged? Think she wasn't *nice enough* to Howard Weitzman?" I observe, invoking the sacred names of The Kim's agent and attorney. "Wouldn't you think that with all the money he makes Howard Weitzman could have his pockmarked face scraped?"

"I think he *uses* it," Todd says.

"Like Pierce uses his size."

Claire's Birthday booms and throbs a block away.

"So this'll be good?" Frankie reconfirms and fishes in her bag for lip gloss.

"The Kim'll have no money," I quip, "but she's got her hands and feet . . ."

• • •

The party's rolling. Hollywood looking but not Hollywood because the guests are (dare I say it?) interacting. Not easy in a town where people slide surface streets in steel coffins avoiding eye contact with other walking-wounded/living-dead road warriors until they've reached their destinations.

"Claire's got a long reach," I observe sotto voce and Frankie agrees. There are more than a few recognizable names in the room.

Chatting up a tall slender blonde Athena, a track star/sports commentator. A model from the cover of last month's *Elle* scarfs down pasta with pesto at the buffet. An artist with a medium rep laughs at a joke thrown by a designer with a big rep. A Star Agent tends to The Star.

"Frankie, there's more interesting women in this room than I've ever *seen* at a party out here. Even ours . . ."

We stroll toward a bar in the kitchen. She nods.

And there's somethin' goin' on here
And you don't know what it i-i-iiiis, I crackwise atonally.

A la The Master.

"We fit right in."

"Oh I'm sure they think we're a couple."

We giggle a politically incorrect giggle. Is there any other kind?

Times being what they are and all.

"We're gonna hate ourselves in the morning for staying so late."

I call Eric Simonoff, the Janklow/Nesbit agent who handles magazines. Sometimes I think he's the only person in the world who cares if I eat. Dinner at least.

I tell him I need an assignment.

"In fact, Eric, what I *really* need is a column. A regular monthly check. Pay the mortgage at least, so I still own the house when the IRS absconds with it."

E. had mentioned in our meeting — en passant but with a

glint in her eye — that she'd seized a couple of 90210 homes the day before the day before but I was too preoccupied with our moment to focus on our future.

"You know how much you hate it when they tell you to cut nineteen lines because they placed a last-minute ad," he protests.

"Eric, I neeeed the money."

He sets up drinks with Kathy Bishop, features editor at the *new Harper's Bazaar,* who happens fortuitously to be winging west next week. Kathy asks if her L.A. colleague Helen Murray, who's read *YNELITTA,* can join us.

Sure fine, I say because it's always nice to have someone at the meeting who's familiar with your work.

We meet in the bar of the Four Seasons Hotel.

ShowBiz/Publishing/News types, wealthy Persians and beautiful young women eddy in quiet whirlpools around us.

"So what did you have in mind?" Kathy sparkles openly after we order drinks and caviar blinis.

"I think I should be a California commentator:

"Sects-and-Dregs-and-Cock-Patrol."

Tentative Title: Adventures in FernoTainmentLand.

"Oh are drugs making a comeback?" Kathy says.

"They never went away," Helen and I chorus/overlap.

"Okay, that's one. What else?" Eeuuuooow, I don't wanna do a think-piece on BabyStuds in rehab at Studio 12.

I three-sixty the room looking for an idea and the model from the other night at Claire's, fawning over a Rich Old Boy at a kittycorner booth, catches my eye and winks.

Thank you God. I wink back.

"Mmmmm. I don't know what I really *mean* by this, but I *do* think that lesbian is going to be the watchword for the nineties out here. Maybe everywhere . . ."

I seduce Kathy and Helen with a recap of Claire's party; titillate them further by confiding that in fact Claire and I have become good friends. They are fascinated.

"But we want you to do some reporting, too," Kathy says strictly, like the schoolteacher she truly is.

"No one's gonna talk for attribution," I say carefully.

"Fine," she says.

And I've got a gig.

I step into my orderly closet in search of something to pair with the Moschino sailor blouse and it occurs to me that I — who think I'm sooo hip for the room — have polished my sophisticated veneer from years of traveling those boys' circuit and my attention to lesbians has been restricted primarily to: Attending a revival of Lillian Hellman's *The Children's Hour*; passing acquaintance with the myths of Gertrude Stein/Alice B. Toklas and Georgia O'Keeffe; and the occasional thought that Tanya (possessed of a sharply evil wit and a short-haired/mustachioed/best-girlfriend nicknamed Bernie) might have been a closet case.

Tanya was before her times-being-what-they-are-and-all.

Tanya was.

How shall I put it?

Heavy Furniture . . .

I phone-pressure Claire into gathering her friends.

And Vera, long-legged and long-maned, a thirtysomething writer-producer — a hyphenate — who appropriately enough swings bi-hyphenate-sexually.

We bonded over herniated discs so I figure a call is within the boundaries of "okay" if not precisely taste.

"I'll put dinner together for you," she says matter-of-factly.

"Claire's organizing a Sunday afternoon and Vera's arranging a meal," I report to David Debin, struggling with his second novel in splendid Woodstock isolation.

Eking out the meager living accruing to Cult Status.

FLASHBACK. Sushi Ko. Fall 1990.

Debin had just concluded a melodramatic Loving Ode to the Female Organ.

"You think you like sashimi because it reminds you of pussy?" I smiled when our order arrived.

"Nah, I probably like pussy because it reminds me of sashimi."

"So you're eating in that town again?" he asks wryly. "Should I be worried about what you're eating?"

I choose to take umbrage at his remark.

"Listen, let's say *you* had the tax problem and *you* got this assignment. So *you* called your *one* gay friend (which, by the way, I doubt you'd have) do *you* think *he* would extend himself the way *my* friends are — "

"You're right you're right!" he laughs. "Don't *say* anymore!"

Debin's pretty elevated. But at fifty isn't it time?

Already.

I head for Ruby, one of the five smartest people I know, to indulge in Socratic dialogue re: Sappho de Lesbos.

I review the past thirty years' sexual politics.

"First The Woman's Movement:

"I want equal pay for equal work *and* multiple orgasms.

"*Which* by the way I don't achieve vaginally . . .

"Half Those Boys' organs had to wilt from stress."

"There weren't that many out here to begin with," Ruby, who grew up in South Central L.A., observes.

"The other half said, 'I can't deal with this, I'm gay!' Major reduction in the male pool. Then AIDS. Further reduction. Of course more lesbians."

"Plus, who understands PMS, menstrual cramps, labor or hot flashes better than another woman?"

"And that's the deal. In a nutshell."

"You've got major chutzpah doing this piece," Ruby laughs, referring to my retirement from The Battle of the . . .

"Sex became so difficult, Ruby, and it had been so easy. Men became debilitating and they had once been *fun*! How'm I supposed to have a functional id with these money problems?" I pout for emphasis.

"I buy it all. Woman's movement. Men out. Hate men. Higher form of love. I draw the line at eating pussy," Ruby says sourly over Precious Pink polish but she is also working the day after root canal, when she should be abed. Lulled into painless torpor by a Vicodin ES. Maybe two.

"Why are you even here?"

"I need the money." Ruby is awaiting word from the L.A. County Art Museum on the matter of her paintings being hung there. They liked her work, warned her she'd have to wait seven months for a final decision.

I ask if the people tormenting her are men.

"No. Prim ladies in sensible shoes."

"Lesbians . . ."

Dalee calls with a number for Jewel Williams, who owns Catch One, where I've danced upon occasion.

In the wee hours.

I query casually if he thinks lesbians are born. Made?

A little of both? Either? Or? All together now?

"They don't *choose* to be that way," he says in his most emphatic Jesse Jackson tone and hangs up.

"Am I gonna have to defend you?" Air says when I inform her of my assignment.

"Oh please."

"Whaddya mean, Oh please. Don't wear that Moschino blouse, and I'd think about the pinstripe suit."

"Are you serious?"

"As cancer."

Air is a Scorpio and I should listen more carefully.

Lee connects me with a lead, a heavy lawyer. She says she has a circle she'll speak to: architects, designers, brokers. She'll get back to me.

"I don't think she wants to talk to me," I tell Lee on the phone.

"Well, she's shy and like you, she hates going out."

"Air's worried she's gonna have to defend me."

Lee laughs.

"Jools, I've been defending you for years."

• • •

Claire's Ladies-Who-Munch Brunch includes:

Sasha, young and beautiful and English, present principally for decoration as she barely speaks. She has thin delicate
hands and she fiddles with them constantly, lets her fingers do
the talking.

Caroline, an angry English club owner who speaks stri-
dently in clipped upwardly mobile Sloane Ranger syllables.
(See Sasha.)

Chloe, whom I met at Claire's Birthday.

"Liked your book," she said, introducing herself. "I'm a
Mount Holyoke graduate, too."

"'Oh Mount Holyoke, we pay thee we pay thee we pay thee,'
we harmonized in the sixties with our gym teachers," I replied
and we laughed. Tall, blonde, slim, chic. An accomplished seven
sisters attorney at a seven sisters studio, she's the most vocal.

But who knows how forthcoming?

Leslie and Anna arrive together.

A producer and another attorney.

Leslie is big and tall and wears her baseball cap backward.

Candy and Liza arrive late. Candy, an art director, is of
hybrid genealogy. Japanese and Portuguese, she informs me
when I ask if she's Hawaiian. Great smile, big white teeth. A
tad dumpy, with that goddamn nosering that always compels
me to ask, But what about the really *big* booger . . . ?!

Liza's quite young and very beautiful.

When I wonder where she was raised she says, "In a lesbian commune in Oregon."

Duh.

The group settles down and I perform my five-minute
pitch. Oscar. Drugs. *YNELITTA.* My haircut.

My assignment.

"I'm probably a closet case," I say disingenuously, and
Candy smiles responsively. I'm a heterosexual on a stretch-
ing-into-permanent hiatus if there isn't a cease-fire between
men and women before the fin de millennium.

Oh, the Bosnia-Herzegovina of it all.

Or is it Hercegovina?

Candy's nosering catches a flicker of afternoon sun and I microFLASHBACK:

Crisco Disco.

Late seventies or was it early eighties?

Me and Victor, twisting the night away.

"Can we go the fifth floor?" I needled. "Where the kinky stuff happens? Can we can we? Can we?"

"You really wannna witness a seven-foot bald guy pissing on his fifteen-year-old pet!? Who'll probably be on a leash . . . ?!"

"Mmmmm . . . from how far away?" I joked and Victor scowled. "I'm kidding!"

"Just keep dancing and don't ask again . . ."

"So tell me," I start — in neutral — "how do people relate to you, say at work?"

"I think the men like us because there's no sexual tension," Chloe says and Anna nods.

"And The Wives looove us," Leslie says.

"Well that helps, to get along with the wives."

"The world's getting more sensitized," Anna says. "When I broke up with my lover-of-six-years, people I worked with let me know they were sorry to hear it."

"That's pretty elevated . . ."

"And there are more of us . . ."

"Are there more of you, or are there more who are out?"

"Maybe a little of both," Chloe says. "And it's weird. I mean, we're *out*, but we're not *really* out."

"As in: you'll talk to me, but you don't want me to use your real names."

"That's a given," Chloe says. Just in case I didn't know the deal. Be nice to the lawyers. "The people we work with *know* but — "

"It's not an acknowledged aspect of corporate life?"

"Exactly."

"Okay, so is there a network?" I push and Claire, who tends to bark, arfs, "No!"

"Why?"

"Because women are too bitchy to each other," Claire says definitely and the others nod.

"Women were never very nice to each other in this town," I admit. "Sorry to hear things haven't changed. Come to think of it though, the men aren't nice to each other either . . ."

And while we chuckle and rearrange ourselves in our seats I think: *people* aren't nice to each other. Period.

Wolves are nicer to each other than people. I know.

"But still," Claire insists, "*They* get along well enough to network and women just *don't*!"

"Did it ever occur to you that might be because they were trained to be women by men?" I challenge. "Jesus, I hate men . . ."

"Oh we *like* men," Leslie says and rearranges her baseball cap. That's because you haven't been fucked by them, I think, reminding myself that I'm easily a decade older than anyone here. If not in the bedroom, just wait'll you find out how they *do* business. "Besides, the big male fantasy is two women with each other," Leslie adds.

Ahhh, the defense.

FLASHBACK: Late sixties or was it early seventies?

Touring the aisles of City Lights Bookstore in San Francisco with PsychoStar, the guy "who bites the baby's ears off and eats 'em," as he once so eloquently stated.

"So, Jools, wanna know what turns me on?" he taunted.

"No . . ."

"Wanna know what — "

"No!" I swear.

"Wanna — ?"

"No no no no no."

"Two lesbians eating each other," he insisted.

I feel Leslie's invocation of PsychoStar's POV is meant to let me know that if it's okay with them, welllll . . .

Waitasecond: You're Those Boys' favorite fantasy and there's no sexual tension?

I wonder.

I'm too shy to ask The Question.

"So what about this book?" I gesture instead to the sample on the table — the one constructed from cheap recycled paper and disintegrating binder. *Sex.* By The The, who thinks she reinvented it. "Does this help the cause?"

"Definitely . . ."

"Right on . . ."

"Yes . . ."

"I know those girls up front," Candy snickers.

"Oh the ones with pierced everything?" I bandy archly and Candy chuckles knowingly. I love a guy with a sense of humor.

"Whadd*you* think, Jools?" Claire asks. I really ponder for a second.

"I think she should seek professional help," I kid on the square and everybody laughs. "Five hours a day, five days a week . . ."

"Ya wanna hit the underground circuit?" Candy offers with a broad smile as the group breaks up.

"If you're there to protect me," I flirt.

"Club Fuck?"

FLASHBACK: Summer 1991. Seeking Crackers, not Sanctuary, on a squirrelly Sunday night.

Me. Niki Harris, the beautiful black backup singer who hit The The's high Cs. Todd. Don and Randy — guys on the circuit — fortified by steak and martinis at a deserted Olive, headed east on Sunset to Club Fuck territory.

Pale boys in tattoos and leather harnesses and girls in underwear danced and performance-coitused in a tight hot space.

Niki and I stood on the bar for a better view. Two feet away a soap opera star swathed in sadomasochistic stretch-leather sipped a sherry.

"What do they wear from the car to the club, I wonder?" Niki smirked.

"Niki, I see penetration with no condoms . . ."

She laughed me off at a disturbingly cynical pitch, but

maybe that was the koo-koo-ka-choo from the ubiquitous boom and throb surrounding — nay, enveloping us.

"They all have AIDS, Jools, they don't care . . ."

"You're too young to have attended so many funerals . . ."

"Welcome to The Future," Niki said noncommittally.

A pale blond boy sidled up to us.

"I loved your book, you should keep writing," he said.

Then another.

And *an Other* . . .

"I thought they pegged me 'homophobic'?!"

"Your fans," Niki grinned, twenty years younger than me and soooo much wiser. "Hey babe, Number One is Number One in this town . . ."

When Todd and I returned to my car we found it had been raped. The passenger door was pried open and the radio stolen. Bummer. The second Alpine in three months, and I was entirely too poor to replace it.

"Why does all the sex happen in these borderline neighborhoods?" I kvetched, fretting over my daughter . . .

The day after the announcement of the second Rodney King verdict Kate breezes in for a layover between the end of sophomore year and an advanced placement poli-sci seminar.

The Authorities keep the jury's decision under wraps for twenty-four hours to deploy troops around town should there be another miscarriage of justice, another riot.

I learned everything I needed to know about poli-sci in a Harvard thesis by Murray Levin about voting for the lesser of two evils in Boston's 1960 mayoral election. THE ALIENATED VOTER. Freshman year. Mount Holyoke College.

It is my turn at Kate-retrieval and I've asked Todd to drive. I often freeze at the entrance to a boutique, so I know I'll probably descend into catatonia at the right turn on Century Boulevard to LAX.

"I can't remember the last time I drove myself to the airport," I whined when I asked if he'd mind and thought, Ou sont les limousines d'antan?

Kate's flight arrives early and her baggage is among the first down the chute. We hustle across the street and she collapses gratefully into 329WOE's backseat.

"You look great!" I say, relieved she hasn't gained substantial weight. Me projecting.

"So what's goin' on, Mom?"

"Doin' this lesbo piece for *Harper's* . . ." Kate chuckles. "Are there lesbian sororities on campus?"

"Mmmm, not that I really know of . . ."

"Think any of your friends are gay?"

Kate leans forward, suddenly intense. "Not gay, Mom, but they're all anorexic!"

"Ah the white-middle-class-daddy's-good-little-girl syndrome." Reinforced by supermodels in relentless rotation hawking cosmetics and diet drinks across the InfernoTainment band.

I flash on one of Kate's pals who's starved herself into such small frailty I fear she'll evaporate into the ether before she has an opportunity to die young.

"I'm the only one who has full meals! I eat *normally* and I feel like I'm pigging out! I'm worried about all of them! All the time."

Todd and I exchange quick glances:

What kind of world . . . ?

Brooke and I T.V.-witness evening-news replays of the Monday Morning InfernoTainment Combustion of the Branch Davidians' Compound.

NearWaco.

"The reporters can't contain themselves! 'Look everybody, Something's Finally Happened! And it's *big*! And it's *bad*! And it's *soooo exciting*!' And it's in *America*, asshole! Grrr . . ."

"Yeah but we're watchin' it," Brooke says and we turn our attention to Janet Reno commencing her Spin Cycle on Larry King Living-Dead, invoking the advice of Experts.

"Well the little children won't be abused anymore!" I talk back to the news.

"Now I know what 'out of the frying pan into the fire'
means."

"These people are too square to be in charge. What
experts!? Their advice sucked from start to finish! Yo Janet
call *me* sometime."

"'I *did* it. I'm *reeealll* sorry!'" Brooke laughs and we head
for the kitchen. "Gay Girls must really be in the atmosphere,"
he says, trying to be helpful with my assignment. "I'm doing
this audition today and the director says, 'Okay, you're in a
bar and you catch the eye of a cute girl across the room. She
comes over to you. Then another one, also a dish, comes over
to flirt, and *cut* . . . and they're *lesbians*, ha ha ha.' Weird,
hunh?"

Claire and I jog from her house to the Monkey Bar. I introduce her to Doug a tad breathless. "Jock meet Jock," I pant
because they're both into racquet sports.

If Claire weren't Jewish and Doug a man I'd swear they're
the same person. Besides Doug loves lady athletes.

"I know they're all gay, Jools," he once told me, "but I
don't care. They have legs like racehorses . . ."

He escorts us to our booth, sits and chats briefly before the
invasion of The Horde: dirty-mouthed middle-aged real estate,
ShowBiz, import-export honchos and lawyers.

Flanked by their twentysomething . . .

. . . escorts.

Claire three-sixties the room on high Jack Nicholson alert.
He's a well-advertised principal backer/patron who frequently
arrives unannounced, and Claire has often confided the one
boy in the world who might seduce her into a heterosexual
frame of mind is The Jack.

I love reminding her that the last time I saw him was at a
Maxfield's private sale. He was pulling a cashmere sweater
over his head to reveal a bulging gut, thin flyaway hair and
a disturbing resemblance to Broderick Crawford from his
Highway Patrol era.

More Optifast than Optifascinating.

"So whaddya wanna know," Claire grins when Doug suddenly departs to seat a high-profile attorney recently axed by a Heavyduty InfernoTainment Firm for sexual harassment.

He's still of counsel, though.

As in: *He* doesn't have a tax problem.

"Everything," I grin back. As little as possible.

"Go ahead," she challenges. "Ask me anything . . ."

"Born that way? Made that way? Political choice? Tell me about your first time."

"I was seduced," Claire grins, "by Athena . . ."

"I knew it!"

"Y'know it's funny, I was with her for three years but she didn't really turn me on. I mean I loved her you know how I love her. She's my best friend . . . I was so mean, I was sooo promiscuous."

"But the promiscuity goes with coming out, don'tcha think?"

"I guess." Claire frowns.

"My friend Victor always tells me that ninety percent of those boys who think they're heterosexual are closet cases." And I often agreed with him. "Same with women?"

I'll bet two clubs . . .

Claire thinks for a minute, grins that grin.

"Yes," she says definitively.

Three no-trump and The Jock wins the — pardonnez-moi — *rubber.*

I call a medium-famous video-producer who jumpstarted myriad MTV careers and doesn't share in the profits.

Recently married. One child.

I last saw her at Steve Antin's birthday party.

She was in the close company of a two-hundred-pound-dyke-on-bike who had a terrible crush on her and I wouldn't say I was comfortable with them but I hit puberty in The Fifties and consider public displays of affection between any configuration but parent and child bad manners.

I assumed she was day-tripping through a hot trend.

"Julia, I'm not a lesbian," she says quickly. Oops!

"I'm not trying to offend you but I know you know some people. It would help if I could talk to them. Off the record. Hey, I've been vibing you intermittently for the last year. You had a baby!"

"Yeeaaaahhhh . . ." Her voice softens and we discuss our descendants for a few minutes. Phew! "I'll call some people for you," she says comfortingly and we hang up.

I fret over her reaction for at least twenty minutes. Well nobody ever accused ShowBiz types of being courageous.

But somehow I thought The Women would be.

Why?

Brad's voice has a forlorn tinge but Brad's like that. When I met Brad a few years ago in June I asked him how old he was and he said, "Thirty. Well, not thirty yet. I'm gonna be thirty in six months. In January," he added mournfully and I fell in love with him on the spot.

"Bad news. I talked to Ms. PowerAgent and I explained 'lesbian, watchword of nineties,' no attribution, off the record. She doesn't wanna do it," Brad says unhappily.

"She said it's time someone did a piece like this, but . . ."

Damn.

Shoulda called myself. But I was being considerate.

I.E.: Cowardly?

A Visit From Athena and Claire.

They repair to the living room for a game of pool on an undersized antique table I purchased decades ago.

From Goldie of the Dank Cheveux.

"Gary Devore took me to Ivy-at-the-Shore and I was seated back-to-back with her . . ."

"What happened?"

"Neither of us knew. Then she got up and on her way out she stopped at a table of publicists . . ."

Athena sinks five balls in a row then scratches.

"And . . ."

"She looked *back*, I looked *up* and she paled out and lost balance. In short, she plotzed. Gary Devore was so engrossed in his Louisiana shrimp he missed the moment."

Claire runs three balls.

I'm no good at pool since I stopped smoking cocaine.

"Did she have dirty hair?" Claire barks.

"Nah, but she had a prominent stain on the front of her blouse!"

We crack up and Claire scratches.

"See what I mean: we're too bitchy to each other!"

"Those girls keep saying women don't help each other but that's not how everyone is behaving with me . . ." I say. "With a couple of notable exceptions . . ."

Athena and Claire express concern that I'm not having it off with anyone.

"I've been reading up on Virtual Reality and any second there's gonna be a program called DILDONICS. I'm waiting till then."

They chuckle pityingly and run more balls.

We hike up to the deck to scope winter's rain and mud damage to the pool, which has been drained but not repaired.

Nine inches of greenish bilge shimmer at the deep end.

A distraught gopher scampers from side to side just above the waterline. His desperate little claws make a hideous scraping sound as he repeatedly attempts escape.

"We have to do something we have to do something," Those Girls rant hysterically.

I've lived in the canyon for two decades and dealt with many vermin so I rush to the kitchen for my trusty broom and butler's pal.

I zip up the stairs and slither down the shallow end's cement slope toward the gopher, who freezes in panic.

"Watch out watch out they have rabies," Those Girls coach.

I shoot them a contemptuous look and open the butler's pal. The gopher walks in. I carry him to the lot next door and dump him. He hesitates: Am I still here? Then bolts for the underbrush.

"Some tough dykes you are," I sneer.

"I don't think you've talked to anyone quite in my position!" Athena spits angrily as we bop down the steps. "You don't know what it's like being on camera."

"Excuse me?"

"I mean as your full-time job. The lesbians think I'm not out enough and pressure me all the time and my boss [she invokes the name of her Telecommunications CEO] tells me that if I don't show up at '21' on some guy's arm some Friday night pretty soon, I'm shaky."

"That's disgusting! I'm beginning to understand why the ShowBiz types are so paranoid . . ."

Vera's crowd convenes at The Olive. These Girls are younger than Claire's and range from pretty to beautiful.

The Wild Ones.

Hazel and P.J., a new couple, sit closest by.

Hazel is an actress. P.J. does hair and makeup.

I recognize their credits.

I tell them I may be prejudiced but I believe that part of the reason I am seeing more women together is as much environmentally induced as biological. As a borderline bipolar being I have a right to make this observation.

I perform my Women's Movement/wilted dicks/sexual harassers-abusers/gay men/death riff.

"You don't think a lot of women are playing with lesbianism out of physical and political fear?" I challenge.

"Oh I think some of my choice was political," P.J. allows.

"Mine wasn't . . ." Hazel says dreamily, reminiscing on her alcoholic/abusive/neglectful Midwestern parents. Her story reminds me of the stories of scores of actresses from the beach days in the seventies. Who ran away from home when they were verrry young, often from Daddy, and landed on their feet in Hollywood. Sort of.

But they weren't lesbians. *They* were mostly whores.

What am I saying here?

Not everyone who smokes pot will shoot heroin.

But everyone who shoots heroin once . . . inhaled.

Not EveryMan who beats his wife kills his wife.

But EveryMan who kills his wife hit her . . . once.

Not every lesbian is a whore.

But every whore . . .

. . . is a thesbian?

I mention Ozone, a sex club Claire checked out a couple of weeks ago. Claire didn't like it.

"I wore a ski mask," she confessed. "Very *Friday the 13th*."

We had an argument anyway.

"I hate the girls doing this stuff," I whined during a Friday afternoon fete at my soon-to-be-repossessed dilapidated canyon pad. The one with the clean closet.

"Why?"

"Because it's just like — "

"Those boys?"

"Yeah."

"So what!!??"

"Well, you see where all *their* fun led . . ."

"They hand out rubber gloves and dental dams at the door," Hazel says gravely.

"I remember working out to Doctor Art Ulene one afternoon in The Eighties. He had all this paraphernalia laid out on a table, lecturing on 'safe sex' and I kept wondering if there were any kinky uses for or fantasies to fulfill with all that latex."

We laugh.

"It's not funny," Hazel says, suddenly serious. "There's a much higher risk for AIDS passing woman to woman than woman to man or vice versa . . ."

"I'm sorry, I didn't know."

They don't *choose* to be that way, Dalee said.

Jasmine and Jane arrive. I recognize Jasmine, a model on the cusp of the seven-figure-a-year salary from the fashion mags and Saturday-morning Elsa Klensch. She looks like an ethnic Macaulay Culkin and has no intention of being Home

Alone. Jane would be a standout in a room without Jasmine. An Amazonian English blond, she is merely attractive in Jasmine's presence.

Jasmine has a baby who was five months old when she left her violence-prone Hispanic husband for Jane, who quit her job as a medium-respected journalist with a medium-respectable English rag to manage Jasmine's career.

They took the baby with them.

Anne Marie, an upandcoming actress who is a dead ringer for Andie MacDowell, arrives late. She is tall and frail, very young, encased in a mantle of despair that exudes a constant erotic glow. It is the kind of despair that would drive Debin and Devore wild and will probably age her quickly. She sits at the opposite side of the table, but eases between Vera and me in twenty minutes.

"She straight?" she asks Vera as if I'm not around and Vera says, Yes.

This interests Anne Marie.

She jams a cigarette in her mouth and waits for me to light it. She pulls on it ferociously. She is fidgety and fretful.

"I haven't had any alcohol or drugs for forty-five days," she smiles. We discuss *that* for a while and she calms down.

I experience a hot flash shortly after, drop a fifty and say good-bye.

It was Fight-or-Flight and Flight won, hands down.

When I get home, there is a message from Ms. Not-a-Lesbian.

"Sorry, honey, I tried, but it's not going to work. Keep on vibing me, though . . ."

Jewel Williams, fifty-three, is a straight-backed strong-chested black woman with an authoritative aura of dignity she wears like a shield. Jewel owns Catch One, the longest-running nightclub in Los Angeles in spite of its wrong-side-of-Wilshire location and has lived over the store for twenty years.

She's brought Karen Ocamb, a lesbian reporter for the lesbian press, who is white. This morning when Jewel said on the phone she'd like to bring her I asked if it were for protection and she laughed because Karen had asked the same question.

"No she's my best friend," Jewel said and I felt honored.

Jewel and I establish midway through brunch that our politics are the same. We commiserate about the breakdown of the system and I say, "It's all the Republicans' fault."

"Thank you," she says.

"I know in my heart that from the time Kennedy was killed the wrong boys got to run things. Like he was such a prize . . ."

"Yeah, but he was just a Bad Boy. They're *really* Baaad Boys," Jewel says.

"Republicans," I muse and we crack up.

Karen, who's considerably younger than me and The Jewel, feels excluded.

"You have to have *been* there!" we harmonize.

"You gonna run for office, Jewel?"

"Thinkin' about it . . ."

I order a drink. Jewel and Karen are clean and sober.

"But is there plenty of drug use in the lesbian community?" I ask casually.

"Absolutely!" Karen volunteers. "More drugs, more alcohol, more suicide, more breast cancer, cervical cancer . . ."

"More abusive backgrounds?"

"Of course," Karen smiles. Duh. "But still . . ."

"You think, 'born that way.'"

"Absolutely," Karen says definitely.

"And the abuse, I think, is much more in our generation," Jewel says quietly.

"I think if anything abuse is on the rise."

"Oh yes, absolutely," Jewel says, "I'm just talking about abuse as a cause. The young ones seem much freer about it . . ."

The young always seem free, I think but don't say.

Until they get older and realize they aren't.

When I tell them the working title HOT ON THE TRAIL OF LES LESBIANS DANGEREUSES, Karen winces and I remind her I'm writing for a mainstream publication. "You need to develop a sense of humor," I say and Jewel smiles.

"So Jewel, in the eighties there were some boys who weren't really gay who I *know* sucked dick for their careers. Same with women . . . ?"

"Oh sure. It's a trend thing."

"But what about this AIDS woman to woman?" I joke. "Bodily fluids?"

"Mmmmm," Jewel says, "and it's the toys . . ."

I, who consider myself the master of the follow-up question, let her sentence hang in the late afternoon Polo Lounge air and return my attention to my eggs Benedict.

I puncture a yolk forcefully.

Oooh gooey . . .

"Oh you have to talk about the strap-ons," Vera laughs on the phone later. "I'm thinking of opening a charge account at Pleasure Chest."

Jewel, I have noticed, is built, like me. "I like the upper body stuff," she said at lunch. "I hate the ones who use it as an excuse to be fat."

I feel dizzy, lie down for a moment.

My head is reeling.

Jewel is heavy furniture and I will make damn sure to pump iron before I see her next time.

"I can't meet you for dinner, maybe drinks, I'm going to this lesbian seminar with Claire . . ."

"Oh, and what are they going to do, teach you to be a lesbian??!!" Frankie says sharply. I am stunned.

So *this* is how it feels . . .

"Have dinner with someone else. I'll meet you for drinks."

We make a plan for me to call her later at the restaurant.

"The truth is," Leslie said at Claire's brunch-is-not-enough, "there are vast parts of this country where if you walk down a street holding hands someone might throw a beer can at you . . ."

I felt a sharp parental pain.

I wouldn't want anyone to treat *my* daughter like that.

I also wouldn't want some dumb boy to beat her or rape her or abuse her so he could feel comfortable with himself.

Me projecting again.

Why can't I shake the recurrent thought that this seemingly ubiquitous female same-sexism is political? That it is as much a reaction to obtuse male brutality as anything. Male and Female people dealt with each other a certain way for millennia until The Movement and that was only twenty-five years ago. After all.

Did We expect Them to cede their dominant position?

With no resistance?

Without a fight?

Did we expect it not to be a war?

Claire and I arrive fifteen minutes late and miss most of Donna Minkowitz, which pisses me off because she is screamingly funny in her five-minute finish, and Helen Zia who follows her is not. She isn't particularly well-organized either, and reads snippets of hate mail to *Ms.* magazine. Excusez-moi, but qu'est-ce que say Le Point? I peruse the line-drawn scrawl on the cover of my program:

WHY IS LESBIAN-FEMINIST STILL A DIRTY WORD?

Why is FEMINIST a dirty word? Or LESBIAN?

LIBERAL for that matter?

Why indeed.

The place is packed and it takes a moment to locate Chloe, who's saved two seats. It's warm and poorly ventilated and when the woman in front of me fondles her girlfriend's long blonde hair I suffer a hot flash and remove my jacket.

I doze through Helen, denying an incipient preoccupation with what might happen here should we experience a temblor of, say, 5-plus . . .

Linda Villarosa, Chloe's friend, is a delicate light-skinned African-American in hip glasses who tells her story in a polished intimate tone. A senior editor at *Essence* magazine, for whom she wrote an article with her mother, the program says, called COMING OUT.

"I came out because I got tired of my co-workers trying to fix me up," she starts and the audience laughs appreciatively. "It happened right after I went to a weekend retreat with my colleagues," she continues and everyone settles down because they know the beginning of a good story. "Everyone was telling about this husband and that wife and this loved one and that significant other, and I was very quiet through the whole weekend, didn't say a thing, because my other was named Jane.

"I was driving back with my boss — her car, her Mercedes — and I just blurted out on the freeway, 'I'm a lesbian,' and after she swerved across four lanes of traffic and regained control of the wheel, she gasped, 'Well' and there-thered me, but not unaccepting, and the next day, Monday, I just went up and down the hall, in and out of people's offices, saying, 'I'm a lesbian, I'm a lesbian, I'm a lesbian . . .'"

And there's something goin' on here
And you don' know what it i-i-i-zzz
Do you, Mr. — excuse me, Ms. — Jooohnnnnzzz.
As The Master never said.

FLASHBACK: Roxbury. Summer 1991.

Researching Crackers' Saturday Night, Todd and I run into Debin and John Herzfeld in the VIP Bowling Alley. We hang out in their booth and survey the passing parade.

Dealers and buttonmen intersperse unobtrusively with high-profile clientele: Male Stars and Those Girls.

In the room the women come and go and ask each other:

Where's the blow?

A beautiful young thing heading in our direction catches our universal attention.

Debin and Herzfeld eye her hungrily.

"She likes me more than you," I taunt. Just kidding, I swear, but damn if she doesn't graze over those boys and settle on me with a full-frontal invitation. The Smile. I smile back, turn away first and she moves on. Those boys shoot me

the same surprised/impressed look they did when we saw
Bruce Springsteen, third row center, and Clarence Clemons
vibed me heavily through a saxophone solo . . .

Tammy Bruce, Los Angeles NOW, speaks next. She is seated
far right, for she advocates mainstreaming — the code word
for alliance with the heterosexual woman's movement (read
homophobic closet-cases). She is not received with anything
approaching the warmth of the previous speakers, including
the soporific Ms. Zia.

Far left, Urvashi Vaid, National Gay and Lesbian Task
Force. Skinny intense charismatic and informative, she seems to
be advocating lesbian separatism, more in sorrow than in anger.

There is still bitterness over Betty Friedan's midSeventies
purge of lesbians from NOW, even though she's since recanted.

Jeez, I didn't even know about that. Where was I? Oh
yeah, producing movies for too little money and too little
credit for star directors who hated me behind my back for getting them everything they wanted.

At least they didn't harass me.

With more (underpaid) women in the workplace the
harassment has escalated. Like men pretty much decided it
was open season on women.

Fanning myself in impatient little strokes with Lesbian-
Feminist strobing before my eyes I decide to blow Frankie
off. I thread my way through the crowd.

Late overflowers fill the aisles and doorways.

I am tempted for a brief moment to yell Fire.

"Too bad you didn't come," I tell her, "you'd relate to the
politics here. You might've met your next husband . . ."

"I'm too tired to wait for you anyway," Frankie laughs.

I return to my tiny little seat. When Urvashi-the-firebrand
winds up the floor will be open for questions.

"Claire, we're two minutes away from a big fight," I say,
and we make a plan to meet the others after the bitter end at
Bienvenuto, a restaurant on Santa Monica Boulevard in the
heart of Boys' Town. We tromp up the aisle purposefully.

It is a profound pleasure to hit the damp night air.

"I need gas," I say when I start the car.

"I'll pump it for you," Claire grins and we turn onto Beverly Boulevard in search of a Union '76 because that's the card I'm carrying.

I pull up to Full Serve and Claire starts to fuss. "Relax!" I say more imperiously than I mean and we chat while a boy in uniform takes care of our needs.

"Boy, I don't have a problem saying that I'm a feminist," I say.

"See, that's 'cause you're straight!" Claire exclaims. I am? "Like you can wear that haircut." I can? "I haven't had anyone pump gas for me since I was seventeen," Claire complains as we ease back onto Beverly.

The good-looking girls at dinner are all dressed in The Uniform: jeans/slacks, teeshirt, blazer. Save one, a woman from LAPD Internal Affairs who's got a gun stashed under an Armani-like gabardine power-suit. She and I are the only ones in makeup.

Beyond her and Claire and me there is Chloe, her lover Jesse, a screenwriter, and their friend Nicky, a powerful programming executive.

"You guys left just in time," Chloe smiles and Claire shoots me a reluctant look of deep respect.

"They beat the shit out of the NOW lady?" The table regards me like I'm God Herself. Of course they did. "Y'know, in my whole life, I never thought I'd be in agreement with the extreme right position, but I'm with the mainstreaming concept," I blurt. "Or the Women's Movement will be Yugoslavia any day now."

Nobody disagrees. We discuss common female issues: health, equal pay/equal work, civil rights.

Health.

Nicky, early thirties, has been admitted into the first large study for women with a proclivity for developing breast cancer.

Thirty thousand women. That's a lot of women.

"Y'wanna hear the most chilling choice, Jools? Number

three? They tell you, 'Well, you can have a double mastec-
tomy, reconstructive surgery optional, *now* — '"

"With no cancer?!" I object reasonably.

"With no cancer."

Jesse, late twenties, failed her Pap smear a year ago.

"Type three," she intones portentously and the other
women "amen." Qu'est-ce que c'est type three? I wonder,
reminding myself to call the gynecologist for an appointment.
"Changing cells," Jesse asides intuitively.

Jesse and Nicky, so high risk, have recently renounced
smoking — gone the patch route — so I puff away at an adjacent table with Josh Evans and his girlfriend, Natasha
Wagner. The only boy-girl combo in the restaurant. Children
of my contemporaries, with whom I've always imagined I
have more rapport. They eye my table knowingly and I dish
with Josh that my talking dog's called Crackers, which I've
read is the name of his mom Ali MacGraw's dog.

I tamp out my butt in their ashtray, we trade numbers we
know we'll never dial and I rejoin Those Girls.

"So Jools, how would you feel if your daughter turned out
gay?" Jesse asks as I sit down.

"Relieved . . ."

We cross Santa Monica Boulevard to Caroline's place, Little
Freda's. It is bright and narrow with a counter serving up fat-
tening pastry and cappuccino.

Caroline's exceedingly butch in a baseball cap and nasty
attitude.

Biker wannabes futz around the pool table in back.

We linger for a moment, order coffee.

Fat-bottomed girls with facial hair, noserings and haircuts
trying-to-be-mine line the counter. They seem not so much a
third sex as an alternative homo sapien.

The Thing, Zoe calls them.

"Calm down, Jools," Nicky laughs, applying gentle pressure to my shoulders, "it's just the college crowd."

"Did I wince?"

"You did," she smiles.

We sit at a small table stacked with a giveaway bar guide. She opens one, leafs through the ads:

Klub Banshee, Joanie Weir — yeah, I'm meeting her.

Girl Bar, Robin and Sandy — yeah, them, too.

Nicky's impressed and I tell her Vera's put me in touch with them.

"Vera's confused," I explain. "So tell me, Nicky, is there a network?"

"Whadd*you* think?"

"I think there's a circuit — "

"There's a lot of circuits — "

"And they intersect. But I don't see a network yet."

"Why is that?"

"Those girls keep telling me women are too bitchy . . ."

"They are sometimes," Nicky laughs softly.

"I like to keep pointing out that might be because they were trained to be women by men."

"Some men can be really wonderful and sensitive, though," Nicky says and recounts the tale of a programmer in another division who sent her a script purporting to portray a lesbian relationship. "He just wanted my notes."

"Did he use them?"

"Yes."

"I suppose there are a *few* good men," I allow ironically, not meaning it.

"See you can say that because you're straight!"

I am? I am? Iam iamb *not* a lezz-bee-anne?

"So, Jools, working title: YOU'LL NEVER EAT PUSSY IN THIS TOWN AGAIN?!" Chloe shouts as we head for the parking lot.

"Clams and honey!" I shout back, quoting from a short story a friend scribed a quarter of a century ago for *Screw* magazine under the pseudonym Jubal Washcloth. Oh it happens to everyone sometimes, I comforted Jubal after his second wilted attempt at consummation . . .

The Girls howl. Way to go, Jubal! We say good night.

"Everyone kept asking if you were straight." Claire grins. "I loved saying, Yes."

"Well, let's discuss *your* self-esteem for a minute," I grin back, alarmed and sad.

"Mmmm, I suppose you're right," Claire says solemnly and we are quiet for the rest of the drive.

Home. Sanctuary.

I step into my closet to find my Moschino sailor blouse. And some retro polka-dot bell-bottoms cut on the bias from years ago. Not bad, I pronounce to my posed mirror self.

Eat your heart out, Karl Lagerfeld!

I sigh and reflect on the perfectly wonderful young women from dinner dealing with susceptibility to cancer and nicotine withdrawal, tossing and turning restlessly through the night dressed only in their Habitrol patches.

Is it my imagination, or are a disproportionate number of women oppressed, impoverished, dehumanized by our current system? Well at least the last one standing in the recent demolition derby posing as an election was My Boy.

With 43 percent, how American.

Even though I didn't trust him, even though I didn't like his starstruck/starfuck-er tendencies — I, the alienated voter, cast her ballot for the lesser of two — make that least of *three* — evils.

Maybe since he's so partial to California he'll use his influence to improve its real estate market before the end of the year.

I freeze on the white dots in the pants and squint them into life-forms, squiggling around on the black background.

Like so many changing cells.

"Those girls think I should call it YOU'LL NEVER EAT PUSSY IN THIS TOWN AGAIN," I report to Debin the day after. He laughs uncomfortably. "Y'know, the weirdest thing, they asked me how I would feel if Kate was gay and I said 'relieved.'"

"You didn't mean that," he says.

"No, I didn't mean it. I was just relating to the well-at-least-she-won't-be-hurt-by-men aspect." Like me. "But if she were, I could deal. Life is too short to sacrifice *that* kind of love . . ."

I bring Brooke up to speed on the title issue. "YOU'LL NEVER SUCK DICK! IN THIS TOWN AGAIN . . ." he objects. "What about BOX LUNCH," he suggests dryly.

"I've got it, I've got it!" Todd's voice exclaims excitedly on my answering machine. "OUT TO LUNCH!"

I'm back in my booth at the Monkey Bar. I've become addicted to their roast-chicken-stuffed-with-mushroom-sauce-and-mashed-potatoes. Besides Joanie Weir, who runs Klub Banshee and Trinity, has heard The Buzz and wants to check it out.

Joanie comes from dysfunctional Catholic stock. Nine kids. Who absconded to The Road where they made music and money as The Weirz when they were very young.

"Michael Damien is my older brother," she announces abruptly, like that's First Credit on The Crawl That Is Her Life. Joanie has long blonde hair, sparkly blue eyes and a husky voice.

She is extremely likable.

Mark, a shark in waiter white, comes over to say hello.

"Julia's doing this lesbo piece for *Harper's*," Joanie says.

"Been hearing about it," Mark smiles. Uh-oh. "Besides, we've always *won*dered about Julia . . ."

He heads to another table.

"Well, you can just keep wondering," I say, and turn back to Joanie. "Harumph. Where were we? Tell me, on the road, so young, all that, were you seduced?"

I am exceptionally confident on this point: it strikes a chord so frequently.

"Oh nooo," Joanie's blue eyes twinkle behind hip glasses. "I seduced her. I was sixteen and curious, she was an older woman and confused . . ." Joanie smiles pointedly.

I disengage and vague past her shoulder and there's Howard Rosenman, schmoozing with the corner-two, and Sandy Gallin, his boss, a senior member of The Gang of Four. He stands an aloof foot away, checking the room with his distinctive Hollywood Glaze, a look that is at once wary and relaxed.

But that could be from too many surgical segues.

"Hello, Julia," he says first.

"Hello, yourself," I reply, surprised.

Joanie and Howard whip-pan to see what they've missed.

Kisses kisses kisses. And they're gone.

"Think he'd have hello'd me if he were with David Geffen?"

Surfing the internet with WFAG:

Bored with InfernoMation predigested and regurgitated into superficial soundbytes, he transfers to DOOM. We chat whilst he kills enemies, collects treasure and earns health points.

"What is your problem? I don't understand!"

"Every article about him starts: He has the power to destroy a career with a single phone call. *That's* positive. Plus he has really great credits! And all he ever talks about is how much *money* he made!"

Boom. Doom. Two hundred percent health.

"Barry Diller and David Geffen will run and/or *own* all communication in five years. I wish you would just make up with him!"

"Well *that's* certainly something to look forward to! I wonder how the ugly middle American would react if he knew the real deal."

Boom. One hundred percent health.

"Howcum they're all still alive?!" I challenge. "Do they eat the hearts of young children for breakfast?!"

The enemy sneaks in a barrage and suddenly WFAG's down to 43 percent health. "Uhhh! Uhhh! Uhnngggghhhh . . ."

GAME OVER. Like that.

"With Howard, the dog at their feet, panting huh-huh!?
Waiting for leftover heart?!"

"I never had this conversation with you . . ."

"I never had this conversation with *myself*!"

"Jools, it's God, pick up the phone," Gary Devore's deep
voice demands.

Someone with whom I can really discuss lesbians.

Gary spent two hours animatedly interacting with Athena
last birthday and I think he has a penchant for women who
swing. Well that's not fair. The truth is Gary's one of the few
straight men I know who is genuinely attracted to strong
women. Anyway, he's not *fearful* of strong women.

I tell him about the disturbing health issues Hazel laid on
me at dinner.

"I didn't know that," he says. "That makes me sad."

"Yeah, me too. And I'm getting exhausted from this circuit."

"And people are talking about it."

"They are?" I can't get used to the fact that there's no way
to do my research anonymously.

"Mostly they want to know if you're a lesbian."

"Here's the party line: I don't know, the subject never
came up!" I bark, somewhat Clairishly.

"Oh adding to the legend I see."

Gary laughs softly and I laugh too.

"It's time to see *Basic Instinct*," I inform Todd.

Every one of my lesbian friends loved the movie, ACT-UP
notwithstanding. My deal with movies is: If I don't see them
opening day I don't see them until they're on a cassette for
Academy consideration. If I *do* see a movie in the theater I
have a tendency to wander after thirty-seven minutes.

"Why shouldn't they love the movie?" Frankie said after
attending the hot *Basic* Hollywood *Instinct* screening on the
arm of a powerful gay *male* agent. "They're gorgeous, they're
powerful —"

"They're rich!" I didn't used to mention money as an attribute. Who says The Eighties are over?

"But I don't like that ultrasex involves ultraviolence. I've asked around and I can't find any women who like being beaten up. You know of any?"

"None who'll admit it. Madonna?"

"*She* probably beats *them* up. Jools, there *is* this one fabulous scene . . ."

"I've heard." Interrogation. Smoking. No underwear. The one about which The Stone's demurred: I didn't know. Yeah right. They had those sun guns pointed up your snatch for the sheer joy of it.

"Jools," Frankie smiled, "it *is* really fabulous."

The last film that really gripped me was *The Grifters*.

I saw it with Corey, who is young enough to be the son of my son, and he squirmed in his seat for the run of the show.

Heh-heh-heh . . .

FLASHBACK: Summer 1990. The Valley. Corey's Pool.

Face to face on the diving board.

Me: Thanks for letting me camp out whilst Forthill
    clears away my sycamore's second suicide attempt.
    I wish they could finish vetting *YNELITTA* for me . . .
He: I'm glad you're back, LadyGod. I missed you . . .
Me: I missed myself . . .
He: I had dreams about you. Sexy dreams, LadyGod.
    Five at least . . .
Me: I'm telling you this now and forever. Never.
    Nevernever-never . . .

Daddy's little girl has her limits and wants to be *GOOD* after all. Although maybe if his skin cleared up . . .

He: Okay, Jools, let's just suppose that it's the day
    after the day after The Apocalypse and there's no
    one left but you and me . . .

Me: Here? In L.A.?

He: Nah fuck that. Hawaii, South of France. Isn't that
 what you like?

Me: So what's your point?

He: I mean, LadyGod, not even then?

Me: Not even then.

He: Not even a spoon, like sleeping?

Me: Lemme think about it. I'll get back to you by the
 close of business January 2. In the year 2000 . . .

He: It'll be over by then. Or we'll be too old.

Me: Hey, baby, I'm too old now.

He: Yeah, Jools. Me too . . .

"This print is so red," I complain. "Is there something else
wrong with my eyes, or is this print very red?"

Basic Instinct's pre-credit sequence. The Rock Star is getting off in a very big, very final kind of way, ooh-ooh.

"'She's dangerous, she's brilliant!' Watch out for that *brilliant* woman!" I critique at our first PAUSE and head for the
bathroom.

"It'll be a movie about her breakthrough," Todd says.

FLASHBACK: *Thelma and Louise*, Opening Day.

Todd and I know nothing about the movie except that we
have to see it.

"They're gonna kiss," he smiled on the way in.

"They're gonna die," I said.

"I'm confused . . . is it a circle of lesbian murderers?" I protest
and press REWIND.

"Nah, Jools, he's just such a hot fuck she's a cured killer."

"That ass. That neck. Puh-leeze. Roxy was the infinitely
better alternative. So is Catherine Trammell Hannibal Lecter
in drag?"

Todd laughs.

• • •

Nicole Conn, who directed *Claire of the Moon*, a low-budget art offering about the evolution of a lesbian love, calls to ask if she can drop off a tape. She is extremely authoritative on the phone, so I'm hardly prepared for the tiny little cute-person who appears the day after. We agree I should view her movie before we talk.

Claire's static and intellectual and not much of a film. Positive qualities after *Basic Instinct*.

And a couple of scenes make me think.

One, an explication on lesbianism as a higher form of love for a woman than she could ever have with a man.

Two, details with some humor the difference in warmth between lesbians hugging and straight women hugging.

I have read in *Scientific American* that the average space requirement for homo sapiens is eighteen inches.

In my case it is a yard.

But I resolve that for the course of my research I will hug warmly. I don't want anyone to feel me recoil, even though I sometimes have trouble squeezing The Kate tightly.

Nicole and I reconnoiter in my kitchen.

"Oh I was Claire," Nicole says. "Drinking smoking fucking men with abandon. I've gotten flack from the politically correct lesbians about the smoking and drinking in the film. But that's part of it, y'know?"

I do.

"The drinking and fucking and — ?"

"And my younger sister came out, so I figured, What the fuck?"

"Back up a second. Let's talk about *Claire of the Moon*."

"Let's talk about before *Claire of the Moon*. I was here three years. I wrote four scripts and all of them were optioned. One, *Cynara*, got pretty famous. But it was a lesbian love story. Everyone shied away from it . . .

"Jodie Foster loved it, said she'd do anything to help get it made, but she couldn't play the lead . . .".

"The homophobic double standard is really extreme in show business. Which is interesting. If *half* the rumors are true, we're talking about some powerful people. You'd think they'd have a little more, pardonnez-moi, *balls*."

Nicole laughs an improbable Eddie Murphy laugh.

"I just got tired and frustrated, Julia. I wrote *Claire* in six weeks, went home and hit up friends and family for cash and credit cards . . ."

"How many?"

"Mmmmmmm . . . about thirty."

"That's a lot of friends and family."

"I raised $180,000 and shot the picture. We couldn't get distribution, so I ended up platforming it myself in nine markets. I've pretty much made the money back."

"Wow."

"We're talking about a niche market with no fare. You wouldn't believe the mail I'm getting from women all over the country. We're going wider at the end of January. I've had a lot of support . . ."

"Your family?"

"My mom and my stepfather . . ."

"What about your real father?"

Nicole looks me dead in the eye and I know that her next words are emblazoned on her heart forever.

"Here's what he said when I told him I was gay. 'There's two kinds of people I don't deal with: criminals and queers. You're sick, thwarted, and perverted and you're no daughter of mine.' That was twelve years ago and I haven't seen him since."

They don't *choose* to be that way.

Dalee said.

"Oh we were that Uptown-Manhattan-German-Jews-who-don't-know-they're-Jewish family," Carole laughs softly the day after over lunch. Carole, who is as small as Nicole and looks in her delicate-featured way like her older sister, is one of the heaviest real estate brokers on the West Side.

We are discussing the out process.

Nicole's story has shaken me.

"I had been married once, long ago, for a short time. I knew, but for some reason the subject just never came up with my family. Very typical: domineering mother, invisible dad. My mother was visiting me out here, and I was throwing a dinner party for her. We were in the kitchen preparing, and I told her.

"She stomped to her room and started packing. I followed her and I said to her, 'If you have to leave, then leave.' I was ready to let her go, Julia . . .

"I returned to the kitchen. After a while I noticed that it had gotten quiet and I walked back to find her unpacking. 'Oh you're staying?' I asked, and she said, 'Well, at least for dinner.' 'What are you going to wear?' I said. She sighed and sat on the edge of the bed . . .

"'A shroud . . . '"

I check in with Fern, another writer, read her some pages. I hear her two-year-old daughter chirping in the background. Her husband's away on location and she's guilty/happy about it.

"Oh don't worry, some of the best marriages are the separate-vacation kind. Could we get back to my lesbians please?"

"Y'know, I did that for about a year, and she took care of me, built up my confidence, but — "

"But what?"

"It just wasn't in the cells. Know what I mean?"

I do.

"Jools, it's Air. There's a message on my machine from Ryan Murphy at the *L.A. Times*. I think you should return the call."

I return Ryan Murphy at the *Times*' call.

He tells me there's a lot of gossip about a piece I'm doing for *Harper's Bazaar*.

"I hear you're outing everyone and outing yourself," he says.

"I'm sooo happy to have my work trivialized . . ."

It's taken me two years to say that sentence.

"Hey I'm on your side. I don't know if you remember, but I did a long interview with you at the Polo Lounge for the hardcover release . . ." Are you kidding? Do you know how many of those I did? And after a while you really *were* all the same.

What's the next line? I can't remember my line.

"Of course I remember, but I don't know how it ended up on paper."

"I wrote nice stuff . . ."

"I didn't read the press."

Or I might have considered homicide. Scored an Uzi from a friend of a friend and wiped out half of InfernoTainment's Elite some Monday night at Mortons.

Suicide maybe, depending on the time of month.

WOMAN KILLS SHOWBIZ, SHOOTS SELF.

"We're going with something in 'Calendar' this Sunday so you might as well talk to me . . ."

I perform spin control for the next half hour.

I'm so thoroughly pissed off by the time we finish I must call Air. "He said the gossip is that I'm outing everyone and outing myself!"

"I told you this would happen."

"Then people are really stupid and small-minded."

"No shit!" Air laughs.

It takes me a day to figure out I should put Eric Simonoff and Helen Murray in the loop. I don't want *Harper's Bazaar* to think I'm the kind of cheap slut who might place this item.

I call those girls I've been interviewing to warn them that a piece on my piece is running in "Calendar."

"Pretty silly, huh?" I say to Claire.

"Must be something that's on people's minds."

Relieved when it turns out to be mainly positive, I check in with Joanie Weir.

"I got a laugh that Whitney's on the cover," she says.

"Please, don't *ever* make me speak to that woman again!" WFAG, expounding from the car. "She read 'Calendar' and

screamed at me that her private life is her private life and you
say women don't help each other."

"I said *they* say they don't help each other!"

Of course out of thirty minutes of decent soundbites a male
journalist *would* choose that line.

"I wish you were doing this article about gay men in the
business, who *would* talk to you and *do* network," WFAG
says.

"But that's the point, don'tcha think? In the pecking order,
gay men are waaay above gay women. Straight women too.
Talk about your Men's Clubs!"

"I didn't hear that, darling. I'm fading out . . ."

"You're the headline *and* practically the whole column!" Julie
Grau exclaims in her ironic/excited voice. *New York Post*.
Page Six. The Uptowners' guilty secret. Like Rush Limbaugh
and Martin Lawrence are mine I'm so eclectic for myself. "I'll
read it . . ."

"Of course there's that women-don't-help-each-other line
again!"

"Just so they spell your name with two *l*s . . ."

W runs an item.

Even Cindy Adams who gets most of her facts wrong.

Save one: I've met Julia.

Joni checks in.

"How's the piece coming?" she asks with a bloodand-
money smile in her voice.

"I'd love you and Julie to see it when I'm done," I say.

"We'll read it right away."

"Another audition!" I tell The Creature crankily after we
hang up, but my heart flip-flops because I smell what George
Roy Hill called A Deal in Search of a Story — referring to a
negotiation that contemplated reteaming him and the *Butch
Cassidy* stars for a movie about Dirk and Serpico, two NYPD
Boys.

On the strength of said Deal-in-Search-of Joan Didion and

John Gregory Dunne had upped their screenplay-ante in a meeting with Dick Zanuck at Fox.

"I wore my fur coat," Joan whispered, "and I kept pulling my sleeves on like I was leaving . . ."

"$25,000 a sleeve," John hardee-har-harred.

"I'll do all the talking and then Redford'll just pull at his earring and I've lost the scene," Paul Newman, who was to play Dirk, complained to the Dunnes over beer at their beach house.

"I knew it was over right then," John said sadly . . .

Nicky and I confer on the matter of rendering her unrecognizable. I reassure her: I have mastered this technique through fourteen months of vetting *YNELITTA*. I can pretty much wring the gist out of any thing. Any time. Any place. There'll be plenty *of that* on this piece.

The conversation turns to The Geff's, "As a gay man . . ." at last year's AmFar benefit.

It was the talk of the town. For a minute.

And wasn't it about time?

Already.

"I hear an-infinite-number-of-hands-clapping."

"Prolonged," Nicky says.

"I'm all for that and it's a good thing, but isn't it mildly ironic that *he* gets a Standing-O for outing himself whilst *we* water your story down so you *don't*? And I'm *not* counseling you out yourself. It would be hazardous to your career. But don'tcha find it a tad double-standardish?"

"Welcome to my world," Nicky says philosophically.

Jody's throwing a Big Bash. I call to explain I'll be leaving early to experience Girls' Night at Jewel's Catch One. We discuss the Yin and Yang of the approaching evening and The Assignment.

"I've been meeting a lot of terrific women . . ."

"Honey, you know I grew up out here in the sixties," Jody chuckles, "and I'm liberal and open. But I draw the line at eating pussy."

How straight women loooove to draw that line.

I do believe I've found something for straight men and women to agree on.

Nobody, I notice, draws the line at having their pussy eaten.

"In fact, if I were a contortionist," Jody muses, "I don't think I'd go down on myself. Sorry, honey, but we took Serafina to Cirque du Soleil today . . ."

FLASHBACK: The Pines. The Seventies.

Victor and me and C.J., an awesomely hung double-jointed bisexual, bet that C.J. can go down on himself.

Victor wanders around the pool, collects cash from doubters in a hat.

C.J. does himself to wild applause.

We win more than a thousand dollars.

Later that night we hear Dr. Ruth radio-counseling on cunnilingus: "Undt duzz it feel like a schmellly und darrrrk und scarrry place?" she asks cheerfully.

FLASHBACK within a FLASHBACK:

Jennifer and Margot and I, who have always worn bottoms before, hit the nude beach fully nude.

The boy next door freaks and we are intimidated into retreat. To search for G-strings.

"See it's fine with the nice pretty titties, but not those dirty cunts!" Jennifer rages and we laugh angrily.

Gee, C.J. didn't feel that way about himself . . .

Jody's party's at full tilt when Todd and I arrive an hour in. Sprinkled throughout, ShowBiz types I haven't seen in a while. Or Neil's DONE them so many times they're incognito. I play Anita Hill to Buddy Monash's Clarence Thomas for a moment too long and become ravenous. I race to the buffet and literally bump into Howard Koch, Jr. who gives me guff about asking for money for the use of my paperback cover for his high-priced upcoming movie starring The Stone.

"They want my face in her lap," I reported to Claire a week before, who claimed to be turned on by the concept.

We meet Jewel and her lover Rue at a vegetarian nonsmoking restaurant on La Brea, A Votre Santé.

Rue is light-skinned, light-eyed and proportioned rather more voluptuously than Jewel. She starts as chilly as the room, rewarding me with ice-pearl half-smiles through the first fifteen minutes. Todd gasps mightily for air and wolfs down a giant salad whilst I try to make friends.

"What do you do, Rue?" I ask, chomping tensely on a refreshing Nicorette, denying a strong desire for a second martini.

"Well I just got the first federal grant, $165,000, for a hospice for mothers and their children who have AIDS . . ."

$165,000. My tax problema equals Rue's grant. Not likely it would go there. "Y'know they're usually separated in the system . . ."

I didn't know that.

I didn't know about lesbian abuse or yeast infections that metastasize into changing cells either.

Jewel and Rue pick up the check and we follow their gold BMW. To Girls' Night.

Catch One is half-filled with obese black and Hispanic women. On stage, a cross-dresser does a fair Michael Jackson. I belly up to the bar and feel a presence behind my left shoulder.

"Buy you a drink?" a raspy voice not dissimilar to Richard Pryor's Old Guy offers and I nod before I turn around.

The person facing me resembles the shuffler in *McCabe and Mrs. Miller*, the dancer on the muddy street. Porkpie hat. Red-rimmed glasses. Androgynous skeletal body hidden beneath a pair of khaki cotton Dockers and a faded red sweat-shirt.

"I'm Pat," it says, and when we shake hands we're closer together than I like. I look at Todd desperately, who shoots me an evil deal-with-this-yourself look.

Sensing my discomfiture, The Jewel peels Pat off.

"Oh you straight little white girl," Pat smiles philosophically. "I bet if the lights were on those baby blues would just pierce my tired black heart!"

I feel terrible about letting her buy me a drink but it's probably more because of the black/white dynamic than the gay/straight.

Nevertheless, I feel like a cocktease and shortly after wend from the large room to the bar near the entrance.

Jewel and Rue eventually join us. They snuggle.

"So Rue . . . for the piece, what's your last name?"

"Same as Jewel's."

"We were married, September 2, 1989. In church."

"Oh yeah, who wore the dress?" They laugh.

"Rue did," Jewel says.

"And you were in the tux?"

"I'm not a tux type," Jewel smiles. "I've got tits and ass, y'know . . ."

On the drive home I decide I will probably be voting for Jewel whenever she gets around to running for councilperson from the Tenth District.

I figure I'll be living in the neighborhood by then if the IRS has anything to say about it.

Vera's got the situation wired. Our cars are parked and we're in the door, and strolling down a long raised walkway interspersed with tables and chairs before I can say, I don' wanna but I *think* I can.

Lights music videos.

Six hundred women boom and throb on the dancefloor a level below. Young and wild and lipstick. Jeans and bustiers and designer jackets strewn in heaps at their feet whilst they bump and grind. I open my mouth to suck in extra oxygen à la Todd.

Vera guides me to the back room which has the requisite

pool table. We order a drink. She introduces me to Robin and Sandy, who live with each other, invented Girl Bar and love each other Maury Povich–out. In that order. Sandy is a beauty, Robin is pretty. They're warm but apprehensive.

We're meeting each other later in the week for a real talk, but I wanted to catch this action first.

I run into people who work for people I used-to-know, two girls two boys. We chat lightly.

They don't ask why I'm here and I don't tell.

Am I gonna have to defend you?

I've been defending you for years . . .

Vera and Anne Marie and I wander into the main room.

Vera gets aggressive with Anne Marie on the dance floor and Anne Marie recoils into unhappiness.

We split.

"The Tea Room?" Vera suggests. Anne Marie jumps in my car.

The place is packed but we see people we know and impose on their table. Vera and Anne Marie indulge in a deep magnetic kiss and soon every mini-machomoviestar deserts his girlfriend and eases over.

They invite us to parties. Latuhhh.

I squint and scowl and drive them away.

"*That* was something!" I say, impressed.

"Yeah it's a power trip," Vera smiles happily and Anne Marie shifts uneasily in her seat.

Home. Alone. Sanctuary.

I scrape off clothes and makeup and plaque in a hot ten minutes and settle into my pillows with my *Bar Guide*.

I peruse the personals.

Of a hundred ads, ninety close with:

No Drugs/Alcohol/Smoking/Bis/Vera/Anne Marie.

So women who love women have their hearts broken on a regular basis by women whose consciousness is often altered and who occasionally love men.

Duh.

• • •

The Girl Bar impresarias know how to have a good time. Robin is shorter plumper shyer and blushes when she smiles. Sandy, possessed of a throaty voice and Cindy Crawford hair, tosses it often, throwing her head back for boisterous laughter. They are extremely pleasant company, a tantalizing come-on for their income-producing venue, The Epitome of The New Girl.

We discuss the sexual spectrum, how All Girls Are Created a little this-way-this-way-please and a little that-way, and how one is nudged by life experience.

"Mommy and Daddy!" I declare and they laugh.

Sandy tells me her parents were very accepting of her gender bent, but that her Hispanic-Catholic mother *did* cry off and on for a year after she told her she was gay.

"Maybe two," she adds and tosses her mane and laughs.

They worry about my hiatus from sexual interaction and I make a broad gesture across the table. "There, that's me!" I point to the floor on my left. "I just fell off the spectrum!" We laugh again.

"So all the straight women draw the line at eating pussy . . ."

"Oh yeah, tell me about all the straight women who love sucking dick!" they chorus. I concede the point and ask them what they think of Ozone. I can't dispel the image of Hazel murmuring of the rubber dispensary at the door.

"Oh it closed in six weeks," Sandy says.

"See women aren't really into that stuff," Robin adds.

"I'm a small cog in the wheel of Nature," Candy tells me on the phone. She's checking to see if I want to hit the Pussycat Revue at Peanuts later.

"How about *much* later!" I josh. Just what I'm dying to see: a stripper doing herself with a dildo. "I don't care if she's performing for other women; to me, it's still exploitive!"

Excuse me, Jools, but what's your point?

I'm thinking I'm thinking . . .

"I'm the answer to the population explosion," Candy says.

"Sex was once for reproduction, part of Nature," Dad offers one afternoon from Florida. "The perk was that it was pleasurable. Or no one would do it, it's so silly. Somewhere along the way, when it wasn't for the survival of the species the pleasure part became more significant than the reproductive part . . ." Artificial insemination: turkey basters, those girls call the babies.

"Candy says it's birth control," I say, thinking paradoxically of Anne Rice's *Vampire Chronicles*.

"Candy's right," Dad says.

"Candy has a nosering and wears bright orange construction worker's parkas."

"Soooo . . ." Way to go, Pop! Well, he's seventy-nine, and it's time. Already. "So, June, are you going to be accused of being a lesbian?" Spoke too soon. And by the way, Dad, howcum you call me by the names of your wives? Did you ever . . . ?

"No doubt. Probably," I say. "I'll be accused of being homophobic as well. There's no way to win in this turf.

"I'll tell you what though. I met some great ladies researching this piece. I think I'm gonna throw them a party at Jewel's place when it's over. And Dad, if you were a guest on my arm, you'd be going, 'Julia, that one? That one? That one, too?'

"Who knows? Maybe I'll start a lesbian network . . ."

I finish EATING OUT IN THIS TOWN on a drizzly Sunday afternoon. It runs sixty-nine pages appropriately enough.

I call Todd and Helen Murray.

Safety and Print three copies.

When they arrive, we split immediately to separate reading areas. Ten minutes. Tick tick tick. A-*chung!*

POWER OFF

"Oh fuck!" I say ritualistically and hand them each a Sportman's Lamp. "Continue please . . ."

"Jeez, it's just a little drizzle," Todd says.

"Yo! Breakdown-of-the-Infrastucture *this*!"

"If I wasn't here I wouldn't believe it!" Todd confesses.

"I got to Print and Safety . . ." I offer, uncharacteristically focusing on the bright silver lining dark clouds.

But that's because I know my Deal in Search of a Story is within eating distance.

"Kathy Bishop doesn't have a sense of humor," Eric Simonoff reports morosely. I've already FedExed a floppy disc so she can cut the piece, which Eric loves and she despises.

"Why don't we just take the kill fee and go elsewhere?"

"We are obliged to let her take her best shot . . ."

"Eric, I neeed the money . . ."

"Lynn says she and Joni have commenced negotiating . . ."

"Eric!" Call-waiting. Lynn.

"I'm having a hell of a time just getting Joni to meet your last price. She's worried it'll be nonfiction essays with no throughline. You need to talk to her . . ."

I call Joni.

"How do you see this book?" she asks and I pitch seven minutes of fake narrative.

Writer's #2 Rule: You have permission to lie.

"How do *you* see it, Joni?"

"Julia Tells the Truth . . ."

"Uh-oh. Puke roll safety? I already *have* five ruptured discs!"

Joni laughs, ha-ha isn't she funny and jumps off.

Harper's kills the piece the day after.

The day after the day after Lynn and Joni close.

When the contracts arrive they're for *Untitled Essays*, which depresses me but the signing money offsets the gloom.

I keep the banks and vendors at bay and messenger another twenty grand to E.

• • •

Lee and I loiter in the kitchen poking at pot-stickers he's brought from Chin Chin.

"I miss the lamb at Mortons," Lee needles. "I'm sure you could go back there by now."

"Never! Never never never!" I spit unreasonably.

We laugh.

"I just love the lesbo piece," Lee says, veering off confrontation. He brushes at his Veronica Lake dip for emphasis. "Pardon me for bringing up another never! but if David Geffen read it he'd wanna make up . . ."

"Oh this is about him? Excuse me I forgot. *Everything's* about him."

"The same could be said of you."

"Solipsistic," Gary Devore muttered one day when I hogged an entire phone call complaining I suffered all symptoms of prostate malfunction and I had to request a definition.

"Priapistic!" I joked when he finished and he forgave me.

Swinging on the stool in the corner of my kitchen, she plays with an ice-cold shot of Jagermeister and nibbles from a bag of barbecue kettle chips I stock specifically for her.

It is the same spot Claire, fiddling with a beer, occupied some months ago.

"You have to get into the psyche!" Claire barked.

In twenty-five hundred words or less.

Standing at the counter near the sink I witness the long lonely trek of a single ant carrying another ant across the brightly painted Spanish tile.

Romeo and Juliet.

Or Romeo and Romeo.

Juliet and Juliet?

"Your first time, were you seduced?"

She convulses.

"How do you know?!" She is genuinely impressed and she's made a career of being unimpressed.

"Mmmm . . ." Claire told me.

"My mother's best friend . . . So Jools, were you ever with a woman?" she asks provocatively.

"Only the two-women/one-man equation. Guess I never had to face it . . ." Hey *back off*. "Also, two men and one woman as in: a deal's a deal. Also, thirteen men and ten women, ya gotta remember, The-Seventies-The-Seventies . . ."

She laughs.

"Did you always know you were gay?" I ask.

"Oh no I was a debutante with lots of boyfriends. Didn't like any of 'em very much though. I probably would *never* have known if I weren't out here. This *is* a freer environment than the rest of the country. Except maybe New York . . ."

From whence I absconded like an Africanized bee. Decades ago. Too uptight for me.

"Whaddya mean?"

"Being in L.A. made it possible to try something I thought would make me really happy. I'd have denied it back home and I would've been as miserable as my mother."

The ant, exhausted, lurches to a complete Stop!

"You think your mother knows you're gay?"

"I think *she's* gay and doesn't know it."

"It's occurred to me that *many* mothers were gay and didn't know it. Girl not enjoying sex with Boy is *still* considered proper etiquette . . ."

She crumples the empty bag and tosses it into the garbage can.

Three points.

"Y'know if I weren't with someone? If we broke up? I don't see myself hitting the bars cruising for a replacement."

I poke at the ant: Start movin', soldier! and it drops its cargo which lays motionless on the orange corner of a tile. The ant hesitates, then races in frenetic circles around its late mate.

A lightbulb flashes on in my brain.

"*You* guys are a real *love* story."

She blushes prettily. The ant faints into a dead heap.

I tickle it with my fingernail. Nothing.

"That we are, Miss Julia, that we are . . ."

I focus on the inanimate ants: *This* is a love story!

Turn the water and disposal on.

And sweep the Juliets into the Great Beyond.

GOOD-BYE.

Good-bye yourselves.

I remind me of a man with the power of voodoo.

"This is distinctly more Rodney Dangerfield than Joyce Carol Oates," I joke tensely and Todd frowns in the periphery of my eyeline. The photographer, a handsome lean athletic woman in her early thirties, laughs me off and continues snapping pictures. I scowl and thrust out my lower lip. "I'm the unhappiest white woman in Los Angeles . . ."

The photographer tells the crew to take five. She eyecontacts Todd and he ambles over. I pull at sweat-soaked Calvin Klein/Fogal black spandex and snap it against my aching midsection. Shoulda taken a Zantac. Maybe two.

"C'mon, Jools, you know what they want. Tighten everything up." Todd strikes a bicep-curled-bent-legged pose, the bodybuilder on the cover of the catalogue.

"This is so undignified," I groan, flex my muscles and check my look in the full-length mirror that borders one long wall of the airless cement enclosure *Allure* has booked for a second shoot, so dissatisfied were they with the results of the first.

"Not any more undignified than selling the story of your liposucked furfel to a magazine in the first place!" Todd grins.

"Hey it paid the rent!"

"Exactly . . ."

"Maybe I'll get lucky and they'll kill it."

August has bruited in on an exceptionally ill 100-degree wind. Notwithstanding the wide-open doors and the giant fans churning at the poison particle-laden air, it's easily 110 in this hot-lit cave.

I glance over at the crew ignoring us, waiting in the corner, perusing the newspaper, gossiping in whispers.

Then, a giant laugh.

"Are you guys making fun of me?!"

"Nah, Jools," the stylist says. "We're all fascinated with the story about this young Hollywood madam, Heidi Fleiss. And her celeb-studded little black book . . ."

She holds up yesterday's front page. Exhibit A.

"You know what they're referring to?" I ask Todd, who always reads the *Sunday Los Angeles Times*.

"Nahh, I went for a looong bike ride at the beach."

"I did the canyon run *and* weights. In preparation for this fabulous day . . ."

"I didn't release enough endorphins for *that*!"

"Me neither."

We laugh.

"Bernie Weinraub asked me last week if I knew anything about this girl everyone in Hollywood was talking about and I pooh-poohed him . . ."

We were dining with Bernie's son Jesse and The Kate at a Moroccan-decored nightspot called Babylon. Ironically situated midway between Mortons and Girl Bar on Robertson Boulevard.

Every once in a while Bernie would stake me to a meal so I'd wire a venture into what he considered The Other Side.

Not so far Other as Clubs Louie or Fuck, but places he'd heard about from Don Simpson and Steve Tisch and Art Linson. Tryst and the Monkey Bar and Babylon. Filled, when they enjoyed their *hot* one-two-three-etcetera, with beautiful boys and girls girls girls who materialized in trendy venues after sunset and didn't stay long.

"Whaddyou think of it?" I'd queried Dalee, who'd conducted a preview.

"It's very clever," he replied.

I had quite a struggle with Kate over this foray. She wanted to attend a Dodgers game instead with a friend. Frustrated, I wrote a letter and attached it to her pillow. The gist: I never ask you to show up at family/friends gatherings and this is *The New York Times* and Fuck the Dodgers and That Fucking Jason!

"I'll have to make sure I can get the night off," she laughed, referring to her summer job cocktail-waitressing at Chiller's on the Third Street Promenade in Santa Monica. There wasn't much part-time employment available by the time she returned from the poli-sci seminar in mid-July.

Michael and I worried about the hours (late) and the drive (far) but felt compelled to be supportive since she got the gig herself.

"Whoa, my legs and calves *huuurt!*" she complained after her first weekend. "Mom, The English don't tip very well and the Europeans don't tip at all."

"Think of it as postgraduate poli-sci."

"What do you think you want to do after college, Kate?" Bernie asked.

"Law school first and then I think I'd like to be a geopolitical analyst at the CIA." Bernie smiled, unsure if she meant what she said, and Jesse, who had been three-sixtying the room in search of a famous face, one-eightied back to Kate and appreciated her for the first time. Don't be so EastCoastSnotty, I thought, just because she's pretty and curvaceous and soft-spoken.

Kate's California veneer was as much a shield as The Pinstripe.

Or Jewel's dignity.

Every girl must have her armor.

Times being what they are and all.

"My daughter the spook," I said and ordered another drink.

"She's so together," Bernie, impressed, sotto-voced curbside whilst we awaited our cars.

"What did you expect!" I scowled, knowing he'd anticipated a high-strung little Julia. "Isn't it fairly typical for wild-and-crazies to spawn conservatives?" Grrrr . . .

"You drive," I told Kate when the valet deposited 329WOE, battered but unbowed, and we smiled and said good night to Those Weinraub Boys.

"Seat belt please," she reminded and lurched into traffic.

"Thanks."

"You're welcome."

Three little words.

More significant even than I Love You.

If manners were precursor to diplomacy and diplomacy a cornerstone of civilization The End must have begun when parents ceased teaching Please and Thank You. And Thank You and You're Welcome. Parked their progeny instead alone at the tube to be sucked into the chaotic thrall of InfernoTainment.

Why did people act surprised by the violo-pornographic results of such alternative acculturation?

"They'll either be the leaders of tomorrow," I told Bernie at dinner, regarding our anachronistic offspring, "Or they'll be marched off to internment camps . . ."

As The Heidi pirouettes centerstage in a slow news month, my phones ring and fax purrs with respectful requests from the press for an audience with me.

Like I'm The Guru of Hollywood.

I'm vulnerable to the attention as I'm having a terrible time searching for the story of my deal so I give print media phone time and soundbites. Fortunately, I'm misquoted and I see the error of my ways immediately.

I turn down Larry King Alive-or-Dead twice.

"I promised myself a long time ago I'd never voluntarily be in a room with the Ivan Nagys of the world."

"But it won't be in a room. It'll be from separate studios, separate states!"

"You know what I mean."

"I do."

Larry King's woman producer excepted, The Fourth Estate is populated by a more annoying protozoan than I recall.

Newsweek snookers me into sparing them precious self-fucking time by pretending they want me to write a Heidi/Hollyweird sidebar.

Even worse, I make the mistake of allowing a primetime newsmagazine producer into my domain.

Previously known as Sanctuary.

He arrives in a black Porsche, thunder thighs encased in too-short tennies. His nasty impulses are only marginally less attractive than his physiognomy.

I take more than a moment to realize he's very high.

Kate and her handsome college friend Greg return from dinner just as he's at the brink of spinning out of control.

Greg, a large Midwestern boy, politely propels him out the door. He stumbles down the stairs to his car.

"Did we just save you from being raped?" Greg kids.

I feel faint. I feel stoopid. I feel rage.

"I hope he dies in a one-car crack-up!"

"What happened to the other guy?" Kate asks.

When Kate departed a few hours ago I was on the patio with a striking blue-eyed twentysomething, tall and smart and stringing for *The Sunday Telegraph*.

"Too bad Josh Young is married," I told Kate after Greg left. "He's great boyfriend material for you."

"I was thinking for you," she chuckled and we headed to the kitchen for PB&J and empathy. "Mom, remember when you said, 'If I'm doing interviews six months after *YNELITTA*'s release instead of writing, remind me I think that's a shmucky thing to do'?"

"Consider me reminded."

"It's not like they're asking you to comment on Clinton's budget proposal."

"Definition of New Democrat: Old Republican.

"New Republican: *you*?!"

"Uchchch Jooools. In white shorts! *Eeeuuuooow . . .*"

"I have no taste for a lawsuit and I can't afford decent counsel anyway . . ."

I'm grinding teeth, phone receiver to a burning ear, smiling mightily. Conversing on the matter of the casting of The Tom as Lestat in Global Geff's *Interview with a! Vampire*, as the exceptionally imperious MikeLevyMikeLevy on the other end persists in calling it.

"Buddy Monash is starting a new law firm and could use the business. He glanced at the paperwork and he thinks we have a good case. He'll work on contingency. You could do this *one* thing. At least. Go to a *meeting*. You *owe* me that much!"

What? What?!@# I owe *you*? This is about *you*?!@#

Donnez-moi un fucking break.

"One meeting, that's it."

"Why don't *you* set it up and I'll just be there."

Same as it ever was.

"That's *two* things I'm doing for you."

MikeLevy MikeLevy ignores me.

"Lemme just find his number."

"Grrr."

"And Jools?"

"Yeah."

"Dress niiiice . . ."

The morning of the meeting, George Rush, a gossip columnist for the *New York Daily News*, calls.

"Buddy Monash tells me you're suing David Geffen," he tells Hi-it's-Julia/callya-back in a smooth radio-guy voice.

I pick up.

"I have yet to *meet* with Buddy and he's talking to *you*?! *Please* don't print this."

He says he's a fan. We chat. We bond.

He says he'll sit on the story if I'll stay in touch.

"Real-soon-I-promise."

I fling open the bedroom doors, step onto the patio for a breath-of-fresh and commence choking. Probably a combination of fury and the noxious effect of fetid-heat-wave August atmosphere.

Funny how they come and go together.

The *nerve* of Buddy Monash! Cough!

The *temerity* of LevyLevy! Cough cough!

Dress Nice *this*! Phfft-tooey!

Learned that from Pauly.

I scowl and search for something inappropriate to wear.

I choose the *Allure*-shoot loot tucked into a Ghost tiered-eyelet skirt that hits about six inches above the knee. Black of course. Accessorized by silver cross earrings and a peace sign hanging from my neck.

Black Dolce & Gabbana combat boots.

I smile involuntarily at the memory of the last time this drag and I went out together. Not so long ago.

It was a Hollywood Night . . .

I'd promised to take Greg and another of Kate's college friends, Amy, and a couple of her friends (in for the weekend) to a cocktail party hosted by Sofia Coppola at the Chateau Marmont pool.

I couldn't imagine why I'd been invited but I RSVP'd Julia Phillips and Party knowing Those Kids would love it.

"I'm so jealous, Mom," Kate smirked sardonically as she took off for another underpaid nightshift in Santa Monica.

By five in the afternoon I'd pushed myself into fragile foreplay with The Creature and abruptly canceled.

Brad, who was to drive, called at five-fifteen.

"They were probably sooo looking forward to going," he said mournfully.

"Not to mention you."

"C'mon Jools it'll be fun. I'm there to protect ya!"

"We'd better go right now or I'll change my mind . . ."

"I'll tell them to meet us there . . ."

Brad deposited the car in the Roxbury parking lot and we bumped into Omar steps from the Chateau. Omar was attired in white sailor pants, a black and white striped sailor tee and matching bright-white smile.

Very strolling up and down the Croisette in Cannes.

"I haven't seen you in forevah!" Omar said.

"Going out as little as possible these days."

"Tell me about it."

"This bash any good?"

"Oh dahling, it's the party of the century," Omar declared.

One of Omar's Men, tanned and blond beyond Fabio, stepped into his waiting car. I'd always *won*dered about Omar. Like people always *won*dered about me.

"Then why're you leaving?"

"I'm not happy with my — I don't have my *look* together!"

We laughed and Brad and I headed for the sounds of merrymaking that floated over the bougainvillea surrounding and protecting the pool.

We told the boy at the door Party would be meeting Julia Phillips and he smiled and waved us in.

"Don't worry, I'll take care of them. When's your next book coming out?"

"Working on it now . . ."

What's the next line? Do *you* know the next line?

Beautiful people lightly sprinkled the walkway but the pool was chockablock, particularly near the bar at the south end.

"Drinks first?" Brad suggested; I stood rooted, dreading threading our way through the densely packed crowd.

"Jools! Jools! Izzat you?!"

Billy Wirth in casual gear.

"Bills! I shoulda known you'd be here."

I introduced Brad and started to chat when a woman from *The New York Times* accosted me: A couple of quick shots, just over there? I insisted those boys be included and carefully spelled their names for her.

The photographer posed Brad and Billy crouched bent-kneed on either side of me seated in a chair and kept instructing I jut jut jut to tighten my neck and jawline.

The picture ran in the Style section several Sundays later captioned: Julia Phillips and two unidentified men.

When the party was covered again in Monday's B section and we didn't make the cut Brad was relieved. Me too, as I was the least attractive person in the photo . . .

Those Kids arrived and instantly geared into mingling mode. $100,000 for a college education and upon completion

the graduates were sure to have refined their social skills so
they could handle any party.

Brad and I chatted up Jon Sidel, one of the owners of the
Olive and Small's. He brushed at his Jewish rasta curls impa-
tiently and signaled a beautifully tanned streaked blond with a
nosering he'd be right over.

The first time I met Jon, he'd abruptly alighted at my booth
in his restaurant.

"You okay?" I asked, he seemed so antsy.

"I don't shoot heroin and speed on the hour anymore. I'm
much better . . ." Jon grew up as one of those well-off
Manhattan boys whom Michael Lindsay-Hogg once described
as possessed of bounteous reserves of "apartment smarts."

Sub-thirty, drug-free and three thousand miles from his
family he'd evolved into an enormously successful restaura-
teur/club owner/trendsetter.

He really wanted to be a rock 'n' roll star of course.

"Where's the hostess?" I asked Jon and he pointed her out.

Green silk dress. Bright red hair. Papa's proboscis.

"With Donovan Leitch by her side," Brad noted sarcasti-
cally.

"I wonder what the occasion is?"

"Probably nothing."

"What's your point?"

"Look around. Very trendy. Heavy press presence."

"Is that what's done now? Not even the pretense of a chari-
table benefit? Just invite the Rolodex to a photo-op in search
of a purpose?"

"Here comes Jools, hurtling into The Nineties."

"Let's go to Orso's and sit down for a while."

Brad and Amy's friends faded after a large meal with a
large party that included a couple of Uptown African-
Americans in development at Disney we picked up at the
party. Trey and Yule.

"I love that," I said when Yule spelled his name whilst we
waited for our cars. "When I leave word I can say, 'Yule it's
Yul-ee-a.'"

"What next?" I asked Amy and Greg. "I'll take you anywhere but you have to drive."

"The Monkey Bar for a nightcap!" The place had become famous since *Newsweek* ran a map of Heidi's hangouts, compliments of me. Which was making it busier than ever.

Another Roadside Attraction.

In a single night I'd run into Jerry Casale, ex-Devo, Nick Wechsler and Sean Penn, who came over to my booth to bum a cigarette. Right in the middle of a Socratic born-that-way/made-that-way dialogue with Those Boys.

"We've met," he said shyly, eyes-up/head-down, and the table smiled at him fondly . . .

Amy and Greg and I climbed out of the car and were walking to the entrance just as Doug swept open the door. Out stepped a beautiful frail blonde girl and Pauly Shore. I knew him pre-MTV through Lance, who'd represented him at CAA.

We smiled at each other and fell into a warm hug.

"Duuude, I'm so *proud* of you!" we exclaimed in unison and everybody laughed. Life is moments. This was one.

"Jools, that was so cool," Those Kids said after we'd been seated comfortably at a booth off the bar and I started to relax. Then, heavy clomping and stumbling and a large familiar figure lurched past us.

"Doug, I need another!" Lionel Stander's familiar rasp, tinged purple with booze, called out.

"*Hart to Hart*, right?" Amy said.

"And the Fredric March–Janet Gaynor *A Star Is Born* . . ."

How d'ya send a letter of congratulations to the Pacific Ocean?

"Is that before the one with Barbra Streisand/Kris Kristofferson?" Greg smiled.

"Before the Judy Garland/James Mason version."

"I'm not familiar with that one."

"I know. History started when you were born." Recently, Kate and I had vagued out briefly to *Wheel of Fortune* during College Week. President Who Served Four Terms was spelled after The Vanna turned all the cards.

"Five hundred bucks extra if you know the name," Pat Sajak told the three contestants, sporting alma mater sweatshirts and hearty enthusiasm. None of them did.

"Franklin Delano Roosevelt!" Kate talked back.

"College students don't know that!?" I exclaimed, shocked.

"Aren't you glad your daughter does?"

Indeed.

Lionel Stander swayed drunkenly at the bar and Doug sprinted to stop a fall.

"I'm gonna try not to get too depressed," I said and Those Kids protested we could leave whenever I was ready. I checked my watch. Nearly two. "Lemme just see if Kate's home yet."

I headed for the maître d's counter in front to use Doug's phone and when I looked up Peter Morton walked in.

"Oh are you working here now? Capitalizing on your celebrity?" He smirked and I smirked back.

"Mmmm not a bad idea . . ."

It was the second after it was time to leave when it was time to leave.

Kate was getting out of her car as we pulled into the garage.

Crying.

"What happened?!"

"Oh this black guy was beating his girlfriend right in front of Chiller's as we were leaving. I started to yell at him and my friends held me back. A lady in a passing car said she'd call 911 and the girl ran away. Then we all ran to our cars. I sped ten miles over the limit all the way home."

"Kate, you're lucky he didn't have a gun!"

"That's what my co-workers said."

"Kate, race relations have deteriorated and hostilities increased considerably since the riots . . ."

"I *know*. But she was *tiny*! And he was *huge* and he was *pounding* her! And people were staring but *nobody* was *acting*!"

"I'm proud of your moral impulses, but don't *do* that again!"

The four of us repaired to the kitchen to calm down with a nightcap of Celestial Seasonings Tea.

I told them I commuted by subway all over New York City when I was less than ten. Attended James Brown concerts at the Apollo in my teens. Knew *all* the presidents. Learned THAT in grade school. I told them I *tried* to make it better but I was getting tired and it was their turn.

They studied me curiously.

As if I were a Space Creature.

"Doesn't it trouble you at all? Aren't you *bothered* by the dysfunction, the ignorance, the *violence*?!" I challenged, out-raged, and nonplussed them into silent pondering.

"Ya gotta understand, Jools," Amy said finally, "we've never known it any other way . . ."

"Let's discuss fee arrangements," Buddy Monash broaches after fifteen minutes of small-talk in his not-yet-decorated conference room.

"What fee? I thought this was on contingency!"

"I can't operate without some sort of retainer. I was think-ing ten grand. To cover costs . . ."

"Ten grand!? Ten grand?! I can't afford ten cents! I wouldn't have wasted *any* of our time if I knew you expected a five-figure retainer . . ."

Squinting for emphasis I shoot LevyLevy a meaningful look. His eyes ricochet off mine into the middle distance. The little turnip.

"Let's put the matter of a fee on hold," Buddy conciliates. "I want you to go back into your calendars."

"Why don't you just read that section of my book!" I bark à la Claire. LevyLevy frowns. Buddy Monash grins.

"I have already but I'd appreciate some serious documen-tation," Buddy says. Oh document this! How is it I'm a name they drop and they *still* address me as if I'm their summer intern. "I called Bert Fields about this already. I told him I'd even played Zulu chants in the background to gain some insight into his bullshit letters of termination," Buddy continues. "I said, 'C'mon you know he's wrong. This is silly!' And y'know what he said?"

"What?" I ask, indulging Buddy.

"He said that David Geffen told him, 'I'll spend my last penny to destroy her.'"

"Wooowww," I say appreciatively. The Geff will have to spend a billion dollars of pennies to reach his last.

A billion isn't what it used to be, but still . . .

"You were much more involved over the years than Mike. It'll be your records that tell the tale."

"Okay. All right. You've inspired me. Gimme a couple of weeks to hand pages in. I need my new money." Again. "Speaking of pages, I'm not constrained in any way from writing what I want, am I?"

. "Noooo," Buddy grins.

"Good. Meeting over?"

LevyLevy and I, mute, inhale fumes curbside in the underground garage. Our chariots arrive and we kiss air.

"If I'm doing the work, you *could* put up the cash," I say snidely as I step into 329WOE.

Feigning deafness from engine-reverb, pretending not to hear, LevyLevy scurries to his car without responding.

TO: Buddy Monash and Michael Levy
FROM: Julia Phillips

August 15, 1993

Sooo Buddy . . .

First, the broad strokes of The Big Picture . . .
. . . as far as I can tell, we assaulted the charismatic Katzenberg, then president of Paramount, for the rights to *Interview with the Vampire* at the end of 1984–beginning 1985. Somewhere in that period, Lynn Nesbit, Anne Rice's agent (and mine), knowing

of my interest in *Interview* (still trapped in a nine-year deal, commencing in 1977) sneaked me a copy of *The Vampire Lestat*. Paramount, which probably had some rights but regarded *Interview* as an eight-hundred-pound-Dick-Sylbert gorilla, passed on *Lestat*, and Michael and I were given the right to run free with it.

We pitched the project to Keith Barish, to Richard Fischoff at Carson Films, to Mark Canton at Warners. I gave the book to Ileen Maisel, a friend of a few years (and who can ask for more in the business of Show). She'd just been toasted by Frank Yablans at MGM, and landed on her feet immediately at the newly created CBS Films under Bernie Safronsky. From then on, the pattern of the action and the deals pretty much coincides with Ileen's career path.

So . . . for the first half of 1985 we were in business with CBS Films, which went under with great dispatch and extreme prejudice in less than half a year.

Maisel landed on her feet at Taft-Barish under Rob Cohen, an old . . . well, call him a friend. We had flirted with Keith from the beginning, so it felt karmically correct to end up with his operation. We suffered there from late 1985 until somewhere in 1987. During that time, the rights to *Interview* reverted to Anne Rice (despite the repeated imprecations of Paramount teevee, which had developed a truly hideous teevee movie, to extend — talk about your oxymorons) and we convinced Rob, Ileen and Keith that we should separate the two properties. Develop *The Vampire Lestat* as a movie, *Interview* as a Broadway musical.

We almost got into the development business with Richard Gere, who led us to Oliver Stone, who stayed somewhat-committed for a week or so. We flirted outrageously with Ridley Scott to direct. We met myriad writers and ultimately went with Stephen Geller, who has the screenplay credit on *Slaughterhouse Five*. He delivered a truly awful script, probably in 1987.

We also commenced a serious-meeting mode (oxy-moron oxymoron) with various musical types, most principally Tim Rice, Barry Gibb, Holly Knight, Bryan Ferry, and Elton John and Bernie Taupin. We chatted with David Geffen about financing a Broadway show.

Taft-Barish reneged on the *Interview*/musical-con-cept/deal and toasted Ileen, who landed, again upright, with Bernie Brillstein, who was then made chairman of Lorimar Pictures; he hired Ileen's old pal from CBS Films over her (you gottit: oxy-you-know-what) Peter Chernin.

1988 brought Barry Krost, David Geffen, and the merging of Lorimar into Warners. Bernie returned to management, Ileen parachuted to Paramount, and Peter Chernin decamped to Fox.

Somewhere between the moment we hoisted our glasses of champagne in Elton John's suite and cho-rused "to the show" and the release of the third vol-ume (*The Queen of the Damned*) of what had become *The Vampire Chronicles*, we plighted our troth to David Geffen, who didn't love Elton John anymore. Barry Krost, he added crossly, was "a loser" anyway.

1989. We informed Warners that we really wanted the project, which was by then all three books, assigned to Geffen. Oh, and by the way, let's forget all that nonsense about Krost and John and a Broadway musical.

We had some really stupid meetings and finally Michael Cristofer was hired. I have a notation that I was given his supersecret superunlisted phone num-bers, but I don't remember ever talking to him . . .

In the spring of 1990, Anne Rice and David Geffen absconded with *The Witching Hour* and by Christmas Geffen was hearing gossip from the network to whom I'd given my book for waivers that I was less than com-plimentary about him. In early 1991, we stopped the presses for him and he freaked. Within weeks, Michael and I were fired.

Following is all the documentation I could glean
from my trusty Week-at-a-Glance Calendars, 1985
through 1990. Assume, unless otherwise noted, that
lunch is at Le Dome and dinner at Mortons and that
with the exception of Ileen and Michael, I picked up
the check. I'm sure my phone logs could tell a tale as
well, but frankly I have neither the heart nor the time.
The truth is I need my next payment on the next book,
as my tax problem seems to escalate daily; I must
therefore return to cranking out new pages the second
after I transmit this opus/fax.

I worry it's an exercise in futility, as I haven't the
cash just now to front expenses and just reviewing all
the wasted work, appropriated ideas and stolen/pre-
cious time reminds me — piercingly — why I left. I
hardly have an appetite for more of the same.

Nevertheless:

1985:

1/18 –	lunch with Keith Barish
1/30 –	lunch with Michael Levy
2/11 –	lunch with Keith Barish
	6:00 P.M. meeting with Jeff Katzenberg
3/14 –	lunch with Richard Fischoff
	dinner with Ileen Maisel
4/17 –	phone conversation with Wiatt/Berg
5/2 –	dinner with Ileen Maisel
5/6 –	meeting with Fischoff
5/8 –	2:30 P.M. meeting with Sue Mengers/Jim Wiatt
5/9 –	lunch with Rob Cohen
5/16 –	meeting with Fischoff
6/3 –	10:30 A.M. meeting with Bernie Safronsky/Ileen
6/17 –	9:45 A.M. meeting with Bernie Safronsky
6/25 –	lunch with Paula Wagner (discussed Tom Cruise)
6/27 –	dinner with Ileen
7/12 –	drinks with Ed Limato
	(agent for Richard Gere, Mel Gibson)

8/9 –   first call to Anne Rice telling her to hang in.
           Beginning of a beautiful friendship
8/20 –   meeting with Safronsky, Alan Levin at CBS (they
           don't close) meeting immediately following with
           Mark Rosenberg (then head of production at
           Warners) who says he'll make the deal. The deal
           closes at CBS the following day
9/6 –   meeting with Ileen and Rob Gurelnick, her
           assistant
9/13 –   dinner with Lynn Nesbit
9/19 –   dinner with Hilary Henkin (potential writer),
           Harlan Goodman (my assistant) and Beverly Ross
           (his girlfriend, Hilary's girlfriend)
9/26 –   lunch with Hilary Henkin
10/10 –   3:30 P.M. meeting with Hilary Henkin
10/24 –   drinks with Hilary Henkin
11/15 –   dinner with Anne Rice and her husband,
           Stan Rice
11/19 –   dinner with Ileen

1986:

1/9 –   dinner with Michael Levy
1/12 –   dinner with Anne Rice
2/13 –   drinks with Ed Limato; dinner with Ileen
2/15 –   dinner with Ileen, Adam Ant,
           Anne Dollard (Ant's agent)
2/20 –   meeting Warner Bros.
           Allyn Stewart, Billy Gerber, Mark Canton
3/5 –   dinner with Carl Parsons, Ileen
3/13 –   lunch with Ed Limato, Mel Gibson
3/25 –   Michael Levy phone call
4/2 –   dinner with Ileen, Steve Reuther, Jeff Wald
4/7 –   4:00 P.M. meeting with Ileen and her assistant,
           Rob
5/8 –   dinner with Ridley Scott
5/13 –   meeting with Wiatt

5/14 –   dinner with Ed Limato
5/15 –   meeting with Richard Gere/Levy/Maisel
         Chateau Marmont
5/17 –   dinner with Richard Gere
5/18 –   dinner party at Ed Limato's
5/20 –   lunch with Rob Cohen, Richard Gere
5/22 –   dinner with Holly Knight
5/27 –   dinner with Ileen
5/29 –   lunch with Paula Wagner re: Oliver Stone
6/16 –   meeting with Wiatt
6/21 –   Gere arrives and I take care of him
6/23 –   dinner with Holly Knight
6/24 –   lengthy phone call with Paula Wagner re: Stone
6/25 –   Richard Gere, Eurythmics concert
6/29 –   meeting with Richard Gere/Ileen
7/2 –   lunch with Paul Michael Glaser, who wants to
         direct *Interview*. His agent, Andrea Eastman, a
         friend, begs me
7/10 –   meeting with Anne Rice, Richard Gere, Oliver
         Stone; dinner at Ed Limato's
7/14 –   Oliver Stone commits, then uncommits a week
         hence
7/16 –   meeting with Josh Donen
7/17 –   meeting with Mark Canton
7/18 –   meeting with Rob Cohen
7/19 –   meeting with Ileen
7/26 –   meeting with Mark Canton
8/1 –   dinner with Charles Melnicker (Bizaffairs, ICM)
8/2 –   lunch with Ridley Scott, Mimi Polk
         (his assistant)
8/6 –   drinks with Ridley Scott and Mimi — he
         commits
8/7 –   meeting with Ed Khmara (potential writer)
8/14 –   meeting with Ed Khmara, Rob Cohen, Ileen, Levy
8/15 –   lunch with Stephen Geller
8/21 –   lunch with Charles Melnicker
8/28 –   dinner with Holly Knight

8/31 –   huge flowering plant to Richard Gere for birthday
9/9 –   meeting with Mike Levy
9/12 –   dinner with Ridley Scott, Stephen Geller, Mimi
         Polk
9/23 –   meeting with Tim Rice
9/24 –   dinner with Rob Cohen, Ileen, Tim Rice —
         Mortons David Geffen comps us a bottle of
         champagne
9/26 –   meeting with Mike Levy
10/4 –   Anne Rice's birthday — more expensive flowers
10/9 –   dinner with Ileen
10/14 – lunch with Stephen Geller
11/3 –   dinner with Ridley Scott, Mimi Polk
11/4 –   lunch with Tim Rice, Barry Gibb, Rob Cohen,
         Ileen Maisel — Four Seasons, NYC — Rob picks
         up the check, oh joy!
11/5 –   drinks Tim Rice, Jim Silverman, Ileen
12/13 – lunch with Stephen Geller
12/17 – dinner with Ileen
12/24 – lunch with Stephen Geller

1987:

1/13 –   meeting with Geller, Levy
1/16 –   meeting with Geller/Levy
2/3 –   Stephen Geller conf. call with Levy
2/4 –   lunch with Geller; lengthy Oliver Stone phone
         call (regarding what? I dunno . . .)
2/16 –   dinner with Rob Cohen
3/19 –   lunch with Levy; dinner with Ileen
4/1 –   dinner with Holly Knight
4/3 –   lunch with Paul Michael Glaser
4/6 –   4:30 P.M. meeting with Peter Chernin
         dinner with Ileen
7/13 –   dinner with Christopher Lambert
7/24 –   lunch with Christopher Lambert
8/24 –   Anne Rice 5:30 P.M., then dinner

9/1 –   lunch with Mary Agnes Donahue (*Beaches*)
9/23 –   meeting with Anne Rice, Peter Chernin, Ileen
         dinner with Anne Rice, Howard Rosenman
10/15 – dinner with Ileen
10/22 – lunch with Amos Poe (possible writer)
11/17 – lunch with Paul Michael Glaser
12/10 – celebratory dinner with Charles Melnicker and
         wife, Deenie (not kidding)

1988:

1/4 –   lunch with Ileen
3/15 –   dinner with Mimi Polk (Ridley's associate now)
4/6 –   dinner with Michael Levy
4/26 –   *Vampire* meeting (I have no idea what this is or
         who was in it, but it was important, because I
         have an exclamation point after the notation)
5/16 –   meeting with Levy/Ileen/Randy (I's assistant)
8/31 –   late dinner with Ileen
9/15 –   4:00 P.M. meeting with David Geffen, Mike Levy
9/21 –   dinner with Ileen
9/22 –   lunch with Barry Krost re: musical with John/Taupin
         3:45 P.M. meeting with David Geffen/Levy
9/26 –   dinner with Anne Rice, Barry Krost, Bernie
         Taupin
9/27 –   lunch et seq. with Elton John, Bernie Taupin,
         Anne Rice, Mike Levy, Barry Krost — Four
         Seasons
10/12 – dinner with Ileen
10/18 – 2:30 P.M. meeting with Bernie Brillstein
         dinner with Ileen
11/5 –   dinner with Anne Rice
11/10 – 3:00 P.M. meeting with Barry Krost, Michael
         Levy; 4:00 P.M. meeting Warners — Krost, Levy,
         Canton et al.
11/13 – *Liaisons Dangereuses* screening re: Stephen
         Frears to direct

1989:

1/19 –	2:00 P.M. meeting with Levy
	3:00 P.M. meeting with Geffen/Levy
2/14 –	dinner with Ileen
2/23 –	dinner with Nick Wechsler, Jon Lyden
3/14 –	meeting with Jeff Berg, Mike Levy
	4:30 P.M. call to Anne Rice
4/7 –	dinner with Ileen
4/13 –	lunch with David Geffen (Il Giardino)
4/17 –	3:00 P.M. meeting with Levy/Sean Daniel/Cari-Esta Albert re: writers — we agree on Michael Cristofer
5/1 –	lunch with Christopher Lambert
5/29 –	dinner with Ileen
6/6 –	dinner with Ileen, Bob Hohlman (writer's agent)
8/8 –	dinner with Ileen
10/18 –	dinner with Ileen
12/14 –	dinner with Ileen

1990:

1/18 –	Geffen call — must be important if on my calendar
2/14 –	dinner with Ileen
2/16 –	dinner with Ileen
5/1 –	lunch with Geffen (at his house)
6/22 –	Cristofer numbers in my book

At some point in the middle of all the actor
approaches, I know I had dinner with Rutger Hauer. I
have no written record, but I remember it well,
because he screeched into the Mortons parking lot on
a verrry imposing Harley-Davidson machine, swathed
in leather and escorted by the police.

It was fun while it lasted.

Love and squalor, as ever

Jools

Concurrent to phone-negotiation with George *The New York Daily News* Rush, I'm T.V.-witnessing Bert Fields's second news conference regarding Michael Jackson in as many days.

The Michael is out of the United States, racing around the world as if he can outpace headlines screaming accusations of pedophilia. He's replaced The Heidi on The InfernoTainment Hit List. With a bullet.

Is anyone really surprised by this? I wonder, bored.

Is it just a matter of milliseconds till *The New York Times* surrenders and runs front-page color photos?

"George, don't you believe what you hear from the horse's mouth?!"

"But Buddy said — "

"I don't *care* what Buddy said, I'm not suing."

"He's about to be indicted in another county," Bert Fields says on T.V. and before he can utter another word Howard Weitzman cuts in. Ooooh. Big Bad Bert just misspoke. Big Time. In front of a billion people probably. I grin.

It's the little things that cheer me up.

"Buddy says you've been wrongfully terminated and that you have a good case. You *should* sue." Be niiice . . .

"George, here's the deal — "

"What?"

"The pen is mightier than the lawyer!"

"Julie, I don't care if you have to swim halfway across the flooding waters of the Mississippi and I have to swim the other half. That money *has* to be in my account by this Friday!"

Pace pace puff puff ooh ooh.

"Oy gevalt meshuggene Julia!"

"Grrr."

"Not to worry. It'll be there today!"

The doorbell rings.

"I gotta go. Todd's here."

"He baby-sitting you?"

"Fuckin'-A . . ."

We hang up and I join Todd, who's already microwaving morning coffee in the kitchen.

"It's bad enough this book's a struggle! I keep losing editors as well . . ."

Alberto Vitale has put the kibosh on Turtle Bay Books. Joni's bailed, set herself up as a superentity at William Morris. Lynn's exerted considerable energy on Julie Grau's behalf and she's moved to Villard, a Random House imprint.

I've moved with her, settled down, and handed in a second stack of pages.

She's released the second half of my first payment.

Where's my fucking deal?! There. *There's* your deal . . .

"Aren't they announcing the verdict today?" Todd says.

"Which verdict?" It's difficult to keep abreast of the trials as lately the last act in every major InfernoTainment drama appears to be set in court.

I'm constantly reminded of a seventies *Sunday New York Times* article headlined GLUT OF STUDENTS IN LAW SCHOOLS.

Think we'll become a more litigious society? I asked my first-and-last-ex-husband, an attorney.

Without a doubt, he smiled . . .

Heidi begat Michael and Michael begat The Bobbitts, John Wayne and Lorena, who made the word penis safe for the world.

The Penis, oddly, seemed central to *all* The Begat Cases.

"Reginald Denny," Todd says and we turn on the tube in time for the announcement, which makes me snort and Todd scowl.

"I'm not surprised. Edi Fahl is hot stuff. Been catching his act on Court TV." When Reginald Denny hugged the defendants' mothers I was so moved I cried.

Then I couldn't help but wonder if his exemplary humanity was the result of brain damage.

"So Jools, are white people gonna go out now and riot?"

"*This* white person will riot if the wire-transfer doesn't go down in the next five hours!"

Yo tengo un tax problema.

Does Damien Williams?

Not likely.

Kate settles under the covers of my bed and flicks the remote lackadaisically. Soon her head will fall onto the pillows and her eyes droop shut.

Kate's just arrived for a brief Vulnerable Season Break and she likes to sleep with me her first night home.

When I've queried crossly if she plans to continue this particular bonding mechanism at twenty-eight (with two ex-husbands and three ex-children sleeping in her wing of Sanctuary) she's chuckled a definitive Yes.

I hardly ever sleep anyway, so why protest?

I'm particularly agitated, since Julie Grau's absconded from Villard. I've been assigned to the publisher, Diane Reverand, whom I've never met. I'm queasy from the sudden turn of events.

Like I'm loaded on a drug imparting the high too many rides on Space Mountain might.

I'm flying without a net and I don't like it.

Kate falls out almost immediately.

I retrieve the remote from her limp hand to press MUTE and she murmurs ILoveYouGoodNight.

Good night yourself.

I open the trades and entertain myself with Industry reaction to tonight's Cocktails with Clinton.

That Valley Boy's guest list *in*cludes his clients, *ex*cludes everybody else — even heavy contributors to the Democratic Party — and people are pissed.

In muted fashion, since he's still Number One on *Premiere*'s Power List and the derivative of Number-One-to-the-*X* more than equals Number-One-to-the-*X* in *this* town.

I switch to CNN announcing the grim postmortem of a pretty prepubescent. Near Petaluma.

"She always feared a man would snatch her from her bed and she always wanted to be famous. She was right on both counts I guess," her father says and I burst into tears.

• • •

Memo to Joni.

Subject: Julia Tells the Truth.

Are the concomitant events of MikeOvitz's exclusionary fund-raiser and the discovery of Polly Klaas's cosseted corpse coincidental? Karmic?

Would she have ripped her hands off to escape the CAA?

Did Phoenix Fellini the River All Hallows' Eve?

I didn't *choose* to ask these questions!

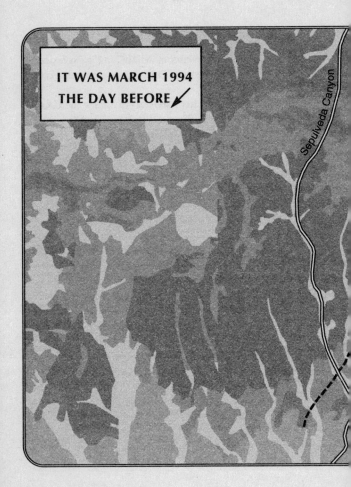

IT WAS MARCH 1994
THE DAY BEFORE

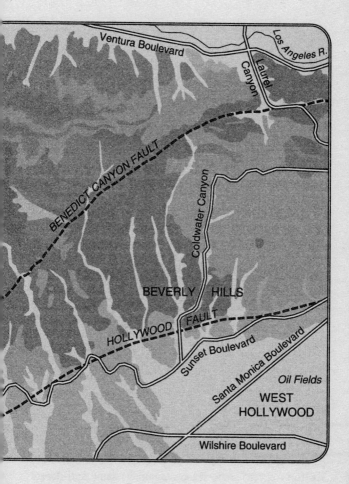

Dick.

"Whatta prick!"

Tearing headphones from my ears I consider hurling the Walkman in protest but I'm too impoverished for property implosion, however gratifying.

"R-R-R-Realpolitik," I stutter instead, plop to the curb and fritz through the black leather runner's codpiece messengered by a Fox T.V. executive the day after drinks at Adriano's, where I'd pitched him and his superior an antitalk show they didn't buy.

DOING TIME WITH JULIA.

Over second martinis I'd entertained them with a précis of my weekend jog through a neighborhood development that was once a neighborhood wildlife sanctuary.

"Three miles. Upwardly tilted thirty degrees. Three Stops! Nicotine break at each one. There's a payphone at the first sign, so sometimes I place a crank call or two . . ."

JULES'S SMOKE AND RUN KIT says the label on the purse. Inside: rolls of quarters, packs of Marlboro Reds, a Bic.

I light a cigarette and switch off La Limbaugh breathlessly confiding he's received a fax confirming Vince Foster's body was moved to the park after he'd been murdered in an apartment leased by Hillary Clinton.

I'd been deeply disturbed by Vince Foster's suicide, it paralleled Norman Garey's so precisely. Same age (forty-six–forty-seven) same season (summer) same anti-depressant (Desyrel) same honor-bound gestalt (perceived shame about deeds with which Those Bigger Boys felt sooo comfortable).

Same ticket to The AfterWorld. Gun.

How awful for the family to hear this banter.

Stalk Radio.

Perpetrated by Rush. Of the big fat tush.

His DittoHeads have brains of mush.

He'd be silly. If not dangerous.

Amusing. If not The Man with The Power.

I stand up.

Pace pace puff puff ooh ooh.

Abruptly, as lately is Her wont, Miz Earth multiple-
orgasms-from-Hell. I roll with it and aftershock into recently-
suppressed memory . . .

HOW I SPENT MY BULNERABLE SEASON,1994
THE SEQUEL TO THE SEQUEL BY JULIO PHILLIPPE

Uh-oh. Sleepless Sunday Night. Homework unfinished.

Too busy chatting up the dead people.

Mom and Machiavelli . . .

Talking Points: Big Issues, Big Questions.

Whaddya want for dinner?

The Marys: Shelley and Baker Eddy . . .

Do you really love me?

Marvin Gaye and Metternich . . .

Didja come? Well didja?

Wolfgang Amadeus . . .

Leaving so soon?

. . . Amadeus-Amadeus . . .

How could you *do* this to mc?

Mozart!

Didja? Well? Didja? Come?

Another trick question. And me without my sides.

Martin Luther King recently.

MLK, FirstandLastEx-Husband dubbed him. Back in The
Era of Those LaceCurtain BostonIrish ChoirBoys: R & JFK.

I missed the visceral connect of MLK's resonant basso

profundo. When he was on a roll, MLK and his voice could penetrate the soul of the crowd. Transport it.

For the length of the speech anyway.

The run of the show.

"MLK being a long-lost Kennedy brother, from one of Joe Senior's trips South," Michael kidded and I laughed.

"I don't think so. Hardly," I added in the icy tone I learned from my mother, Tanya, who used it on me.

Tanya cast her ballot for John Kennedy as the lesser of two evils because she always cast her ballot. She abhorred Joe Sr. for his Nazism and distrusted Bobby for his service to Joe McCarthy, but my mother came from another country and considered electoral participation her honorable obligation to democracy.

She'd *never* vote for Richard Nixon, whose anticommunism was more repugnant than the Kennedys'.

Wrapped in a considerably less attractive package.

Tanya always waaas openly partial to pretty.

And as ruthlessly ambitious as the Kennedys were in pursuit of high office, they hadn't paraded around a woman who'd recently been released from a mental institution and fobbed her off as political opponent Helen Gahagan Douglas, which my mother claimed Richard Nixon did in his first California congressional campaign.

Tanya was preoccupied with these matters in 1960.

The year before she'd been wrenched from a semisophisticated New York existence to Milwaukee, Wisconsin.

DittoTush Territory.

A Polish/German bastion, populated by the bodypolitik that had sent Senator McCarthy to Washington.

A foreign place — America — where The Bund operated openly in 1943. She was still in shock.

She never recovered.

"West of the Hudson, you could burn it," her best friend Ann said when my mother told her we were moving to the center of the country, thinking she was just topping a joke. Then realized from my mother's brimming brown eyes it was true.

FLASHBACK: Eavesdropping on one of Tanya's afternoon

dialogues with Miriam, her Milwaukee Ann (not as slim, not as pretty, not as bright) the day before the day before the first televised Nixon-Kennedy StandOff.

"How could you have voted for McCarthy?!" Tanya hollered.

"You don't understand, La Follette was getting crazier and crazier. We thought he was a fascist. We thought McCarthy was —"

"Evil incarnate. Equaled only by the grocer's son."

"Oh say his name, Tanya. It always makes me laugh."

The hateful-little-man/evil fuck.

Tanya probably hated that he had the power and she didn't.

"Hasn't changed a bit. Actually it's worse," I said out loud to Mommy, who'd been gone almost fifteen years.

Whaddid you expect? I felt her sneer knowingly.

I talked to the dead people more and more as I aged.

Reluctantly, I flung back hotflash-sweaty sheets, rattling quantities of *Sunday Times*es and a *Scientific American* folded to an article I'd been scanning for days.

WHAT IS THE COLD DARK MATTER? Indeed.

Ask MLK.

Ramona rustled from under the papers, fixed me with a cold stare, then ambled off the bed, a dark beast slouching toward the kitchen.

POWER OFF/ON/OFF/ON/OFF/OFF/OFF/ON

DWP. Après-midnight relaying.

Separating red-white-and-blue clown-pajamas from sopping skin I lit a cigarette and contemplated the deeper meaning of my persistent surge situation.

Why had I chosen to live for twenty years in a poorly wired home/office encamped in the conflagration of three intersecting networks? Why? Because I was a science brat?

Because every time my family settled in after a move and I made friends, we'd pick up stakes? Move again?

I'm staying here for Kate, I'd rationalized, but I knew I was trapped by antipathy to physical change, emotional inertia and the IRS.

A phantom breeze chilled me to beneath-the-bone.

I wrapped myself in a moderately motheaten cashmere bathrobe, shoved my freezing sweaty feet into worn velvet slippers.and schlepped into the kitchen for microwaved Grapenuts 'n' milk.

I fumbled through the odds-and-ends drawer, found a small swirled sepia candle from someone else's birthday long ago and lit it off a gas-fed flame on the stove.

I planted it firmly in the center of the viscous glob.

It listed starboard and fizzled but I sang:

"Happy birthday to you . . .

"HappyBirthday to you . . ."

Ramona looked up from her Friskies and harmonized:

"Rrreeent rrreeent rrreeent rrreeent rrreeent rrreoww . . ."

"Happy Birthday, dear Marrr-tinnnn . . ."

"Happppyyyy Birthththdaaaay tooooyooooo . . ."

"Rrreeeowwwoooowwww."

I serenaded the dead people too.

On their dates-of-birth if I remembered them.

Usually, though, it was the dates of their deaths that stuck in my mind.

Just the opposite with MLK. I never recalled until this past year when the memory was jogged by a two-day InfernoTainment orgy commemorating the twenty-fifth anniversary of his murder that it occurred just in time to provide riots for my twenty-fourth birthday.

Fuck IHaveADream. Everybody hasadream. What about: I may not get there with you but I have been to the mountaintop and I can tell you that We As A People Will Get! to the promised land . . .

The one I knew by heart. Delivered teary-eyed the night before the day he died because he knew someone was gonna make him a martyr. Martinize him.

Maybe he knew James Earl Ray was gonna martin him.

Maybe that was the deal. Like — hypothetically of course — the one between Jesus and Judas?

$Sudden Violent Death: Retail for Fame Everlasting.

E.G.:

Jesus to Judas: (flapping a tablet in the air) Did you
    see *The Times*'s lead editorial today? They say I'm
    (reading from tablet) A dangerous demagogue. A
    deranged dilettante. A menace to the masses.
    Who writes this shit? (smashes the tablet on the
    ground)

Judas to Jesus: We're slippin' in the polls. This guy
    Barabbas is catching up fast. We gotta *do* some-
    thin'!

Jesus: Hey Jude, there's alot of fucking *Messiahs*
    comin' round my way . . .

Judas: And that Mary Magdalene rumor keeps pop-
    pin' up.

They bark harsh laughter. They can't help themselves.
They're just a couple of those boys after all.
Loitering in a corner of the marketplace. Silence.
They pace, thinking. Then:

Judas: They'll never notice if we make a Big Bang.

Jesus: Excuse me, but what is walking on water? heal-
    ing the terminally dead? chopped fucking
    Caviar?!@#

Judas: I know I know, but people today got no atten-
    tion span.

Jesus: Mmmmm I suppose you're right. Why do I even
    care? The Way Things Are we could be gone
    tomorrow.

Judas: That's it! That's a brilliant idea! That's It! (kisses
    Jesus on both cheeks, then pinches them)

Jesus: (grimacing, wiping his cheeks) Eeeeuuuooow!
    Don't *do* that! I *hate* when you *do* that!

Judas: (unfazed, beaming) Such a bright boy.

Jesus: (confused) What's brilliant? What's *it*!!?@#

Judas: Okay, this is rough, y'understand, but what if I
    betray you. (Jesus reacts) Stay with me here. You're
    crucified, along with the other guy, who's a petty

thief, so that's easy. Crowd demands your freedom,
other guy dies, melts into dim memory . . .

Jesus: (thinks) Flat. I'll have a hot opening weekend,
then it's outta the living room and into the toilet for
good.

Judas: Sooo The Rabble votes for the other guy. You
die . . .

Jesus: That's a little extreme, don'tcha think? And
what's your motivation anyway?

Judas: How about *I'm* the vilified villain? Good thing
I've been working on my self-esteem.

Jesus: Oh this is about you?

Judas: (ignoring him, on a roll) Let's come back to
motive. We'll thinka somethin'. There's always
filthy lucre.

Jesus: (getting into the spirit) Let's assume we *did* pursue your concept, I'm just saying *if*!
We would need a . . . a . . . *bigger* ending . . .

Judas: Okay! Okay. That's where I'm going. Verrry
rough, y'understand, but what if you die and come
back? Resurrect yourself? Think you could do it?

Jesus: With the right drugs and a decent stunt double . . .
They laugh mordantly.

FADE OUT.

FADE UP:

THE CRUCIFIXION

Jesus: (pinioned, muttering)
    Oy gevalt meshuggener . . . OW!
    Ow ow owwww.
    I'd rip my hands and feet off to . . .

This is good this is good, Jools. Go to work.

But I stayed in the kitchen and blew out the candle.

A wish on MLK's behalf for an end to racism, sexism, jingoism, terrorism and the necessity for onanism.

The Salvation of Mankind. Not that He deserved it.

Ramona brushed against my legs and wandered toward The Creature's room, stopped, glanced back: C-O-M-I-N-G?

Deadline pressure from the family pet.

I nibbled MLK's birthday treat and followed her. Maybe I *could* make a dent in my homework, even though I'd gotten stuck on the first sentence: So here's the deal.

Knowing there WAS no deal.

No deal in search of a story even and it had made *YNELITTA TU*? hard to write, hard to finish and I'd taken so long events were superseding prescience.

"Ahh shit, Victor," I said.

What was left of him had won the second-chick contest, ceased its struggle for existence more-or-less a week ago.

He is. He was.

The transitional stage could last years.

"Go see him," Debin had advised. "For closure."

"Foreclosure is right! Do you understand I have *no money!*"

Harumph. Closure.

I didn't need to bear witness to VS's final ravaged AIDS-induced coma to accept his passing.

I phoned it in, two lengthy lucid conversations before he drifted permanently into dementia. Years of long-distancing with my father's hoarse whisper had prepared me.

"Hard to speak or hard to breathe?" I asked.

"Haaa'd t' *pppreathe* . . ."

"Tell me key words and I'll figure out the rest," I instructed.

"Smaaa't *grrr'* . . ."

"VS I love you," was the last thing I told him.

"Lufff . . . *tooo* . . ." he gasped.

I flicked The Creature's switch.

POWER ON
Search Search Search.
Scroll Scroll Scroll.
YNELITTA TU ? Screw the deal in search of a story.
I'd rather fuck with the story in search of a deal.
Work in Progress. WIP. Crackers/Talking Dog.
And his people. Shari/Cheri/Klaus. Scroll.
Writer's Rule # 3: When in doubt go further out.
Ramona dug ferociously at the sand in her catbox whilst I
perused THE MOGUL KLAUS FENNIG.

Klaus had fattened Hannibal McCannibal on caviar, prosciutto
and goose pâté. Leftovers from his opulent life.

The carnivorous turkey resided in an outbuilding on the
back four acres of the Stone Canyon compound and had
taken to walking the estate with him early in the morning
and late at night.

McTurkey was not an easy secret to keep.

Given The Staff. The Wife. Her Kid.

Not to forget The Friends. The Guests.

Those Persons who rooted through his garbage seeking
something embarrassing. Something incriminating.

Something to pry open the fingers of his wrenching grip on
Hollywood's balls. Always difficult to locate anyway.

With The Cowardice Scale soaring there was no sport in it
anymore. His waddles with Hannibal were often the high
point of days. Sometimes weeks.

Which would disturb Klaus Fennig . . .

Née Menom Shvartzerfergerberger.

The *rich*est most *power*ful *lone*liest boy

In FernoTainment. The King of Hollywood.

Although some nasties whispered Queen.

. . . if something more compelling weren't on his mind.

Klaus cut through thick marine-layer smog and Hannibal
McCannibal trucked the requisite ten paces behind.

Freddie Mercury *rock*ed Klaus along in his headgear,
strapped tightly under his chin for maximum alienation from

his surroundings. A bicycle helmet with speakers earside, so he could really power walk his Stone Canyon estate.

Survey his fief. Keep in shape.

Keep Hannibal robust.

His best friend. For the year anyway. Long-term relationship, by Hollywood standards. By any standards.

His fourth sacrifice. Working The Program.

The Thirteen Steps of Sacrifice.

Chaz McGuffin's club. Effete. Effective.

More exclusive than The Senate.

Which wasn't saying much these days, but still . . .

We will we will rock you/We will we will . . .

Hannibal struggled to catch up and Klaus slowed his pace fractionally. Hannibal nuzzled him.

Rock you . . .

Klaus quickened his pace.

Walk walk. Life.

Power POWER. Death.

Hannibal and Klaus power-walked to their destiny.

"Phew. This stinks!"

Ramona had produced an evil-smelling dump.

I swiveled, vaulted from the chair too suddenly and stepped on her tail.

She screeched and glared and jumped atop The Creature.

With bated breath, I kept the malodorous vapors permeating the room at bay and glared back. Marching furiously, I toted the catbox outside, stomped back in and grabbed an air freshener I kept handy for such emergencies.

I sprayed the enclosed space noisily.

Ramona, deep into zen-washing-cycle, startled briefly then settled down. She didn't like the aroma either.

I continued to read THE MOGUL KLAUS FENNIG.

The few who knew the shack would hardly be surprised to find ghosts there, or four generations of eyesore-marsupials (mutated possums for example) or remnants from The Dawn

of Man buried two feet beneath the haphazard slab of cement
upon which it had been built.

Even brand new it was that kind of place.

Klaus pushed the door gently and Hannibal wuffled past and
there was Chaz. Tall and tan and blond and blue-eyed Chaz. A
charlatan if Klaus had ever seen one and Klaus had seen everything. Who could channel The Power of The Death to . . .
accomplish things.

I know a man with the power of voodoo.

"Hoo-doo?" Chaz smiled beautifully and Klaus shrank
before him and remembered that he believed.

Goddamn, he beee*leeeved*.

"Nice hat," Chaz taunted.

Klaus's hands, stressed-out hummingbirds, twittered about
his helmet, then flopped to his sides.

Klaus drew near, moth to a flame, an excited boy.

Anything. Any. Thing. Just make me younggggg.

Klaus closed the door.

Chaz grabbed McTurkey abruptly from behind and for a
moment of life-and-death struggle, Klaus imagined Chaz was
fucking Hannibal in the ass. Huh-huh.

"The knife!" Chaz pointed imperiously and with a violent
lurch Hannibal broke free. He ran in frantic concentric circles,
clapping his beak open-shut open-shut.

Klaus's hands sprang involuntarily to his helmet.

"I don' wanna die," Freddie Mercury wailed.

Sweat oozed from every pore of his body and Klaus wondered if he could really *do* this and knew he could.

He lunged for the knife he and Chaz picked up at a swap-
meet months ago and sliced the heel of his right hand on the
newly-sharpened blade.

He didn't feel it.

He tossed The Knife to Chaz, who caught it midair and
thrust it at Hannibal's throat with a Vogue-ish flourish, nick-
ing him superficially on his left shoulder.

Blood flowed but McTurkey was far from dead.

For a moment Chaz and McTurkey did a spin, stood each

other off, a flashback to a Fifties cha-cha, and Klaus *was* young but then Chaz jabbed Hannibal again, deep in his chest and blood spurted everywhere and Klaus was old again.

"Gimme a hand here!" Chaz screamed and Klaus bolted into action.

They ambushed Hannibal and wrestled him to the ground.

Klaus noticed the slice on his hand. He sucked the wound and wondered if he drank his blood or McTurkey's.

He didn't care.

It was thick and warm and salty-sweet, like cum.

It tasted nourishing.

"That's all, she wrote!"

Ramona stirred sharply, stood up and arched her back.

A pause for interspecies mindlock.

S-P-O-O-K-Y/S-I-L-L-Y . . .

"From Julia Phillips to Stephen King."

B-I-L-L-Y C-R-Y-S-T-A-L S-A-I-D . . .

"From our lips to God's downloaded memory."

G-O F-U-C-K Y-O-U-R-S-E-L-F . . .

"Okay I will."

Ramona smiled and melted into catnap position but she twitched her whiskers and fixed me with unblinking eyes.

My fingertips caressed The Creature's keyboard . . .

BluppBlupp

Bluppbluppblupp

. . . and then they cruised.

THE MOGUL KLAUS FENNIG. THE MOGUL KLAUS FENNIG.

"Don't let go!" Chaz hollered, but Klaus couldn't hear him over the thrub-thrub-thrub of his heart — or was it Hannibal's? — flanked stereophonically by Freddie's soprano.

Klaus took a deep breath and looked down at the thrashing beast that was once upon a time his best friend.

Hannibal's pale eyes locked him in a deathstare.

Et tu, Klaus?

"Ohmigod!" Klaus shrieked.

Née Many ShvartzersFuckYerMother . . .

"What?! What did you say?!"

Hannibal extricated himself from his executioners' grasp and hobbled to his feet. His head listed heavily to one side. His chest spouted blood.

"Say the words! Say the words!" Chaz screamed through Queen. "Focus on The Power of The Death!"

ShvartzersFuckMyMother!?@# Who writes your dialogue?!

Klaus scrambled around the shack in search of a more definitive weapon.

Wait a second, what am I doing here? Seven figures each to ACLU, Pediatric AIDS and MOMA this year . . .

Klaus found an ax.

This will serve nicely as Hannibal's ticket to immortality! was his next irresistible thought.

Klaus grabbed the ax and aimed it and Hannibal's glazed eyes pierced Klaus for the last time.

Ramona bolted upright, blew out her fur and hissed.

I-M O-U-T-T-A H-E-R-E . . .

She flew through the air and landed with a thud on the other side of the room, licked her shoulder strenuously for an instant, then stormed across the hardwood floor to neutral territory and parts beyond.

She sounded like a herd of elephants and rattled the house a bit.

Y-E-R O-N Y-E-R O-W-N . . .

Weird.

Back to blupping FENNIG.

Klaus reeled through a moment of overwhelming nausea and lost his footing.

"You hit a wire! The power's going!" Chaz shrieked. "Say the words!" Sparks flew and crackled and Chaz shut up.

Klaus breathed deeply. Fucking Christmas Eve!
Scaramouche Scaramouche
Can we do the fandango—
Queen cut to black and Klaus was engulfed by white noise.
Hannibal was more still than still.
Then a terrible low rumbling and The Earth moved.

The 7.0 (later reduced to 6.8, probably so the insurance companies wouldn't be required to forgive their policies' 10 percent deductibles) started in the middle.

Like Quentin Tarantino.

God, catching forty winks deep in the bowels of the Earth, awakened in a sudden baaad mood and pummeled its crust roughly, like a frustrated parent shook the shoulders of a persistently recalcitrant child.

And God said, Let there be GRRRRR.

Or maybe MLK had tossed the shackles of peaceful demonstration from his spirit and was celebrating his birthday in ultraviolent Nineties fashion.

Memo to the Living-Dead from the Dead-Dead People.

Yo. Suck this!

"Oh Fuuuck!" I bellowed because the floor was erupting and my knees were crashing into The Creature's table and there was nothing stable to grab for balance or to keep the fear on hold.

I knew I should run for cover, but where?

Roaring and clanging going and coming around and around and expensive glassware from my late lamented opulent life hurled itself from the hutch in neutral territory.

Committing suicide, which I'd heard Jack Kevorkian's increasingly-blowdried/increasingly-recognizable lawyer refer to as "a soft exit." Tell that to the battered Baccarat, the shattered Steuben, the wasted Waterford.

Tell that to Norman Garey. Paul Rosenfield.

Vince Foster.

The rumbling ratcheted up some decibels — thunder clapping from a thousand storms and the tremors intensified.

Videotapes and books and bibelots in the bedroom clattered and crashed cacophonously from precarious shelves.

Throughout the kitchen magnetic doors flapped open-shut open-shut, like Hannibal's beak, and cupboards spewed plates and cups and bowls and platters.

Tacky effects from *Poltergeist X*.

In The Creature's room the baker's rack vibrated tenaciously and the mirrors shimmied ominously and peripherally, through the slats in the shades on the glass doors, from the corner of my left eye, I saw an orange and green explosion arc across the sky.

A transformer toppling.

A miniature in a shot. A speck in The Scheme.

A subliminal cut on The Universe's gag reel.

People in glass houses shouldn't live adjacent to blind thrust faults, I despaired. And just as I panicked:

Will this never end?

It did.

POWER OFF

Solipsistic with portfolio, I thought and reached for a flashlight I kept on The Creature's table.

Dark night. Very dark.

And silent. Sooo silent.

"Dear God," I said.

Didja come? Well? Didja?

Hum a few bars and I'll fake it.

Sanctuary hosted a steady stream of claims adjusters and contractors, but the only approved work so far was temporary tarping of my leaky roof, which had nothing to do with the earthquake. Days later, I'd become desperately ill from carbon monoxide poisoning, because that boy on the roof in the too-short red shorts and the too-blond mustache and the too-bright/broad grin encased an air-conditioning unit with a crack in its gas line.

Another five thousand dollar surprise.

Hammering noisily, that boy on the roof accompanied his gyrations with an a capella rendition of *I'm a Gigolo* almost

on key. He'd been swiveling his hips for some ostentatious
hours and it was starting to get me down.

Would I warrant this performance if I were a man?

Probably.

Times being what times were being. And all.

Crankily, I cranked the volume on CNN and turned my
attention to the first delivery of mail since Saturday.

Resident/Occupant/Bill/Bill/Bill. Some glossy mags. A plain
white envelope addressed in a shaky scrawl that looked to be at
fifth-grade level. A giant manila Viking/Penguin number.

When I flipped it over, nearly a hundred letters fell to the
floor. Some postmarked 1992. Lost, then Found when powerful seismic activity shook them loose from whatever crack in
which they'd been lodged.

I could tell from the first ten missives they were unlikely to
provide happy distraction from the 5.0 aftershocks rattling
Sanctuary, hourly it seemed, so I opened the plain white envelope with the gradeschooler's handwriting.

A personal letter from MikeLevy MikeLevy.

Re: *Interview with a! Vampire*/The Geff.

He doesn't want to settle with you, LevyLevy wrote in
childish penmanship. Without prejudicing any further legal
action I might contemplate, LevyLevy continued, he'd come
to his own agreement with The Geff.

Translation: The also-ran was to be *kissed off.*

The principal *offed.*

Later, in a lengthy phone call when I queried if his comfort
level with this moral stance was sufficient to gaze in the mirror with untroubled brow, he replied Yes in a voice resonant
with self-esteem.

Dear-Jools-Thank-you-and-fuck-you-and-have-a-nice-day.

Kindest-personal-regards-MikeLevy.

"I'm a gigolo gigolo. I'm a gigolo gigolo . . ."

Todd and I were returning from the first night out, a
roundtable consciousness-raising session with those boys and
girls at Hamburger Hamlet. Re: Earthquake Anxiety.

"It was the end of the world in The Valley!" Brooke proclaimed. "Fires and water shooting fifty feet in the air. Guys
patrolling the streets with unregistered handguns . . ."

I'm the second chick.

"At least you were on the ground," Fanny said. "Try four
stories up. Everything's in motion — up and down side to
side. And I was butt-nekked!"

I'm the second chick.

"I had to crawl out of my bedroom window with my dog.
You could hear the gas — fsssst. The guys in the neighborhood capped it!" Mara exclaimed.

Her Sanctuary had torqued three feet from its foundation
and she'd been rendered homeless.

I'm the second chick. Hands down.

"Here's my earthquake preparedness kit," Ruby said.
"Twenty Seconal . . ."

"Ruby, why?!" we gasped because she'd been sober more
than fifteen years, although her AA attendance dipped drasti-
cally in The Eighties. She couldn't abide the So Here's the
Deal yuppie infiltrators and their Scene.

*I preferred AA when it was smelly old Skid Row bums and
me,* she once confided.

"I just don't wanna be under fifty feet of rubble squeaking
'help-me' like The Fly, dying slowly and painfully because
nobody hears."

"Or nobody cares," The Bartender added.

"There's one decent effect," I said. "People seem nicer,
helpful even. At least they're giving each other forty-five seconds before they hate each other. Plus, the infrastructure was
restored pretty quickly considering how decrepit it is . . ."

Astonishingly, my first two flipped-out calls after the big
event were from Kate in Switzerland (where she'd just arrived
for second semester Junior year abroad) and Dad in New York.
Bad news had traveled globally within minutes via CNN.

They both got through before 5 A.M.

Kate in fact phoned a second time to request that I tread
through the debris to check her domain. There was little

apparent damage. I found Ramona sandwiched tightly between Kate's bed and the wall but I couldn't coax her out for another day, after POWER ON.

"Something more horrible is still to come," The Psychic, a friend of Brad's whom none of us knew, pronounced portentously after we'd paid and were standing up to leave. "No, I don't know *what*! I just know *worse*!" she responded to our universally raised eyebrows.

"Y'know what bums me out about this earthquake?" I said to Todd on the drive home. "Aside from its negative effect on my daily wrestling match with The Creature?"

How Will This Affect My PageCount? was the way I coped with World Events. Personal ones, too.

"What?"

"The Word won't be 'penis' anymore."

"Well *that's* a relief!"

Since the news anchors stopped tripping over it, I'd been working 'penis' into any and all conversation. Tormenting those boys. We were often surprised it was so frequently pertinent to the matter at hand.

"How happy is Michael Jackson that Tonya Harding and Nancy Kerrigan popped onto the scene?"

Todd laughed.

"Ever wonder if Les Scandals are created for InfernoTainment consumption to divert The Population's nanoattention from the real deal?"

"Like . . . ?"

"Like the latest government report estimates 40 percent of the homeless are under the age of seven. Like one of every three abused children is under the age of two . . ."

And that's what They decided We should know.

No doubt the situation was considerably more grave.

Like The Population gave a shit.

"Jeez. In thirty years they're wild roving packs."

"Todd, try five."

"So the world is accelerating to its end in a derivative-of-*e*-to-the-*x*-equals-*e*-to-the-*x* kind of way."

"Logarithmically. At a less is more and more sort of pace. Wow, what a brilliant note!"

"What a depressing thought."

"Not entirely. The roving packs will be much better able to cope without water and power, which will also be more or less more and more."

"How do you know?"

"How do you not?"

329WOE jiggled expressively.

"Earthquake!" Todd shouted.

"Penis!"

Cutting his right turn onto Alpine a tad tight, Todd lurched off Sunset and a tire kissed the curb. I FLASHEDBACK to an identical moment on this very intersection.

The inception, actually, of Todd's investiture as 329WOE's principal wheel-man.

And I jolted to another earthshaker.

Not long enough ago . . .

HOW I SPENT MY BULNERABLE SEASON, 1990
THE PREQUEL BY JULIO PHILLIPPE

Daddy's-little-girl bounced into my room for final Thanksgiving outfit-preparation. The Kate often checked in for a pre-game pep-talk, trolling The Cabinet of Dr. Caligari for the perfect jacket before dances dates and expeditions to FirstandLastExHusband's.

Early after our splitup he'd carved out Thanksgiving for himself. A relief, since his family was close and large and good with holidays, and my family was distant and practically nil and mostly botched celebrations.

Kate posed in the mirror critically, then recited:

There was a little girl who had a little curl
Right in the middle of her forehead

And when she was good she was very very good
And when she was bad she was . . . mahhhvelous!

We cracked up and then Michael pressed the gatebell and she was out the door with a confident flourish.

If there was a God and Pearly Gates, building my daughter's self-esteem was in The Good column, but I wasn't surprised, certainly, that I opted for Thanksgiving in bed, vaguing out to the Twilight Zone Marathon.

Grinding teeth and smoking smoking smoking . . .

PostTinaFair/WendyStarkContrast Party, November's Final Week, my Vulnerable Season activities escalated to emergency root canal.

Performed by Rami Etessami, an Iranian (funny-you-don't-look) Jewish endodontist whose star clientele's framed and autographed eight-by-tens lined his expensively appointed waiting room. Small bright and cheerful, expensively appointed as his surroundings, Rami tch-tched and worried out loud he might not be able to save the tooth.

With a certain flair, he and his assistant performed a battery of x-rays. He lectured whilst studying them.

"You grind in your sleep," Rami said in an accusatory health-care-professional tone.

"I grind all the time."

I had my reasons:

Did *he* just say that to me?

Did *she* just do that to me?

And vice versa. More. And less-is-more.

"Do you have a biteplate?" Rami pressed.

"I do."

"Do you wear it?"

"I try. But I've broken so many . . ."

Afraid I'd choke on them, given my breathing skills.

"The grinding provokes the decay that leads to this."

Rami pointed to an x-ray.

I was no expert but the roots looked ablaze.

"I will try to bisect the tooth," Rami said gravely with a twinkle in his eye.

I insisted on gas and he charged fifty dollars extra for the tank. He didn't keep nitrous around, he said, because of "office abuse." We thrust-and-parried for control of the dials, but I was sufficiently weakened to forfeit sooner than I would've liked.

"Julia, I have performed heroic med'cine!" Rami proclaimed when he was done and handed me a mirror so I could inspect the tiny trunk that was once my tooth nestled in swollen bloody gums.

Whoop-dee-doo. Never thought I'd be so glad to see a piece of myself go.

I scheduled an appointment for the following week, charged it all to MasterCard and exceeded the limit.

I filled the script at Rox-San, where I had a house account.

Popped a Percodan in the car but I was throbbing with trauma by the time I entered Sanctuary.

I took another and was constipated for days.

This looked to be an especially Vulnerable Season.

Which provoked reasonably sane people into urgent feelings about warmth and family and meaning anyway.

If not in *life*, at least in *their* lives.

Even the artists and the atheists. The gangsters and the cynics.

The jivers and the jokers and the junkies.

Even the hipsters and the hypers and the hip-hoppers.

And the intelligentsia. All fifteen of them.

Even the cool people. Fresh people. Dope people.

Even me.

A shower for negative-ion/positive-attitude boost.

Shoo Wop Dee Dooo Bah Bah Bom

Shoo Wop Dee Doo Da Dom Oooohh yeahhh . . .

Better. I toweled off lotioned deodorized perfumed and blow-dried expeditiously. Brushed teeth vigorously and prayed for no more periodontal peregrinations. Hoped the hackers developed a User-Friendly Virtual Sex/Vulnerable Season program I'd find affordable when it became available.

Was the word weltschmerz invented in Vulnerable
Season?

It was my third decade in Los Angeles and I'd adapted to
The Vulnerable Season here. Its more bizarre West Coast
aspects canceled out its inherent weltschmaltziness and I was
starting to appreciate the decorations up Santa Monica
Boulevard and down Wilshire Boulevard which ended
abruptly at the now-leaving-Beverly-Hills cross-street and
were only lit in one direction. West.

Where the money was.

I applied blusher, mascara and lip gloss and rubbed my
swollen jaw. Too large a territory for Preparation H.

"I'm the unhappiest white woman in L.A.!"

Half a Percodan. Maybe two.

I brushed at bummer vibes floating in on a nasty tempera-
ture-inverted-first-stage-smog-alerted Santa Ana, took a
breath of the air with no air in it and flung open Caligari's
Cabinet for a heady whomp of leftover perfume.

I selected a subdued stone-green and slate-black animal-
printed spandex Yohji Yamamoto shorts, tube top and turtle-
neck. Katharine Hamnett tights under.

Long black Jasper Conran jacket over.

Low-key and covered but naked if necessary.

Hanging in front, from a couple of nights ago.

Dressed and made up but I blanked on the shoes.

Is it the shoes? It's gotta be the shoes.

Settled on the tasty black suede Alaia elf-boots from eons
ago.

Attacked the toes hurriedly with a toothbrush, because now
I was running late and I had An Evening coming up, filled
with complicated I'll-call-ya-back plans.

Places to go. People to see.

What were their names again?

Michelle. Brooke's ex-girlfriend. A tall Phoebe Cates type,
but also the Richard Dreyfuss character in *The Goodbye Girl*
who always had several jobs.

I loooved people who started with little and made something of themselves. As opposed to me. Or was it trined?

I was setting her up with —

Lance. Who'd eyed her hungrily from time to time over the years and had suffered a long dry spell between reliable fucks.

Not as long as mine but then whose was?

Mother Theresa's. Beeep. Good-answer.

And Stephanie Tifani.

Stefff, as she called herself, seemed more Staph-Infection-in-the-Rough than Epifani.

Stefff spoke forcefully and stood too close. She thought it her charm. I knew mutual friends confused her aggressive delivery with my . . . animation.

Probably the innate anti-Semitism of Those Non-Jews.

A secret thought I sometimes didn't even tell myself.

Stefff was perfect casting for The Vulnerable Season.

A Baaad Influence. Worse even than me.

We were attending a one-off conducted by Matt Robinson.

Matt was the son of Dolores and brother of Holly.

Holly was a singer/actress and Matt a slacker.

I'd made their acquaintance through Brooke.

Dolores — Mrs. Robinson — was a personal manager and I knew her from frequenting the same InfernoTainment eateries.

Black people who grew up in Malibu. The Oxymorons.

The last time I'd seen Dolores was at Morton's, squiring rapper Big Daddy Kane to The Other Side of Town.

Big Daddy Kane was handsomely overdressed, resplendent in too much 22 carat crap. He remained seated and scarfed a Caesar Salad whilst his date and I chatted.

Dolores finally introduced us and BDK tilted his eyes up with a look so distant it wiped the smile from my face.

A glutton for punishment, I stuck out my hand to shake.

BDK glared as if willing its painful disintegration.

"Looove your work," I lied and he squinted and stared, even chillier than before.

Wordless, BDK wiped dressing from his lips and I noticed for the first time he was wearing brass knuckles — gold knuckles, strictly speaking.

"I work out to you on MTV," I said and beat a hasty retreat as he returned his evil eye to Caesar . . .

Brrring brrring. BrrringBrrring.

Beeep.

"Jools, it's Brooke. Ya there?

"Are ya there are ya there are ya there are ya —?"

"I was just thinking of you."

"What're ya doin' later?"

"I'm hooking up Michelle and Lance."

Eeeuuuooow. Daddy's little girl was too old to be this mean. Daddy's little girl had heavy furniture around her eyes and plucked gray-white pubes from time to time. Daddy's little girl was morphing into a California workout type: old face, young body.

At least I don't dye my hair.

Brooke exhaled heavily.

"You don't mind, do you?"

"Unh-unh," he said in his tuned-out way and I believed him for the length of a top quark's struggle for existence. It passed. "Matt Robinson's club's at Helena's tonight —"

"That's where *we're* going!"

"Uh-oh. I was gonna ask if we should go together."

"That would have been an infinitely better plan than the one I'm locked into . . . Duuuude, you always call too late!"

And what am I? Her fucking *understudy*?!@#!

"So what're ya doin'?"

"Me Michelle and Stefff, dinner at Morton's. Then hook up with Lance and his friends at Helena's."

"Stefff . . ."

Brooke and Corey and I had met Stefff the preceding summer. We were tightly squashed into a VIP Bowling Alley/Roxbury Booth. I turned and opened my mouth to speak and she lobbed in a hard round bitter pill. 3 Points.

Zee Bee? Not like-leeee.

I bit it and considered slipping half to Corey, tongue to tongue, because he'd recently lent me enough money so I could breathe almost normally for a week and I was grateful.

I swallowed it dry.

I'd just completed my first big interview with Nancy.

Julia-do-you-think-you're-hard-to-love? Collins.

Not as hard as The Geff.

Not as hard as Stefff.

B and C and Me departed quickly because she crowded us.

"I'm not that high," I kvetched as we flopped down the stairs and through the doors.

To Sunset Boulevard.

Too bright too crisp too clear.

On the drive to Sanctuary, Brooke and Corey told me how much they despiiiised Stefff.

"Can you say lezzz-bee-anne?" Brooke laughed.

"Soooo unfair. She's just another borderline-attractive insecure Jewish girl with an aggressive delivery."

Those Boyeeezzzz rolled their eyes fondly.

"Naahhhh," I Joan-Riversed them and they chuckled condescendingly.

"Oh she wants to do nasty things to you, Jools," little Corey said knowingly through a lopsided grin as old as knock-knock/who's-there?

"You too," I scowled and he patted my knee . . .

"Brooke, you know you can't be around Michelle. She'll go psycho."

"I know I know! I just haven't been out in a long time. I thought it'd be fun."

"Oh hunnnaaayyyy . . ."

"Okay," he sighed, lowering his voice. "I won't go."

He sounded like a man and I believed him.

"How about I get them there by ten-thirty and out by midnight? And you don't show up before midnight-fifteen?"

"Perrrr-fect," Brooke said, still sounding like a grown-up.

"Perfect, what."

"I'll meetcha there at twelve — midnight — thirty."

"Not a second sooner. Swear?"

"Swear."

Stefff lived in a security gate/maid service condo in a border-line neighborhood off Sunset.

I rang the bell and she materialized in an urgent trail of dust, like a cartoon. She popped into the car, dressed most particularly in the sunny smile from the perfume ads where she started out.

It begged: I'm there. Pick me.

She reached for the large bottled water rolling around on the passenger side.

"That's Dalee's," I cautioned.

She laughed but didn't drink.

"I can't swill tonight either," I scowled.

"Oh dear. Still?"

"Look." I turned so she could inspect my swollen jowl.

"It's nothing," she lied.

"I took a Percodan."

"So eat first. *Then* drink."

"What a good idea! Ya Ha!"

329WOE swerved into Mortons' parking lot, deposited itself abruptly into the tender care of ThirdWorldValet (T'engYou MissyFi'Dolla') and we linked arms and brazened through backswept doors held conveniently ajar by Doug, who'd been keeping Michelle warm for fifteen minutes.

"Jools, you okay to drive?" Doug asked solicitously some hours later when I detailed plans for the evening.

I shot him a condescending grimace.

I headed for the car.

We arrived early and the crowd was scant.

I kissed Matt, introduced Michelle and Stefff and searched for Lance's party. They were in the back room, still awaiting their main course.

"Happy to see Helena's service hasn't changed," I smiled, easing Michelle toward the empty chair next to Lance. Stefff and I hovered, three-sixtying the room.

"Uh-oh, Jools. Isn't that Brooke over there?" Stefff whispered and I followed her eyes. He was waving his arms for attention from fifty yards away, circling anxiously at the edge of the empty dancefloor.

"I'd better deal with this," I whispered to Lance, hoping Michelle didn't see or hear anything. If I moved quickly, maybe I could abort a . . . a . . . situation.

"Brooke," I spat crossly. "What're you *doing*!"

"I just got bored and antsy, Jools."

"Let's put some distance between you two, at least."

I grabbed his elbow sharply and propelled him toward the entrance away from Michelle.

Stefff whirled behind us, a hyperactive caboose.

We camped out at the bar where Jack Nicholson used to sit, back in '86. Or was it '85?

Rebecca, mother of his children, was a waitress here.

She was so blonde and blue-eyed and thick-lipped and long-limbed and pert-breasted we forgave her incompetence. One night after a particluarly fucked-up order, Paul Mones turned to me and smiled his straight-toothed cynical smile.

"Don't you just know that girl's whole life story?"

"Live fast die young have a beautiful corpse?"

"Whatever," Mones scowled.

"You gonna save her?"

"Lemme getcha a drink," he laughed and we eased up front where Pauly poured vodka for me and water for him.

Pauly, what was it like? HalfBlack/HalfScot?

Verrry rufff, lasss. Verrry rufff.

"Jools, you're my hero," Mones cracked over burgers at the Hamlet. "A martini before and chocolate cake after . . ."

"We'll be here for a while," I informed the bartender and he threw three napkins on the counter.

"Cuba libre," Brooke ordered.

"Sex-at-the-beach," said Stefff.

"Three vodka martinis!" I exclaimed and the bartender grinned and whipped up a double.

We were about to raise our glasses for a toast when Lance touched me lightly on the shoulder.

"I'm gonna get her outta here," he said. "She's freaked . . ."

"That makes me feel so baaad," I said and sucked down a soulful swig. "Better! Ya-ha!"

Lance looked deep in my eyes.

"You just had root canal and Percodan and you shouldn't have too much fun for too much longer," he cautioned.

"I'm deeply committed to despair, deeply rooted to The Jack's spot," I joked and slurped my Stoly.

Lance shrugged, shook his head and split.

I finished my drink and waved for another.

What did Lance know about a girl and his bar?

The doors whooshed open and people whooshed in. In. Out. Good. Bad. More people. Suddenly, three exceptionally large black men dominated the tiny corridor.

Their leader spectacular in black sequins.

Black leather.

"A Booyah boy!" I blurted and he eyeballed me sharply. Those Booyah Boys were a Samoan rap group who met in jail, male bonding with extreme prejudice. I backed up a bit.

"Sorry," I smiled. "I work out to MTV."

He smiled but he didn't mean it.

I blew out the front doors for cement-patio freshair on the Doo/doo-doo-doo/Doo/doo-doo-doo-doo of Prince's *Erotic City* and flew into the middle of something between upand-coming studio executives that passed for communication.

One of those boys. One of those girls.

Draped in rumpled black Über-Armani.

Black baseball caps. Bill forward. Bill back.

Gary and Mary.

How *did* one distinguish Gary from Mary these days?

And who was I to be so snotty? Old-faced/young-bodied.

Armored in drab-elf camouflage?

"Jools," they smiled, because even though they weren't

elevated enough in FernoTainment's infrastructure to have
warranted xeroxed bootleg *YNELITTA*'s they knew an
Africanized bee-buzz when they heard it.

"Discussing the meaning of life?"

"How did you know?" They chorused/overlapped.

You . . . fuck . . . my . . . ?

"Prince always has that effect on me too."

"*I just want your creamy thighs,*" Prince crooned from
inside.

"Life isn't always a movie," I said, "but always soundtracked!"

We cracked up. Seasonally socializing.

"You're both new parents," I said, taking the easy
smalltalk route and they brightened perceptibly.

Phew. Didn't wanna scare 'em.

Not until that Booyah Boy left or I could drive.

Whichever came first.

"Parenthood makes you think about it all," Mary said.

"The last time I really pondered The Meaning of Life was
the day Kate was born."

"And . . . ?" Gary needled.

Life? Nothing. It means nothing.

And yadda yadda yadda yadda.

My life? I'll get back to you. Close of business.

The day after. The day after.

"Here's what I think," I said. "We're born touching the
face of God and then Mommy and Daddy (not to mention
Civilization as We Know It) grind the image away. "Our last
pure information is about the dinosaurs. "Y'ever notice how
all kids get crazy for dinosaurs between the ages of two and
four?"

Gary and Mary nodded.

"Maybe when we're really old, drooling and grinning, we
know It again but we die before we can tell anyone."

Did I just define Alzheimer's?

OldTimer's Corey called it. Which made me lawff.

Which made me scared.

Gary smiled. "I have to tell you this story. I have friends. A couple. He: shrink. She: artist. One little girl/three-or-four/Caitlin. Wife pregnant with second child . . .

"Three weeks before the baby is born Caitlin gets an idée fixe: 'When the baby is born,' she says, 'I have to be alone with it. I have to spend time alone with the baby.'

"She's tenacious but they figure it'll pass.

"The baby is a boy. Nine pounds, seven ounces.

"Jeremy.

"Caitlin doesn't let up: 'I have to be alone with the baby I have to be alone with the baby I have to be alone with the baby.'

"'If we don't trust her it'll have a profound negative effect on her psyche for the rest of her life,' the shrink says. The artist is hesitant, but he reasons with her until she relents.

"The artist stations herself outside Jeremy's room.

"Shrink's in the nearby den, intercom on full volume.

"They let Caitlin in. She locks the door.

"Tiptoes across the room.

"They hear the mobile over his bed swinging.

"Silence.

"Then they hear her little voice over the intercom:

'Jeremy, quick! Tell me about God, I'm forgetting!'"

The Booyah Boy lightning-bolted out the door. And.

Prince, the heatstorm's downstroke, thunder-clapped.

"*Erotic Citaaaay . . .*"

I searched for Brooke but he'd bailed on God, which I took personally, since he'd more critically bailed on me.

"I'm starved. What about you?" I said when I found Stefff still perched like a mannequin on a front barstool.

She didn't disagree.

I duked that boy in the parking lot, eased right onto Beverly Boulevard and accelerated gently.

A boy and her car.

"Ben Frank's?" I suggested and Stefff laughed.

"Where else in this town at this time?"

She reached for the large Evian rolling around on the floor in front of her and unscrewed the cap thirstily.

"That's Dalee's bottle," I reminded.

She hesitated, then laughed again.

"Fuckit," she said and sucked down a sizable gulp, " I like living on the edge . . ."

I recapped Jeremy/God over scrambled eggs, French toast and bacon. Coffee and OJ on the side.

Smoke and Run. Tomorrow for sure.

"So whaddya think?"

"I think he was fucking with you."

"Grrrr . . ."

"Whoa," she laughed and jiggled her hands expressively over her scrambled eggs. I noticed her plastic nails were painted red.

"What's your point?"

"I saw all the letters, one by one, flying out of your mouth and lilting through the air into my eggs . . ."

She smiled brightly and took a bite.

"Then you'll appreciate this. I wanna do a whole book about God is an anagram for Dog. And vice versa . . ." Duh.

"Jools, you're not a dog person."

"I know it'll be a stretch. But I thought my voice would be good in a dog. Maybe a ten-year-old dude who's a movie star and addicted to quaaludes?"

Stefff laughed, soooo hip for the room.

"Retro honey. It should be heroin."

"Eeeuuuoooow, I wanna call him Crackers."

"Maybe retro'll be back."

"It never left."

Stefff thinks for a minute.

"God . . . Dog . . ."

I watched her watching The A-B-C's divebomb into her eggs.

"What?"

"What if it's not God or Dog, but like, Gdo, nah Dgo is better."

"Some Vietnamese person place or thing that we blew up in The Seventies — to save it — and that's coming back to haunt us."

"Oooh that's smart."

"I know. I think I just made it up out of letters from your words."

"That's very smart . . ."

I invited her to Sanctuary for a nightcap.

Heading for WOE, we intersected with Harry Dean Stanton hustling a Drew Barrymore clone in an insistent ohbaby ohbaby monotone. Everybody smiled.

De rigueur for this time of night in the parking lot outside Ben Frank's. Adjacent to the Union '76 station.

It's One-Etc. Do you know where your daughter is?

Stefff's red-plastic nails strobed violently before me.

"It's a tear-down, Jools!" she yelled spewing nasty drug-and-alcohol breath up my nostrils and my instinct was to caution.

It's Home, Sanctuary, even if there is a For Sale sign at the base of the driveway.

She flailed her fleshy arms and inch-long roots for emphasis, pitched forward and her too-brand-new silver-toed Tony Lama impaled the resuscitated right instep on my tasty little black suede Alaia elf-boot.

Ow. I deserve that for inviting this *thing* this Stefff to Sanctuary.

OW. I was juuuust introducing two friends. I didn't know it would get weird. Oh yeah, when's the last time you introduced friends and it didn't get weird?

OOWWW! Why do I bother? Nobody says ThankYou.

"Ooh sorry," Stefff declaimed disingenuously and backed off.

How is she still here?

I eased my eyes ninety nonconfrontational degrees starboard for a status report from 1-2-3-etc.

"It's almost a quarter to three!" I exclaimed and she halted her gyrations momentarily.

"What should we do?"

"You could stay in Kate's room," I allowed reluctantly. "She's sleeping out tonight, back tomorrow. But you gotta be outta here before she gets home."

Waitaquark. No waaaay I'm arising with any Sunday company but *The Times*es. Certainly not this trash.

And what does that make me?

"I'm taking you home!" Like I'm doing *her* a favor.

"You really okay to drive?"

"I was always the one who got us to The Dead, no matter how wasted we were," I bragged. "And everyone was very grateful."

I located my keys, wrapped her up, and moved us swiftly to the door, the car, the driveway and down the hill to drop her off at her security gate/maid service condo.

In a borderline neighborhood near Hollywood. Off Sunset.

I knew I was embarking on the kind of journey I'd warned Kate against. I knew I was entirely too old to be engaged in this sort of enterprise at this sort of hour.

Ignoring myself I cranked the radio.

Opened the windows. Lit a cigarette.

Hit the brights and inhaled deeply.

I knew I was an asshole and should turn back, but I sneaked a peek and she was an even bigger asshole.

To be strictly fair, though, most people were assholes.

Except when they were very young and were only assholes in training.

As the Catholic Church said, Give us a child until he is six and he will be ours for life. No one admitted that was because half the choir boys had been diddled by their priests and would be haunted by guilt until they died, prisoners of the church that betrayed them.

Nobody seemed compelled anymore to protect and nurture the young. Made me wonder why so many adults I knew were searching for their inner child.

It had pretty much come down to Caveat Baby:

Yasserrrr, Caveat Baby

Nasserrrr, I don't mean maybe, Yasser, that's my . . .

I exhaled forcefully and every muscle tweaked the corners of my mouth upward, protruding my cheekbones, tightening my jaw.

Jeez I didn't know you were this high, RightBrain observed appreciatively to Left and I focused fiercely on the newly-painted center lines in the road.

On the lights sparkling in the middle-distant city-that-wasn't.

On depositing this detritus at her security gate/maid service doorstep within fifteen minutes.

And I kept going.

"Thank you so much for understanding." She smiled and opened the valise she called a purse to fish for her keys.

The Janitor. Calm down, Jools, it's almost over.

"Understanding what?" Did I miss something?

"That I'd want to wake up in my own bed."

Not as much as *I* want you to.

She jumped from my car, slammed the door.

"Drive carefully," she called over her shoulder but I barely heard because I'd already executed a screeching u-ey, zoomed toward Sunset and hung a left without really looking.

Away from her.

Toward Sanctuary.

I pulled out to pass a timorous red Porsche doing twenty as I approached Hamburger Hamlet.

We were neck and neck pushing west of Doheny when some surprise Eurotrashies exited Bar One drunkenly.

He veered left and I veered too and accelerated.

Then the night darkened and it was only estates on Sunset, Christmas lights newly-installed. I noticed the one with tiny white bulbs outlining the house and the trees and most particularly the fencing — a fleeting image — and I was one with the car and the road and nothin' was gonna stop me now. Ya ha!

It started in the middle like Quentin Tarantino.

Like an earthquake.

Outta *nowhere* Red strobed brightly in my rearview mirror and for an instant I thought Stefff's plastic nails were in hot pursuit but then I saw Blue, too, a FLASHBACK to an ancient nightmare, and I knew it was BevHillsPD and as my heart collided with my stomach everything I'd ingested for the past 24 hours kicked in and I kissed the curb with my right front tire pulling onto Alpine.

Outta the car and walk the walk and flashlight in eyes and I Swear Officer, A-B-C-D-E-E-E.

Could you wait right here, Ma'am, whilst we summon West LAPD?

Ooh Officer, I don't know. I have to pee-eee-eee . . .

The three of us stood on the street.

In the old days I'd have made conversation to keep panic at bay but I didn't feel the need, what with wrapping myself in a cellophane bubble where I could scream Fuck You Pigs! and they wouldn't hear.

The other jurisdiction arrived, two more boys in pale skin and dark navy and mustaches. Breathtest at the copshop or blood test at the hospital. If deigned drunk I'd spend four hours in jail. No bail. I selected bachelor number #1, the safe breath-test guy.

Who knew what lurked in my limpids?

They ma'amed me profusely, requested I put my hands behind my back and cuffed me too tightly.

Please let these be real cops.

Times being what they are and all.

They had the good taste to lower me into the car without touching my head.

We drove to the West Hollywood jail in silence.

Wonder if any other girls will be there. Not likely . . .

A smiling Negress in khaki ushered me into the breath-test room. She removed the handcuffs.

"How much you weigh?"

She uncoiled her tube and I worried whose lips were

wrapped around the mouthpiece last time. I *was* in the heart of
Boystown, after all, my gums were raw and I felt the beginning of a canker sore on the inside of my right cheek.

I *knew* not through saliva or I'd have tested HIV-positive
a decade ago, if only from all the joints shared with Victor in
the past . . . generation.

But what if they're wrong and my luck's run out tonight?

Ah hell, I like living on the edge.

"One-twenty," I lied.

She pulled one exaggerated Jasper Conran lapel aside and
viewed me critically.

"One-ten, I'd say," she observed, but I was wearing an
especially point-concealing outfit.

She smirked. Gir'frien' *enjoyed* her job.

"One-twenty." Hey babe, *they* scared me but *you* don't.

"Let's call it one-fifteen," she said, adjusting her dials.
"Okay, you get two tries, and we go by the lowest number."
She handed me a tube. It looked like the kind they probably
stuck down Marilyn's throat to revive her the night before the
day she died.

"Okay, deep breath, and blow . . . and . . . it's . . . .08!"

Gameshow Host to Leading Contestant.

Ms. Bust-Me smiled broadly.

A uniformed Negress is a happy Negress!

I'd love busting me too if I were she. Which I was,
metaphorically speaking, but she didn't know that; we'd only
just met, after all, and she saw me as a symbol.

I couldn't hate her for it. But I could try.

I wondered why I took a deep breath, why I followed
instructions so precisely. To show her what a good girl I was?
how smart? I resolved to go shallower on the next go-around.

Take control of the situation.

"Zero Eight!" she exclaimed again.

Congratulations, Jools. You've won a . . . DUI.

Merry Christmas!

And did she see my shoulders sag?

And did she looove saying, This way this way please . . .

• • •

They took the silver Tiffany moneyclip Lee had given me for
making it to forty-five. They ma'amed me into removing the
tasty Brevort Maltese crosses from my ears, a prize for com-
pleting *YNELITTA*. The stainless-steel/eighteen-carat-gold
Cartier watch with which I'd rewarded myself for the loss of
post-coke weight, the only real boo-hoo so far.

Then they asked me to unlace my shoes.

The shoes, officer? Is it the shoes?

It's gotta be the shoes . . .

Oh well, Less is more. Tanya said.

You look beautiful, Tanya. Daddy said.

Daddy's little girl's the worstpieceofshit biggestdisap-
pointment of Daddy's life. But Daddy will never know.

"Do I get to make a phone call?" I queried crossly.

Yes, they said and installed me in a holding cell with a pay
phone.

I dialed Stefff via AT&T credit card.

Her voicemail answered and I left a hostile it's-all-your-
fault message.

Lance. His machine. Left a helpless I'm here/Pick me up
message.

Lee. Again and again and again until he answered.

He instructed me sleepily to call when I was released.

"I'm glad I'll be seeing you at a police station instead of an
emergency room," he said sourly.

Alone in a freezing cold cement locker for four. Double deck-
ers against the walls flanked a stainless steel toilet with a
clean roll of paper at stark attention center stage. I was overjoyed to see the toilet as I had urgent urinary requirements.

I peeked through the glass to see if anyone was looking,
like that'd make a difference, tried the door for the hell of it.
Locked.

I put my ear to the door, which amplified the thump-pound
of my heart. In the distance, those boys expressed themselves.

Koo-koo-ka-choo.

I peed at least a dozen times in the next hour.

Now you evacuate. For all the good it'll do.

I lay down on the lower cot, but the mattress was thin and the bed tilted. My head was at least a foot below my ice-cold sock-clad feet, which made me high again.

I wiggled my toes to see if they still worked, missed my shoes.

Bonded heavily with Mike Milken, deprived in prison of his toupee.

I chuckled at feeling any kinship to Mr. X-Desk Ex-Drexel Burnham, but then the gravity of the situation took the fun out of the concept and I stood up to pace.

Too high. Another piss.

Paced some more and I started. Coming down.

Wondered how much longer incarceration would last. Not good at judging the passage of time without a watch. Not good at circumscribed circumstances. Coming down down down.

Cold breezes wafted through my lonely cement room.

I shivered convulsively and I was.

Stone. Cold. Sober.

I set about the task of making the bed work, pulled the mattress from the upper cot and stacked it on top of the lower bed's mattress. Lay down. My head was still lower than my feet.

Why is this night different from all other nights?

Is Barbara Bush the Antichrist? Is Millie?

Is Michael Jordan the bionic Negro?

Did Bobby try to save Marilyn or did he kill her?

And then Those Kennedys paid ultimate price after ultimate price? Joe, Sr. in his wheelchair, mute, through his grief?

Stone. Cold. Sober.

I closed my eyes and slept until another uniform with pale skin and a mustache awakened me with coffee.

Shortly after, he ushered me from the cell to retrieve my belongings. I laced up my shoes and checked my watch. Eight-fifteen. I asked if I could make a call and he coldly advised there was a bank of payphones right outside.

Harumph. I marched purposefully through the door.

Free at last free at last.

Thank God Almighty I'm free at last.

"You need to get laid," Lee said dryly.

"Oh yeah, who'd you have in mind?"

"I was always in favor of you and Corey, two little elves bouncing around together on a waterbed . . ."

He laughed wickedly but his baby blues searched my face.

For what? Meaning?

I was distressed to see him on foot.

"Where's your truck?"

"In the shop with the Mexicans."

Lee possessed a cherry '54 Ford truck.

The Mexicans loooved feexing eet for 'eem.

"Uuuugggghhhh . . ."

"Oh please, we'll go across the street and call a cab."

"My car's on Alpine."

"Poor baby. Just moments from home. This'll give me an opportunity to point out these posters I've been telling you about."

"That'll cheer me up."

I lit a cigarette and inhaled deeply. Mmmmmmm-Goooood.

As Frankenstein's monster liked to say.

We walked to Rage and Lee called a cab, gesturing for me to check the turquoise pink and white poster on the kiosk on the corner. Pictured: David Geffen and Barry Diller, with girls' names. Not pictured, Sandy Gallin.

The copy, which I'd have tightened a bit, is a diatribe.

The gist: your generous contributions to AIDS research means nothing if you don't come out.

Thank-you-and-fuck-you-and-have-a-nice-day.

Kindest-personal-regards. Queer Nation.

We're here. We're queer. And so are some of you.

"It's not very nice. But I see their point . . ."

"Well they're making the same point as you. Sorta."

Beverly Hills Cab arrived and we swept smoothly through the flats toward Alpine. Toward Sanctuary.

"Where's my car???!!!" I exploded as we approached the corner that was my moment of truth. Or was it gist?

"Turn around," Lee instructed the cabdriver. "We're going to Beverly Hills police headquarters. They towed your car. I know how to do this . . ."

Hours later, I dropped Lee off at his house. We'd shuttled pretty much all over town and he'd had to lend me half the seventy bucks required to spring 329WOE.

"I'm driving under the affluence, koo-koo-ka-choo," I smiled wearily.

Morning sun burned through marine layer and last night's spandex reacted spontaneously with sweaty skin.

I pulled at my threads anxiously.

"Good thing you're not famous yet," Lee smirked as he stepped from the car.

I played my phone machine. Something Sunday-morning normal to do. Calls from last night, the Booyah boy, Lance.

David Geffen at the beach. 9:30 A.M.

Why now, Dgo? Why today?

Stalling, I called Lance.

"Boy am I glad to hear your voice. Where are you?!"

"Home. Finally."

"Y'know, I showed up at nine, per your instructions. Freaked after half-an-hour when you didn't come out. Thought maybe they'd started to grind you through the system, shipped you off downtown by accident. So I went inside and they said they'd released you an hour ago . . ."

"Dude, I'm sorry. When I couldn't reach you I called Lee. They let me out early. I think I annoyed them."

Lance giggled.

"'I'm cold, could I have another blanket? another blanket? another blanket?'"

Lance howled.

"The perfect ending to a perfectly weird night."

"How'd it work out with you and Michelle?"

"Ahhh I drove her to her car at Mortons'. We sat in the parking lot for hours and talked."

"You talked to Michelle for hours? Well, that's a propitious start. At least something turned out well."

"Nah, Jools, there's nothing there. Y'know, she was so upset about Brooke; and the weirdest thing was she decided you'd planned it to happen that way."

"Michelle's been hurt by love."

"Yeah, Jools. Me too."

The Geff answered first ring, right away, just like that and I fantasized he knew it was me.

"Julia, I've been hearing some distressing reports from people who've read your manuscript that you're not very nice about me."

"What?! Who?!"

"I'm not saying who . . ." I *knew* this would happen the second first serial pieces hit the stands. Not to mention the bound galleys sent to interested parties whose signatures were needed on waivers.

I was still line-by-line editing with Julie. Three hours a day by phone. Joni and Julie were indulging me because I'd indulged them all along and Joni had admitted that *YNELITTA* was improving by that last little three to thirteen percent that made a difference.

Something to throw myself into, since I probably wouldn't be going out for a while.

"You occupy under twenty pages in a six hundred page book."

"What I don't understand is why you would have anything insulting to say about me."

"Maybe not entirely flattering," like you're used to, "but not insulting —"

"But how could you have anything negative to say about me at all! I only ever liked you!"

I had to smile.

In Global Geff's world He liking You defined the relationship.

Hadn't David Geffen's mother taught her son that just because one liked somebody didn't mean that body had to like one back?!

"Lemme look at it again. If you have friends who say it's insulting, I have to take the note seriously."

Why did I do this? I'd asked Air after returning from an Il Giardino lunch with him in such a fury I pummeled The Creature for an hour getting it down. Word for word. Talk about insulting.

You were compelled, she'd said.

"Then I shouldn't read it?"

You haven't read it?

Get real.

"Lemme look it over. I guarantee you'll see it at least a month before it's shipped."

He seemed relieved. We traded good-byes and hung up.

I immediately called Joni in the country to apprise her of The Deal in Search of A Story with The Geff.

"Shit," Joni said.

"We have to show it to him sometime. Later is better than sooner, don'tcha think? Especially since I won't change a thing."

Joni laughed and hung up.

I considered removing the Yohji/Katharine/Conran ensemble. Not yet. I didn't deserve relief. Not yet.

At this moment, the only person I hated more than any-or-all of my more-or-less selves was David Geffen. Daddy's little girls and Mommy's little boys rarely got along.

Maybe that's why I'd had such a tough time. Oh well.

Pretty soon I wouldn't be worrying about *that* anymore.

I heard the key turning in the front door. Kate.

So soon, Dgo? You are sooo strict!

I shuffled to the front door to spew unwelcome gist.

"Moooom, with all the lecturing you give me. You could've been killed!" Kate sounded frustrated but her eyes were wide with fright.

"I could've killed someone else."

I didn't think it necessary to add that the former alternative seemed infinitely the lesser of two evils.

She might've thought I was rehearsing a one-liner.

Jerry Chaleff's offices were adjacent to the courtyard of a hip little enclave on Ocean Avenue in Santa Monica. Down the block from Chez Jay's, where wannabe*mores* had been reconnoitering with their — ahem — managers for a drink and exchange of goods-and-services for easily two decades. Sawdust and checkered tablecloths and a line, but a decent steak and a tall cool one when the wait was over.

I hadn't been to Chez Jay's in years. Last time was the Early Eighties. Before the Second Coming of Ronald Reagan. With Andrea Eastman and Paul Lazarus, who were married at the time. And Jan-Michael Vincent, who was more attached to his crack pipe than me. Can't say I blamed him. I was in my I've-given-up-blow-and-I'm-going-to-be-very-fat-for-a-while era and looked about as attractive as he behaved.

He was trying to be clean, i.e. pretending to be clean, and Andrea and Paul, who were enthralled by his performance, thought some interaction with me would inspire him.

He was at that stage of trying to give up smoke-coke when he needed to talk about it constantly. Liked to make the sucking sound of The Pipe, which I'll admit, gave *me* a quiver. Every once in a while, craving a bong-ful, he'd grab me lasciviously and I shuddered to think what my extra pounds felt like.

His desperate conversation finally degenerated into a graphic description of his latest girlfriend/cokewhore's most memorable puff: inhaled, he claimed, through her cunt.

Vagina, I corrected, and thought, Is that one of the ten silliest words or what?

Cunt, he repeated, and I let it pass. Hell, I'd used the word myself, but mostly to other women. Cunt was like kike and nigger and gook and spic. Those Words. You used them casually among Your Own Kind to describe yourselves.

But just let The Other Side invoke them: the pricky Gentile Caucasian Round-Eyed *Greeengo* and you were infuriated . . .

I shook remembrance of insults past and bridled into the moment. Parallel-parked in the last metered spot adjacent to the Pacific Ocean and ran across traffic, backlit by a bubbling postapocalyptic neo-orange sunset bouncing off a brackish toxic sea.

Armored in two-seasons-past black Alaia.

A high-key shot from a *Halloween* They'd never release.

You can take that girl out of film but you can't take film from that girl. Or is it cunt?

Jerry Chaleff's ceilings were low and the help reassuringly multicultural. Overqualified black and hispanic women buzzed about efficiently.

Oh oh oh those girls!

The receptionist smiled, put me on hold with an uplifted index finger and forwarded Incoming to an unseen consiglieri situated in a cool carpeted cave down the hall. I focused on the long chipped iridescent nail under lavender-tinted-but-still-unforgiving fluorescent light.

Ooooh pretty. Pass the Ecstasy and crank up Depeche Mode.

Pet Shop Boys. Dee'lite. Iiiii'm there. Pick me.

But someone else'll have to drive.

In her left front tooth a gold inlay, AMOR, it said.

I love Elll Ayyyyeee.

"L.A. is where you get old and die before you even notice Winter came," Sue Mengers snarled at our last lunch at Le Dome. Before she left show business the second time. Or was it the third? Before Michel, one of Le Dome's glamorous owners, died of AIDS.

Or was it after?

"You should go to New York for a while. Return in your sixties, when it's time to be here," Sue advised.

"But what about the weather? I hate cold. Although at the

rate we're burning carbon fuels Nome-Alaska will be L.A. by the turn of the century. I don't think I'll last 'til then anyway. You either."

"We're too mean to die young."

"Think Bobby Darin . . ."

Jerry Chaleff waved his hand and I lowered myself into a chair, the disciplinary problem in second grade, reduced to sitting obediently in a front row seat by nonverbal commands from the kind-but-strict teacher. Jerry Chaleff leaned back against the desk behind him, soooo casual.

"Gotta hangover?" he twinkled.

"Do I still have prison pallor? I applied blusher . . ."

He twinkled some more.

"Not as bad as some I've seen . . ."

"Those Menendez boys, for example?"

They were a big credit and his twinkle ascended to a beam but he didn't say a word.

"Breath or blood test?" he began.

"Breath."

"Goood. What was the count?"

"Point zero-eight. Both times."

"Great! That's just great!"

"Why?"

"Zero-eight is the minimum! With a margin of error . . . of .065 on a breath test —"

"I could've been drunker?"

"A hair. Or a hair less . . .

"They never should've booked you with that reading."

"I waaas doing sixty on Sunset at three ay-em."

Jerry Chaleff smiled thinly.

"With the new zero-eight law, at your weight — if the bartender likes you — one drink qualifies as too drunk to drive for at least an hour."

"Of course the bartender likes me."

"Of course. Okay, here's the deal. I'll set up a hearing for you, but most likely I'll have to plead it out, get the charge reduced to reckless driving. No matter how convincing you are, they almost always suspend your license four months."

He pressed a buzzer and summoned his partner, Paul Catallano.

"Paul's the DUI guy. He'll hold your hand at the DMV."

Paul and I shook hands and he left.

"So when's the book due out?" Jerry asked.

"Couple of months."

"Christine says it's gonna be huge," Jerry twinkled.

"It better be, or I'll never be able to pay your bill."

"I'll be in touch," Jerry said. "Don't worry, we'll take care of this."

I thanked him profusely.

"Do some work on the next book," Jerry smiled.

Go fuck yourself, Jools.

"And remember, be nice to the lawyers."

Okay I will.

Lee and Catallano accompanied me to a 3 P.M. appointment at the Baldwin Hills DMV. We were the only white faces floating on a sea of black and yellow and brown.

In a tiny enclosed cubicle with peeling tan walls, an empathetic African-Americaness with long iridescent red nails conducted my hearing. It lasted less than half an hour and I consumed two pieces of Nicorette gum.

Chomp chomp. Next line, please.

"Look, it's her job to suspend your license," Catallano said when we were dismissed. "But you were goooood . . ."

"My performances are for the smallest of rooms . . ."

The day after, a heavily-armed highly-disgruntled ex-employee entered the Baldwin Hills DMV at 3:05 P.M. and shot the place up pretty thoroughly. By the time LAPD took him out, he'd wounded three. Two critically, one mortally.

"Timing's everything, Lee," I joked nervously in an abbreviated post-local-news call.

"Just another two-step from the dance of life in the big city," he said . . .

• • •

"He doesn't understand the rhythm of words, the principle of a joke, or the waltz of people!"

E. Graydon Carter's aleady insisted I excise 221 lines of a piece I wouldn't have agreed to if I didn't suffer financial imperative. A review of *Prozac Nation: Young and Depressed in America.* I know it's anticipated I'll excoriate the author, but Elizabeth Wurtzel's a mere twenty-six and I'm not being paid enough to eviscerate a kid.

"By the by, where's my paltry check!" I bark at Aimee Bell, who coproduces the Vanities section of post-Tina FairMarketValue and has only been supportive.

"Being rushed through accounting," Aimee sighs tiredly.

"Aimee, there's War which is simple but hard. And there's Comedy which is hard but simple. Set-up, call-back, pay-off. 1-2-3. Can't he add? I thought those boys prided themselves on their bottomlineness. Does arbitrary editing elevate his self-esteem? Or is this War? "Did E-E-E run out of Things-To-Do-Unto-Others Today?"

Zoe tilts the stool she's pulled from the kitchen to visit in The Creature's room and smiles a secret smile.

"I'm on my way to Graydon about your line now," Aimee says pointedly. "I'll callya back." She hangs up.

"I'm breathless with anticipation."

Zoe laughs.

"What're you so uptight about? This is fine."

Zoe represents what she calls my TrailerPark read. I never send pages unless and until she's enthusiastically approved. She hands me the galleys.

"Zoe, fine isn't fine."

"It'll fill this annoying between-money week."

Those Girls and Boys have been spelling each other, babysitting until the big check lands in my account.

Two weeks ago, Memorial Day weekend, Lynn Nesbit sprinted across The ABA convention floor to corner Diane

Reverand who further sprinted to pry a delivery-of-first-draft payment from Alberto Vitale.

I was so overjoyed that when Frankie suggested we attend a hot publishing party hosted by Morgan Entrekin at the Chateau Marmont, I agreed. We hadn't been there ten minutes when I ran into Sydney Pollack chatting up a tall, toned brunette with a baby strapped to her chest she claimed was sired by Sylvester Stallone.

"You know Janice Dickinson?" Sydney said, and I extended my hand to shake.

"Oh you're my idol!" she exclaimed and several guests gravitated curiously in our direction. "I took your picture at Club Louie. Steve Antin's Birthday Party, I think."

"Did I behave?" I asked brown eyes behind blue glasses.

"You tried but after a couple of shots you growled, 'Got it?' and I gave up."

She'd done me well and our little group laughed easily.

"Telling them about your liposuction?!" Frankie sang across the pool. To put me at ease, I suppose.

The money still hasn't arrived and I'm starting to hyperventilate instead of breathe.

Every night my final incantation is WireTransfer-WireTransfer. The prayer, the mantra of The Financial-FuckUp. HiI'mJulia. Hiiii-Julia . . .

The slaughter of Nicole Simpson and Ron Goldman has provided serious distraction, though hardly relief.

"What kind of drugs, y'think?" Zoe wonders.

"Definitely not Prozac!"

"Or too much Prozac!"

"Freebase first occurred to me. Or that lovely cocaine/alcohol combination that makes men psychotic."

"And women compliant. Probably some kind of speed," Zoe says and I listen. She's two decades younger and sooo much wiser. "Crystal Meththththth," she adds.

Give me Librium or give me Meth! said The Sotherner.

What goes around comes around, said The Don.

"I thought heroin was chic these days," say I.

"Oh they were chic? Mezzaluna? I don't think so."

"Beautiful people doing beautiful things."

"It disturbed me, how they treated Kato."

"Ahhh Kato . . ."

Debin hung out with Kato at Bar One the night before the night before what my firstandlastexhusband once dubbed The UI. The Ugly Incident. Inspired by the extremely-prejudiced assassination of Medgar Evers if memory serves.

Debin reported in the day after the day after.

"What was he like?"

"Entertaining," Debin said.

"They always are," I observed wryly. "Expensive, though. Like drugs."

"Funny how they come and go together."

"So whaddya presume he fetched for The Master?"

"Not drugs. Girls."

"Funny how they come and go together."

We lawff.

"So what was O.J. doing?"

"I think freebase, Debs."

"Why?"

"The only reason Ron Siegel knew enough about it to cure me in 1979 was that he'd been expert-witnessing for major dealers strung out on their product. He told me they didn't just kill the girlfriends, they *hacked* them into teeny leettle pieces . . ."

"Were *you* ever violent?"

"I was verbally abusive."

"How's that different?"

"Now I'm pencil-ly abusive. And I did throw my cat, Ray, against the wall once."

"Didja kill him?"

"No but I'm sure I used up several of his lives."

"I hear forty-one knife wounds."

"Exactly. I'm glad I can't afford a Kato anymore."

"Look at you looking at the bright side of destitution."

"That's me. Going UP! Toward zero . . ."

Zoe snorts disdainfully.

"Not Kato The Guest, Jools. Kato The Dog! Tied him to the fence all day. Poor thing."

"Didn't do such a good job protecting The Mistress, did he?"

The Dog howling through the neighborhood reminded me of those boys' scoffing at my newly-installed burglar alarm system.

1976. Maybe '84.

So you push the panic button and The Patrol arrives in time to find your still-warm but dead body? one sniffed.

Jools, you need a twelve-gauge shotgun, another offered.

"Gimme some ol'time Timothy Leary acid," I volunteer. "Put me in a room with the Akita for eighteen hours. *I'll* tell ya what happened!"

Like we don't know.

The phone rings. Aimee Bell with my line restored.

"Will you sign off now?"

"When I see coin and final proofs."

"I'll FedEx the check tonight and fax the proofs tomorrow."

She hangs up emphatically, no doubt wishing for this gig to end as much as I do. Call waiting. God.

Several years ago Gary Devore met OJ Simpson on a project whilst he was in Oakland, near his *Roots*.

Running through a Hertz commercial.

OJ Cut! and requested an immediate reshoot.

"Ah been hangin' with ma homies three days an' I soun' too black," he explained to the frustrated director.

"And the next take?"

"Perfect. Night and Day . . ."

Zoe signals she's repairing to the kitchen for sandwich preparation whilst I chat with God.

"Jack Gilardi's devastated," God says, referring to The PrimeSuspect's black-haired/cap-toothed/buff-nailed/heavily cologned ICM agent.

"Long-term personal relationship. He's been carrying those Louis Vuitton bags for twenty years."

"That Kardashian boy's carrying The Vuitton."

"Kardashian's Gilardian?"

Gary chuckles reluctantly and we disconnect.

Kardashian/Gilardian/Kevorkian/BranchDavidian.

David Koresh was thirty-three when he was toasted.

Same as Alexander the Great. Same as Jesus Christ.

It's all the Same Fucking Day, said The Janis.

Who also died young.

"Jools, c'mere!" Zoe calls out sharply. I've been in revery at least thirty-three seconds and I'm rarely quiet. Everyone, even softspoken Kate, talks over me. Zoe and I often develop laryngitis during lengthy editorial discussions as she's hard-of-hearing and I'm a passionate articulator.

Sometimes I wish I still felt as certain as I sounded. Duh.

I head for the kitchen.

"Are you obsessing on your wiretransfer again?"

"Nahhh. The dead people . . ." I'd read a wiseguy mathematician recently calculated the number of expired homo sapiens since The Dawn of Man during some computer downtime.

120,000,000,000 souls. Give or take a billion.

A billion here a billion there, Everett Dirksen said.

Pretty soon it adds up to . . .

A lot of fucking fertilizer. Yo chip this!

"Ron and Nicole?" Sure. Why not?

"Twenty-five and thirty-five. Their ages add up to what people would say was appropriate boyfriend material for me."

"Oh this is about you?" Zoe laughs.

"And you. And Kate. And all those girls! If you're pretty or smart or special in any way men love you/fear you even more than they already do! Which is alot. And it doesn't take much to intimidate them. Look at the hatred Hillary inspires with piano legs and an overbite!"

Zoe nibbles her sandwich anxiously, sips her beer and frowns.

"They keep running the same slo-mo tape, Jools. Looks like a sporting event or a concert. He's in a dark cashmere blazer. She's in an umber knitted vest, cross bouncing between full breasts. The perfect photogenic couple. Clean. Sleek. Toned. She turns to him and smiles and whispers something private . . .

"And I keep fixating on those implants!"

"Probably his idea. Looks like he knows his way around a tasty rhinoplasty."

A year later, as The Trial drags past its halfway point and The Dow powers past 4500, it'll occur to me when I leaf through a glossy rag that Pamela Anderson *got* InfernoTainment stardom for having her boobs *done*, Demi Moore *doing* hers *got* $12,000,000 for a single picture and Melanie Griffith *got to do* Antonio Banderas.

Nicole, the second chick, just *got done*.

"C'mon, Jools. He coulda been set up. . . ."

Debin. He's working a mystery centering on a frame, churning out the hundred pages necessary for an advance. Exiled himself to utter Oregon seclusion at The Other Gary's place, the only venue where he can make a substantial dent.

I'm prepared to forgive him.

If both checks hadn't landed and the Prozac piece closed this morning I wouldn't be so charitably inclined.

"I think you're imposing perspective from your novel."

"Zero teevee'll do that."

"See you're all imagination! I on the other hand will spend the entire day in the tube's thrall. I plan to work out to the arraignment."

"What time is that?!"

"Eleven. Want me to report in?"

"If you feel like it," Debin says in his cynical whisper, feigning disinterest.

"Why're they doing it downtown anyway?"

"What's it matter?"

"A jury pool's assembled from residents within a twenty-mile radius of the court where the indictment's filed. It's The Law. I think I might've voted for it."

"So?"

"Sooo he scores a downtown jury. The homies he ran away from. Don'tcha think he'd be more apt to draw his peers in Santa Monica Superior Court?"

"You mean rich white sorta-famous people?"

"I think Gil Garcetti's IQ's in direct proportion to the size of his button nose."

"Later . . ."

"A.W.O.L. Press conference. Those InfernoMongers expelled an audible gasp when Gascon said he was at large, actively being sought by LAPD."

Debin expels an audible gasp and whispers the news to The Other Gary whom I've come to regard as Tog.

"I gotta call Frankie. I'll broadcast breaking developments."

"Please," Debin whispers. Call waiting.

God.

"He's on his way to Mexico . . ."

"Too late. Had to do that the night of the switch at Rockingham."

"After the funeral . . ."

"Isn't that how you'd action-rewrite?"

"Mmmmmm . . ."

I reach Frankie in her car.

"Where are you?"

"Cruising The Neighborhood. Sticking my nose in the air at all the lookie-loos, pretending I live here . . ."

"Isn't he down the street from Stanley Sheinbaum?"

A decade ago I'd arrived at Stanley Sheinbaum's Rockingham estate with Baskin/Streisand for a Democratic fundraiser but we never made it in.

Curbside The Barbra, nervous, requested I crack the limo's window a scooch to scope the scene.

A horde of paparazzi oozed forth in an assault of flicks and flashes. One of them stuck his camera through the partially opened window, shoved it five inches from our faces and fired off several rounds.

Flick flick flick. Flash flash flash.

"Can we get outta here?" The Barbra implored.

We damn near tore the photographer's arm off as we sped from the scene of his crime . . .

"Orenthal-J didn't show up, Frankie."

"Waitasecond, I gotta lower the volume."

"Amadeus-Amadeus?"

"I've progressed to symphonies."

Ever since we read he elevated IQ, Frankie and I do daily doses of Mozart. Sometimes I wonder why we might want to feel even *more* distant from our fellow Ammur'cans, as Lyndon Johnson used to call Us — excuse me — Them.

"Turn on the radio! OJ's a no-show."

"I'm gonna have to swing by if this gets any more exciting . . ."

"Press conference at Robert Shapiro's office in five seconds. I'm gonna crank the volume so you can hear, okay?"

"Okay," Debin and Tog chorus/overlap.

We breathe into our receivers heavily.

"Robert Shapiro looks like an owl."

"Joools . . . shhh . . ."

"Think they told him to make a run for it?" Debin inquires, ever in touch with the sleazy path, compliments of a lifelong buddyship with Peter Locke.

Of Kushner-Locke, purveyor of InfernoShlock.

Verrry prosperous.

Peter counted himself among OJ's closest friends.

The Lockes hosted the New Year's Eve Party The Simpsons attended the night before the day before Nicole fled The Big House screaming, He's gonna *kill* me! He's *gonna* . . .

Peter coined the caveat: Beautiful people doing beautiful things. Peter would know.

"HE was an abused husband?!@#"

"Joools, shhh . . ."

"Y'think 'Craig' is 'Baumgarten'?"

"Joools, *shhh* . . . !"

And yadda yadda yadda. YaddaYadda. Yadda.

"Sounds like an apologaeia to me," I say.

"Sounds like bullshit to me," says Tog.

"He's gonna kill himself," Debin declares.

"Never," Tog pronounces definitely.

"Sounds like a suicide note to meeee," Debin wheedles.

"He's not gonna do himself," Tog intones tiredly. "Too big an ego. I'll betcha ten bucks."

Tog's ten bucks equals the $150,000 a gold-encrusted high-roller booked into a showy highfloored Vegas suite might crap out on a Friday night.

Tog must know what the hell he's talking about.

"I wouldn't wanna dwell too long on what the last three minutes of *those* two people's lives were like," Tog says dryly and we hang up.

Three minutes. Two people. 32. OJ's number.

Equals 5. Like 7. A number of ShowBidness.

S-P-O-O-K-Y/S-I-L-L-Y . . .

Ramona said.

"Dad, hard to speak or hard to breathe?"

"Haa'd t' pppreathe . . ." Chechechechchch . . .

He passes me off to June.

"Think he's gonna kill himself?" I ask her.

"He's gonna show up in some Third World country spouting off how a black man can't get justice in The United States . . ."

Frankie and I are on second martinis and every answer-phone message is Oy gevalt meshuggener shvartzer. I'm conflicted about reinstating a phrase Frankie and I fled years ago. I did it.

I didn't *choose* to be compelled.

Hour three of The Bronco Infomercial.

"They're exiting the freeway ten minutes from here," I note flatly. "We could go . . ."

"We'll see it better on TV. Although this is awfully small, Jools."

The bigscreen that was first but not state of the art has finally died. I've set a smallerscreen on its cabinetry. The television within the television. Initially amusing. Currently depressing.

Yo tengo yo tengo . . .

"But we always bear witness to this shit together."

The Oscars. Elections. Presidential Conventions.

Life is moments / This is one, I told Frankie when we sobbed over Elizabeth Glazer and she didn't disagree.

"The abuse cycle is a nightmare, Jools," Frankie says.

"He got a slap on the wrist because he was The Juice with the juice."

Pace pace! Puff puff! Ooh. Ooh . . .

"You don't need to be a star to warrant a mere slap on the wrist."

We're alone but Frankie lowers her voice to an urgent murmur, as if she's imparting the most secret of secrets at a party where the walls have ears and the guests are spies.

"The beatings go on for years. Years! If She gets a restraining order He's more enraged. The beatings get worse. If She finally screws up her courage and self-esteem which are low low low and *leaves* him He stalks Her.

"And the cops don't wanna be involved . . ."

"'Cause they get *killed* in domestic disputes!"

"And the courts don't take it seriously."

"'Cause they're too busy and too Republican."

Fifty-four percent of sitting federal judges are Reagan/Bush appointments! I keep reminding friends who still believe there's a forum for redress. For justice.

"And if he can, he *murders* her. Battered women are at highest risk the first two years after splitting."

"She divorced him in '92 . . ."

A message from one of those boys:

He's on the 50, the 40, the 30.

He's on the twenty the ten the I-95, the 405.

He's in the 619, the 714, the 818, the 213, the 310 . . .

"I'm not continuing this conversation. You're in denial . . ."

Like Orenthal James Simpson. Jock meet Jock.

"I know I know," Claire whines. "But he was such the greatest football player!"

"Spoken like a true sportsfreak!"

"I can't bear to think he done it."

"I can't bear to think it was DONE."

"Pretty ferocious attack."

"You don't think he might've transported athletic ferocity from the field to real life? Spelled r-e-e-l."

"Duh, Jools. It just bothers me."

"The whole thing bothers me! Mostly Ron Goldman."

"Straight club kid, I hear."

"That could've been *Kate* returning the glasses like a good Scout!"

"Nah . . . the glasses would *always* be returned by one of those boys." Call waiting. Speak of the —

"Mommy?" Kate squeaks. Uh-oh.

"What's wrong?!"

"My head kills and everyone's in Palm Springs . . ."

"Lemme get off the other line." Ohhh Fuuuck!

POWER OFF

"Claire? Kate from the other house with a migraine."

"She alone?"

"Duh."

"Call me back if there's anything I can do."

"You wanna drive her to celebrity parking at Cedars?"

Claire barks harsh laughter. I switch back.

"Kate?" She's whimpering.

"Bad?"

"Verrry," she says, her tiny voice cracking into sobs.

Kate frequently develops headaches, takes them in stride. I have a hennache, she'd announce throughout her terrible twos. And down an Advil dry. Maybe two. In the course of her young life she's also experienced three maybe five heavy migraines which far exceeded her tender coping capacities.

They always commence over weekends.

The last one played on and on and on eight terrifying days and delayed her return to the University of Michigan for the start of Junior year. A major bummer for Kate. After relentless hounding, I'd scored two MTV Awards tickets for her from one of those boys. When I thanked him, he lawffed: It was my pressure, dahling.

Kate had planned to beat the shit out of Sharon Stone, an event presenter, on my behalf.

The Stone, a stranger, had dismissed me as "a Hollywood idiot" in a *Movieline* interview which irked me enough to flirt with the concept of composing some pointed Go-fuck-your-self/0kay-I-will for their letters column.

Dear Sharon: If I'm a Hollywood idiot, then you're a Hollywood c—t and it rhymes with runt and I'm not talkin' about pool.

I got over it.

We sent Kate's friend Mark instead, who cellphoned from the floor excitedly: I'm sitting here between Digable Planets and Arrested Development . . .

I call the doctor I found after Sellers retired last year. A woman both Kate and I like. Out of town. I explain to the exchange I'm combat-ready in defense of my daughter. The operator suffers migraines, promises that boy who's covering — Dr. Dude—will phone within fifteen minutes.

I encapsulate Kate's situation and Dr. Dude says he'll pre-scribe state-of-the-art migraine-medication but he'd also like to speak to her directly. I explain her joint-custodial living arrangements and he takes her number. We chat briefly about the events of last night, bonding I hope.

"I was on the Freeway for three hours," Dr. Dude com-plains.

"He did it. He's reeeaaalll sorry," I kid.

"I hear she pulled his chain," Dr. Dude says quickly.

She. Pulled. His. Chain?!@#

I'd looove to confront him.

She. Pulled. His. Chain!? Define your terms, Dr. Dude.

Mano y mano as it were.

But.

I'm motivated to promote his personal involvement with Kate's hennache. Some hours hence, I'll need him to arrive at

the hospital expeditiously when his prescriptions don't work
and she's blind in one eye, vomiting projectilely.

I deep-breathe and remain silent. Sooo silent.

Woos out in the service of . . . Service!

I don't wanna go there, as Those Boys and Girls say.

I don't wanna go to The Emergency Room either. But.

True to form, we're doing fifty on Sunset in 329WOE.

Heading for Century City Hospital which Dr. Dude says
will be emptier than Cedars. Not to mention closer to him.

Kate, moaning, cradles her head precariously between
shaky knees. I brake gently at each light but half a block
from our destination, on yellow, her skull grazes the dash-
board.

"Owwwwww . . ." she wails.

"Kate! Honey! I'm sooo sorry."

"Mom, I know you used to get these. Whenever did they
go away?"

Translation: I don't *choose* to ask!

"You don't wanna know."

Translation: I don't choose to . . .

"Tell me!"

Translation: . . . answer!

"After Daddy and I split up."

Translation: I don't choose The Gist.

I'm compelled. I'm Mommy. It's my job.

"Owwwwww . . ."

Translation: OWWWWWW . . .

A fax from one of those girls: A real estate listing.
Nicole's BundyCondo circled. Scribbled across:
Heard you were looking for a more affordable place.
This oughtta be within your price range . . .

"So it was on the news he's feeling claustrophobic in his
tiny little cell. How'm I supposed to react to that information?
Am I supposed to feel bad for him?"

"Mara, that's rather dyspeptic for you . . ."

"This just gets me mad, Jools. Think Ron and Nicole might be feeling a bit cramped in their new quarters?"

"You've been mad since The Earthquake."

"I was A Homeless Person. I had to live with The Daughter for a month, you try that sometime!"

"I remember . . ." Every time Mara and I were on the phone for more than ten minutes, her daughter would snap, Whozzat? Who you on the phone with?! Oh you get to be the kid now!? I'd bark from my end and Mara would sniffle.

"Later," she says.

Seven o'clock straight up, so. I flip the channels to CNN.

To be ambushed by Nicole's unedited 1993 911.

All thirteen-plus minutes.

I repair hastily to the kitchen, pour a drink and find myself sobbing into the kitchen sink.

PMS? MenoPMS?

Kate's migraine's finally subsided and she's chirping happily on the phone from her side of the house, organizing evening plans. I don't wanna stress her into relapse.

Additionally, I'm meeting Peg Garrity with her new client, Sondra Locke — Clint Eastwood's discarded paramour — for dinner at Orso's in an hour.

I don't need to look any more tormented.

I pull it together quickly. Retrieve a Prep-H suppository from the refrigerator, rub it hastily around my eyes, blow my nose loudly and sip vodka through a straw.

It tastes bitter, so I decide to add tomato juice and Rose's lime.

Fumbling through a utensil drawer for an opener I stumble on a large butcher's knife.

I grasp it firmly and stand at the sink.

Stab at the air.

One two three etc.

Accompanied by Bernie Hermann's infamous chords.

Rrreeent!Rrreeent!Rrreeent!Rrreeent!

Twenty. Two three etc.

Rrruuuunt!Rrruuunt!Rrruuunt!Rrruuunt!

Thirty. Three etc.

Doonnn doooonnn DOOOONNNNN . . .

"Mom, what the hell are you doing?!"

"You have to stay *psycho* a really long time to inflict so many knife-wounds."

"That shower scene runs only forty-five seconds . . ."

Four and five is nine. The number of completion.

I calculate the date of The UI 6/12/1994.

6+12=18/1+9+9+4=23. 1+8=9/2+3=5.

9+5=14. 1+4=5.

ShowBidness. Again.

Is O O O J's number up?

Not likely.

"Put the security company out of business, got the parents a low seven figure settlement," Peg smiles thinly. "They'd rather have their daughter alive . . ."

"Given that they don't . . . Congratulations," I say and we clink glasses grimly.

Sondra Locke, whose performance in *The Heart Is a Lonely Hunter* is one of the twenty best in the past twenty years, has no idea what we're talking about but she clinks too. That girl Sondra seems a fragile go-with-the-flow flower who's been struggling for sun all her existence.

Peg's representing her in a suit against Clint Eastwood/Warner Bros. who are reneging on a three-picture deal conceived and executed when Sondra and The Clint were parting company.

I'd heard he packed her clothes, changed the locks and sent her belongings to storage whilst she was directing *Impulse*. There's a disquieting whiff of victim paranoia-aura that hangs upon her like day-old perfume but the gesture seems unnecessarily nasty given their eleven-year cohabitation and his clear-cut man-with-the-power position.

Hollywood Adage:

This place makes whores out of the women and sissies out of the men.

Is that why Those Big Boys are so mean? So cheap?

Those Little Women so meek? So Bopeep?

Is that why L'Affaire Simpson cuts so deep?

Are they all afraid: That could be me?

"Hate myself for bringing it up, or relating to OJ in any way, but I wasn't thrilled with the cops climbing over the wall or their tardiness in getting a search warrant. Were you, Peg?"

I don't need to mention that my heart flutters every time I see a shot of El Juice handcuffed. Me projecting.

But you didn't kill anybody! Frankie pointed out when I brought it up. I'm sooo lesser of two evils, I riposted . . .

"Illegal search and seizure," Peg growls.

"I felt: Whoa, if they'll do it to OJ they'll do it to me. For sure."

"We've been a police state for some time," Peg glares.

"Republicans," I kid.

"Republicans . . ."

A fax from one of those boys:

Absolutely 100 Percent not guilty. A secret confession?

Don't great athletes give 110 percent?

"Fanny, I can't help myself. Some detail of his last two years comes up — salary cut, tax problema — and I identify with him for a nanosecond."

"Jools, can you pronounce cab? Spelled t-a-x-i!?"

"That's what you said after the dreaded DUI."

"Stefff . . ."

"Stefff . . ."

"I was stabbed in the chest by a crazed black man —"

"You're kidding!"

"In an underground London hotspot. Climbing a tight spiral staircase after-hours. The sonofabitch just descended on me. The Angel of Death. Fortunately it was a short blade. I'll show you my scar next time I see you."

"Jeez, Fanny, sometimes I think you've led a more eventful life than mine . . . mebbe a little too eventful . . ."

"I'll tell you something about being knifed, Jools, and my experience wasn't nearly nearly decapitated . . ."

"What?"

"It really really hurts."

Socratic Dish with Ruby.

"I hear Jason suffers major child-of-celebrity syndrome," she whispers.

"And he knew Ron Goldman," I say.

"*And* he hated Nicole."

"He hated his father."

"How do you know?"

"I heard he beat the shit out of a lifesize statue of OJ with a baseball bat . . ."

"And he's awfully pudgy for an athlete's son."

"Exactly. Imagine the ego to have a lifesize statue of yourself in close proximity to your person."

"Must run in the family, beating personal property with baseball bats. Didn't OJ do the same thing to her car?"

"And what about A.C. Sidekick?"

"Or maybe a hit."

"Please, Ruby, we could go around and around playing with all the alternative scenarios, but in your heart don't you think OJ did drugs, got mad —"

"He got mad did drugs got madder did more got maddest."

"'You . . . fuck . . . My . . . wife?!@#!? Grrrr. Gonna kill a person. Maybe I'll do two . . .'"

"Jesus, Jools, sometimes you go too far."

"He did it. He's reeeaaallll sorry."

"For himself."

A year later, Jason's taken control of the Rockingham manor and custody of the dog, Kato, whom he renames Sambo.

What does he mean by that? I wonder and wonder further how Sydney and Justin might be coping, having lost their mother, their father and their favorite pets, The Katos, in less than a minute of rapid heartbeats.

A fax from one of those boys:

Robert Shapiro to OJ: I've got some good news and
    some bad news. Which d'ya wanna hear first?

OJ to Robert Shapiro: Gimme the bad news.

RS: Your blood's everywhere. At the murder scene, on
    the gloves, on the cap, in the Bronco . . .

OJ: What's the good news?

RS: Your cholesterol's 160 . . .

I move a television from Neutral Territory into The
Creature's room for the preliminary hearing, convince a
neighborhood cable boy to hook it up in exchange for my
Academy VHS of *Scent of a Woman*. *Smelly Lady,* I call it.

"If I were doing a book I'd start with Sukru and Bettina.
How they traversed the globe and got to be on that street at
that time . . ." Trailing the distressed Akita, Sukru and Bettina
were led to Nicole's river of blood oozing down the pavement
to the curb.

I look and see and then I look away and I never look at it
again, Sukru's testified, referring to her gruesome corpse.

"I was thinking this morning how many people are
affected by a murder," Todd says.

"With the possible exception of Dr. Irwin Golden."

We've been howling over his testimony for two days.

"Irwin Golden's a very large example of the effect of
Proposition 13/ budget cuts," Todd observes.

"Irwin Golden's a very large disturbed child."

"The videotapes running over and over have an insidious
effect, Debs," I complain during a late afternoon writers-on-a-
break phonecall. "It keeps them alive and they're *not* alive.
Maybe the autopsy photos *should* be televised."

"Unprofitable. What Advertiser would wanna buy *that*
commercial time? They'd be too disturbing, even for the
bloodthirsty American public . . ."

"Denise looks like Nicole. *That's* disturbing!"

"It's a hard look," Debin says.

"It's a hard life."

"Whaddya mean?"

"White Slavery . . ."

Blupp. Bluppbluppbluppblupp.

Foreplay with The Creature.

My first creative foray in a week.

Feeling sanguine because I've voted and most of the day still stretches before me.

This morning, at the upscale garage around the corner that served as an electoral polling place, the white-haired Republican lady and the pouf-haired Democratic lady and I tsk-tsked over the low turnout. They turned pages and pages, computer printout of eligible voters.

Lists and lists of names.

Nary a signature in sight save mine and the elderly gentleman's in a nearby booth poking holes in his ballot.

"I'm beginning to think we should pass a law that your driver's license is revoked if you can't show proof that you voted in the last presidential election," I joked and they looked at me as if they were torn between wondering if I were certifiable or senatorial. Or both.

Times being what they are and all.

Bluppbluppblupp. *Brrring brrring.*

Hi-it's-Julia and yadda yadda yadda. Beeep.

"Jools. Jools. If you're there pick up!"

Frankie.

"Jools! Emergency emergency!"

"I'm working!"

"Shit I'm sorry, but I'm stuck here on the street. I need a ride."

"What happened?"

"I was driving back from a luncheon with another woman and she said something that made me so mad, I jumped out of her car. I'm in Beverly Hills."

"What did this person say?"

"'Nicole was no angel.' A *woman* said that!"

"She. Pulled. His. Chain."

"Exactly."

"He did it. He's reeaalll sorry for himself."

"He's not sorry. He goes to sleep every night secure in the knowledge she's not fucking anyone else!"

"We can watch the election returns at my place," I offer.

"Something to depress me even more . . ."

Frankie and I appear to be the only Hollywood liberals bracing for an impending rout.

Probably because we're more liberal than Hollywood.

"The Clintons have made life very difficult for the Democrats."

"Don't start, okay? I'm not in the mood right now," Frankie says crossly.

For two years we've harangued over the timing of the gays in the military move. He needed to establish his presidency first, I'd argued and postulated that he'd been pressured into the early gesture by large contributors.

The Gang of Four, par example.

"A woman said Nicole was no angel?! I'm on my way . . ."

A post-electoral post-mortem with Debin.

"How dare They interpret this as a mandate for The Contract On America? They won with a scant 38 percent of the lumpen electorate getting off their asses and turning off their TVs long enough to vote!"

"Washington is just another Newtist colony," Debin whispers cynically and we laugh.

"I'm the same age as Newt. Why do I feel so oldt?"

"Tenks Gutt you don't look it."

"The Gingrich, on the other hand, looks pasty and overweight and un-worked out. Maybe he'll have a heart attack . . . or an aneurysm . . ."

"Look at you looking at the bright side of the rise of Fascism and the fall of America."

"That's me. Going UP! Toward zero . . ."

Both Frankie and Brad have extended invitations to Thanksgiving but Kate and I indulge in a high-pitched welcome-home fight instead of attending either.

It takes an hour of free-flowing tears for us to forgive each other. We tear off our party duds and makeup and don boxer shorts torn tees and woolly socks to dine on Lean Cuisine in Neutral Territory.

"So'd ya bother to cast your absentee ballot?" I ask.

"I was the only one who did," she says softly.

"Yes!" I exclaim proudly. "Who'd you vote for?"

Kate studies the carpet, murmurs something.

"What? I didn't hear you."

"Pete Wilson," she whispers. Looking down looking guilty.

My mouth drops open.

"Chechechehchchch. Did you vote for 187, too?"

She nods. I am stunned.

"Aaarrrrrgh . . ."

Kate jumps up from the table waving her hands.

"I voted for Feinstein! I voted for Feinstein!" she cheers defensively.

"Congratulations," I say in an icy Tanya-tone. "You didn't waste your ballot on an empty suit."

But I smile quickly, pretend I'm kidding.

I understand: That which you fear you learn to hate.

After two weeks of Left-Words, I finally connect with my insurance claims-adjuster. Sanctuary's sustained $65,000 of earthquake damage. I will net $10,000 out of a $12,500 payment.

The mortgage company will hold onto the remaining $2500 pending completion of repairs. What repairs?

Can you spell rip-off? I chuckle to myself and wonder why I bother to pay the exorbitant premiums.

"It's been ten months and we're not talking big money here. When may I expect to receive this check?"

"Oh four or five years," he teases.

"This may be funny to you. It's dead serious to me."

"Maybe by Christmas," he says sourly and hangs up.

After two days of Left-Words, I connect with The Hoff.

"This bastard needs to hear a male voice," I complain.

"How's the book comin'?" he asks.

"Slowly . . ."

"You write eighty pages over the weekend and I'll pursue the ten grand," he kids and we hang up.

The day after, an appraiser I've danced around with on the matter of selling rugs jewelry and movie memorabilia conveys a confidential offer of fifty thousand dollars for my Oscar.

I call The Hoff for consultation.

"Sell the fucking thing," he exclaims, no doubt tickled at the prospect of my solvency being sufficient to pay his mounting bill. We hang up. I hate myself for being attached, but I don't wanna go there. The Hoff probably wouldn't wanna either, if the fucking thing belonged to him.

Depressed, I turn the
POWER ON
Work in Progress. Scroll. WIP. Scroll.
FENNIG.
BluppBlupp. BluppBluppBluppBlupp . . .

It was generally acknowledged that Crackers, who would turn ten this Christmas, gave the best head in Hollywood.

"He found my G-spot . . ." Shari, Klaus Fennig's fourth wife, confided to her twin-sister Cheri during their morning phone call. Just to get her goat. Cheri gasped with shock and inhaled a small chunk of the half-cantaloupe she dined on daily for breakfast. Cheri was always on a diet; Shari ate anything she wanted.

In the end, they looked the same.

Gorgeous.

Those Girls, everybody called them.

"That dog's the safest sex in town," Shari added and convulsed with laughter, covered the receiver.

"Chechechechechchch . . ." Cheri said.

"Cheri, Cheri, are you okay?!?!" Shari giggled.

"Chechechchechch . . ." Clunk! The receiver dropped.

Thud! Cheri's body hit the floor.

Shaking with dread, Shari dialed 911 from another extension.

Paramedics Bobby and Sandy (BS their detractors in the department called them) arrived at Cheri's upscale 90210 address within minutes, but the recently-acquired Filipino couple didn't understand English and refused to open the security gate.

By the time BS gained entry and found her on a fake rock overlooking her fake-lagoon/black pool, Cheri was blue and bloated and beyond redemption.

Blood spurted in little fountains from her eyes and nose and ears. The cellular phone still clutched in her right hand was covered with the stuff, which was congealing into a gooey mess.

"We should clean her up," Bobby said after a futile half-hour of CPR and Sandy concurred.

They had completed the task by the time Shari arrived — escorted from the Fennig Fortress by two of L.A.'s finest, mounted on their motorcycles as if they were steeds from the Old West — but it didn't improve her appearance much.

The gore, had provided an explanation for the horror.

Shari caught a glimpse and lost it.

"Cover her face cover her face cover her face!" she screamed and Bobby and Sandy did after some hesitation, since they were both overwhelmed by Shari's arrival.

Shari was a verrry big movie star and under more propitious circumstances they'd have requested autographs.

Bobby, a star-fucker supremo, for sure.

Saving Who? What? Where.
    Saving When.
    Saving How?
    Saving!

why . . . ?

Writer's Rule #4: You have permission to say GoodBye.

Good-bye.

Didja come? Well? Didja?

Good-bye.

I'll get back to you on that.

Good-bye.

Close of business. Tomorrow for sure.

Good-bye yourself.

POWER OFF

Spic.

That's The Word on all Those Other Girls' minds.

I see it on their faces, in their eyes.

I wonder if I look like them. If I *am* like them.

I've struggled against that grain all of my existence.

But Rosa Lopez' testimony broadcasts from portable black-and-whites stationed throughout Ruby's Easy Street Salon and it's hard not to respond stereotypically.

"Chee eeesss lyeen'," Amalia, a Salvadoran, had emphasized this morning. In case I didn't know the deal.

"Jools, you're scowling."

"If she wrings her hands and makes one more reference to the wonderful Mr. Chonnie, I'm gonna lose it. Am I being too racial here?"

Ruby laughs and shoves the fingers doing the talking into warm soapy water.

"You're just overreacting to the father figure aspect."

"Since I haven't got a father anymore . . ."

"Still feeling like an orphan?"

"I am an orphan!"

I'm *nobody's* Daddy's-little-girl.

"Takes a while but you get used to it," Ruby says. "You don't get used to it, actually. You accept it."

Life is pain. Lynn Nesbit said.

"Thanks for not using that yuppie word."

"Closure?"

"Shit! You went and said it."

"Grist for the mill, right?"

"Referring to the neverending book? *How I Spent My Bulnerable Season* by Julio-Phillippe-not-Harold-Brodkey?"

Ruby, one of the last people in L.A. who reads for pleasure, gets the joke and laughs even though it's unfunny.

"Drive carefully," she admonishes when we air-kiss goodbye.

Among my messages, an invitation from the JULES'S SMOKE AND RUN Fox executive to Kato Kaelin's birthday party.

I can't manipulate anyone into serving as a traveling companion, although everyone agrees it's good material.

"Is Kato Kaelin Forrest Gump?" one of those girls snickers when she turns me down.

Frustrated, restless and a tad bored, I inflict a teary flashback-laden night on myself instead . . .

HOW I SPENT MY BULNERABLE SEASON, 1994
THE SEQUEL TO THE SEQUEL TO THE SEQUEL
BY JULIO PHILLIPPE

Seated in the color-coding corner, chortling corrosively, Dalee and I took turns reading Anne Rice's love letters to her cast, her crew, Herself re: *Interview With A! Vampire*/TheMovie.

Starring some really pretty clothes and jewelry.

I'd saved the trades in which they'd appeared.

They were starting to form quite the little stack.

"Bet *she* doesn't tengo un tax problema!"

"Still, Jools?"

Dalee lived in the moment. If you didn't complain about an ailment for a while, he presumed it had passed.

"More!"

"Maybe you should become a Scientologist. They seem to intimidate the IRS," Dalee suggested and I sneered disparagingly.

"Jools, will there *ever* be a final solution?"

"An unfortunate choice of words from black to Jew . . ."
We laughed.
"You're the only one who's had the nerve to ask."
"I don't *choose* to — " he started and the phone rang.
Hi-it's-Julia/Real-soon-I-promise.
Beeep.
"Julia, it's June . . ."
I picked up immediately for I could tell from her frazzled
tone that Dad had gone into a state of extreme
chechechechch and was sucking on a respirator again.
Freebasing pure oxygen.
Struggling for existence.
She ran down the particulars in this latest of increasingly-
frequent emergencies and I had to strain to hear her over the
thrub-thrub-thrub of my frightened heart.
It was haaa'd to *pppreathe* . . .

Friday the Thirteenth 2:30 A.M.
We'd become so accustomed to Dad's miraculous recover-
ies that even though he'd been on and off a respirator twice in
three weeks and even though June sadly told us he'd aspirated
food and faxed his living will, when my brother Matthew
called to inform me Dad had slipped through our fingers his
voice was surprised and I was shocked.
It's a long way from dying to dead, I'd written in the
Prozac piece but E. Graydon Carter cut it. Now I know what I
meant, I thought, sobbing in the shower some hours later.
"Whomever will love me like Dad did?" I inveighed, and
then I focused on him and felt relief.
At least he hadn't suffered a long painful decline.
Unless I counted the past five years.
"Whomever will I discuss the quarks with?" I cried.
The up/down top/bottom strange/charm of it all.

"New York has the greatest restaurants in the world. You
want room service?" I challenged and Kate rolled her brown
eyes heavenward. She'd arrived hours before me and knocked

off an interview at NYU Law School. Together we'd visited June in the apartment she'd shared with my father.

We'd be holding his memorial there tomorrow.

"You're on California time, Mom. It's late. Besides, wouldn't you rather tear off that catsuit and lie in bed?"

Kate fiddled with the menu.

I hung up Don't Ask/Don't Tell, my all-purpose traveling companion, pfumpferred through the pockets, found a tasty leftover and lit it defiantly.

"I suppose I should be offering you a puff?"

"No thanks. But thanks for asking, Jools."

We feasted on scrambled eggs and stayed up most of the night watching *The Firm*.

I closed my eyes firmly at 5:30 A.M.

Hoped Kate had, too.

Short sleep. Short dream . . .

THE QUILLMEISTER'S QUAGMIRE—PART III

Seeking SANCTUARY, searching for TUPAC, the WOMAN WRITER hurtles through the downstroke of a restless Santa Ana Windy Night. Approaching bright white spots at the speed of light, she's dropped unceremoniously into their midst.

She brushes herself off and scopes the venue.

A television gameshow and she's in the wings.

That Girl Nicole leads her to the set.

This way, this way please, That Other Girl Denise says.

The woman looks up and knows from the sea of white faces in the audience she's not at a meeting of FFA.

"I wanna go home," she says.

"Only one way to do that!" exclaims the host, The Tom.

"Be nice to the lawyers!" the audience screams.

Woof woof woof.

That's the next line?! Phooey!

"I don't wanna go there," she says.

Then she is running running running.

Faster and faster but The Host is gaining on her.

She's neck and neck with The Tom.

And I was awake, wondering what to wear to the wake.

More than a hundred people. Old family friends: Tony Randall and Belle Cooper. Matthew and Mae and their two children, Alex and Katherine Anne. A troop of Matthew's Harvard Mates. My contingent: Phyllis Levy. Julie Grau and her assistant, Nicky Weinstock. Roger Friedman and Bruce Bibby and George Rush and Diane Reverand. Josh Young.

Joni never made it and neither did Connie, and I vowed not to miss any more memorials because their absence hurt.

Kate and I couldn't have attended ourselves without financial aid from my brother, my publisher and God, who'd picked up Kate's planefare.

Diane Reverand, who'd moved from Villard to HarperCollins and taken me with her, staked us to cars and hotel and my brother used advantage miles to roundtrip me business class. I was grateful, but I also felt like everybody's mercy-fuck, which only added to my sadness.

If I held to my pattern, I'd be subsumed by flu in three days.

Taking ill, getting sick. How The Jew grieved.

I'd spent the morning of Dad's death composing my memoriam, but I was unable to catch a breath for the first couple of sentences until I focused on Roger, perched precariously at the edge of a couch, which calmed me. I started over:

"My father — my best friend, my favorite teacher — seemed to me a powerful physical embodiment of words like dichotomy and paradox. He was a thinker, a mathematician, a man of reason. With a scientist's brain and a poet's heart. A cynic with a capacity for moral outrage. A serious man who loved a good laugh. A feisty scrapper with an enormous wellspring of humanity. Principled, almost strict, and stubborn sometimes, but remarkably nonjudgmental, open and accepting.

"Which was lucky for me, given what a bad kid I was for at least a decade past when anyone has a right to be a bad kid. My father took my triumphs in stride with pride and was steadfast and loyal when I was at my nadir.

"I was a fortunate Fifties daughter, for my father was a true feminist. From an early age, I noticed I wasn't treated with the same condescension most of my girlfriends were by their fathers, and I believe that imbued me with a confidence that kept me at best productive, at worst intact, all my life.

"My father taught me the trivial — how to pitch a baseball so I wouldn't 'throw like a girl' — and the sublime — 'Whenas in silk my Julia goes . . .' He even tried valiantly to help me overcome my math anxiety, probably inflicted on me by teachers in school not nearly as gifted as he was.

"Conversations with my father have been a precious pastime for me, particularly as I have gotten older. At least once a week we'd indulge in an End of the World discussion that generally started with my father quoting from the Gospel According to Mel Brooks: 'They can all go to hell except Cave 17!' Ended with his encouraging call to arms: 'Up the Rebels!' And always cheered me up.

"In between we'd cover guns and drugs, ethnic cleansing and racial injustice, popcultural headlines and headhunters, quarks and cold dark matter.

"Our last argument, in fact, revolved around the quarks. I'd been reading about a new theory of cold dark matter in *Scientific American* and didn't quite understand it. I called him for an explanation, but he was a bit cross that day — breathing had become increasingly difficult — and wanted to postpone any serious discourse.

"When I complained about his recalcitrance to a friend, he said, 'But Jools, who else do you know in Hollywood who could have an argument with her father about the quarks?'

"My father was possessed of a remarkable intellect, which

I'm proud to say he exercised until his dying day. In his late
seventies he wrote and published his first book, and he was hard
at work on his second when he died. It has occurred to me more
than once in these past five years of his struggle with declining
physical health that he continued to survive as much from his
brilliance and sheer will as from any medical ministrations.

"And a great reluctance to leave June, or me and my
daughter Kate, or Matthew and Mae and Alex and Katherine
Anne.

"He loved us all with a big and generous heart and I think
that I shall miss that part of his spirit most of all.

"Several weeks ago, I joked to June that a friend of mine
had declared he was sure my father had one simple elegant
equation to complete before he could pass on.

"I hope you finished it, Dad. Up the Rebels!"

Japan's second poisoning incident's yesterday's news.

I've been losing sleep over it. What kind of world . . . ?

"You tapped out my card!" I bark into the receiver.

$39.00 to tapped out in point of fact.

The Limit. A record low.

Todd mumbles something that sounds a lot like Grrrr.

"Todd, I need to call you back!" I hang up.

The Oklahoma City Bombing InfernoTains today, amping
my adrenaline, depleting my endorphins. April 19, anniversary of The Big San Francisco Quake. 1906, I think.

It is also, as I've repeatedly reminded the phone installer
(he of the cap and beard, the fifty extra pounds and the sibilant
S) the second anniversary of The Waco Debacle. He argues.

He spends weekends in the wild shooting assault rifles,
rehearsing no doubt for the coming revolution. With his
Vietnam buddies, he says.

I don't think so, unless he was in country when he was ten.

We head to Neutral Territory where he calms down.

He admires some semi-precious items in the hutch that
spewed most of the good stuff to its demise during The Sorta
Big One and I casually inquire if he's married.

Lives with Mother and two cats.

I head to The Creature's room and he follows.

We pause to absorb more live FEEDME FEEDME.

Beirut. Sarajevo. Downtown L.A.

He says we should reinstate the neutron bomb and instead of confronting him about what he might mean I again recall The Anniversary of Waco.

Times being. And all.

We agree The BranchDavidian Incineration pissed us off and Janet Reno still has time to resign if indeed she was responsible.

Phew!

He volunteers kindly I might wanna check out Michael Reagan's radioshow for information and I volunteer nothing.

Overstuffed ignoramus!

I wonder if he wears Mommy's panties under his camouflage.

Faux fatigues for the faux warrior.

I don't wanna go there.

I wanna call Todd and yell some more.

Fat phone installer heads for Kate's phone, which is giving him trouble and I punch keys on my portable, which I must rent because I don't have enough cash to buy.

There are homeless people who have more money in their pockets than me.

"I apologize," I say when Todd picks up. "You were just guaranteeing plane ticket and hotel for Kate's graduation."

"Accepted. I already calmed down."

"How'd you manage that?"

"I invented a mantra."

"Oh yeah?"

Todd chants.

"Yokohama. Oklahoma. Oklahoma. Yokohama."

Call waiting. God.

"At least this has blown The Trial off the airwaves."

"For a minute."

"I think it's moving to the backburner anyway."

"Why?"

"People don't wanna bear witness to the — "

"Shitstained pissy corruption?"

"Pithy as ever, Jools . . ."

"Sydney's phone message: 'Mommy mommy please call me Mommy please call.' Broke my heart," Sharyn says.

Sharyn's the first new friend I've made in five years.

I still tread softly with her, though, because she reminds me in look and inflection of Gail Parent and that relationship didn't turn out so well.

"I've heard that message in my life. Only my daughter was younger and the guy who held a gun on me fell asleep instead of blowing my head off."

"Joools . . ."

"I'm so glad I can't afford a Kato anymore."

"The little shit."

Sharyn shared A Guest with her first and last ex-husband. When they split up he retained custody.

"His footprint's on Nicole's back just as surely as OJ's," Sharyn says.

"Kato. The *Ultimate* That Boy," I say.

"I hear he's represented by Buddy Monash."

"Perrrfect casting . . ."

WFAG had downloaded the computer-animated rendition of the murders for our viewing pleasure one recent afternoon. We were shocked by how quickly Ron and Nicole were dispatched.

One slaughtered like a large bird, the other cornered like a frightened gopher.

Remember last year, when They told us he put up a hell of fight? I remarked.

Despite her superficial GailParenthood, Sharyn and I have cleaved on a number of issues. Today it's the outing of Jann Wenner. More specifically, *New York's* piece on the outing of Jann Wenner, which she's just finished reading.

She tosses the magazine on the color-coding table and it flies open to a smiling shot of The Jann with his model-boyfriend, quintessence of Omar's Men. Distributed by Joop! Parfums?

"Is that love in the Nineties?" Sharyn snorts.

"Love in The Nineties is me flying coach to my daughter's graduation!"

Sharyn laughs lustily.

Sharyn's been hurt by love.

Who hasn't?

"Wayne, this is Michael and Juliana and you have to tell them you bumped me to First Class for old times' sake!"

Memo to Sharyn: This Boarding Pass is Love in The 90's.

So's the pretty threesome before me. First and Last X.

Third wife Juliana. Third daughter Natasha.

They shoot me a wry three-part harmony look and Natasha reaches out to touch one of Don'tAsk/Don'tTell's shiny gold buttons.

"That's a hell of a jacket," Michael says.

"I'm never worrying about you again," Juliana grins.

We board the aircraft and go separate ways.

She right. Me left.

Follow our bliss, as it were.

"Why couldn't you have worn The Suit?!"

Saturday P.M. Graduation Weekend and I'm still standing.

The Child has inflicted a fight on Each Parent and I've drawn the short straw tonight. The Kate is The Pissed!

"Long ago, this drag cost four thousand dollars on *sale*. I can't believe you're giving me guff about it!"

I've armored myself in asymmetrical Yohji Yamamoto.

The Red and The Black.

Paired with over-the-knee Romeo Gigli stocking-boots.

Not the best choice for social engagements in a Conservative County, but I packed in a hurry.

Teary-eyed I light a cigarette on the terrace of an upscale AnnArborMichigan Restaurant and refract my psyche off all the tickachung I expended to be this miserable.

How could Kate know I last donned The Suit for Pauly's funeral? That Mike Maday, who recycled it to me, had recently died — alone — of undiagnosed cause?

There was a three-thousand-case backlog at The Coroners' office and his wife was still awaiting the results of an autopsy performed months ago.

"Did he commit suicide?" I blurted when she called.

"I don't think so. He was trying to give up alcohol for the billionth time. In his solitary-confinement basement room. An aneurysm . . . an embolism maybe . . . ?"

"Vietnam killed him!" I exclaimed before I thought.

"I don't wanna go there," she muttered.

As Those Girls and Boys and Boys-and-Girls say.

The Possessed, The Obsessed, The Guest, All The Rest.

"That's a hell of a jacket," the cabdriver said last night/this morning in a voice raspy with cigarettes and bourbon. He looked to be computer-generated from the parts of dead people.

Skinny. Bearded. Baseball-capped. Dark-Glassesed.

We chatted. He: Viet Vet. Me: *Taxi Driver.*

Travis Bickle to Travis Bickle.

"Very typical. Drug-addicted alcoholic drifter," he volunteered. "Deepest relationship lasted four years."

"Long-term these days."

He laughed, lit a cigarette and hit the accelerator, merging easily onto I-95. I checked the meter.

This boy's gonna cost half what that boy who brought me to Ann Arbor did. Another Vet. Gulf War. He scoped me and figured, Hey rich bitch let's take the *scenic* route.

Finally, I held up one of my precious twenties and said, This is it! and he deposited me hastily at the house Kate shared with seven other girls. I was the final arrival and there was much sidewalk conferencing.

Natasha made a sudden run toward the street as a car lurched out of a neighboring driveway. Several adults, me included, jumped to pull her back sharply from the curb. Back twinge back twinge.

"She's too old to be doing that," I opined crankily.

Kate's best friend, Meri's father, Michael, clasped my hand and walked me to the bar where we were meeting The Group. He took a wrong turn on the main drag, but we were rescued by: "Jools!"

Greg and two friends. We ambled to the teenage/townie bar, absconded with a large table and ordered watered-down martinis and a couple of pitchers of beer.

Kate joined us, tossed me two graduation ceremony tickets off-handedly. If you don't care I don't care.

"You wouldn't wanna go . . . ?" I pleaded with Greg and he promised he'd make sure I attended if I called him at 7:30 A.M.

He wrote his phone number on the corner of a napkin. When I tucked it into the top left snap pocket I thought I felt a roach.

Pace pace puff puff ooh ooh.

A leftover from my late lamented opulent life . . .

The cab swished smoothly into the driveway of the Ypsilanti Radisson and I extended my hand.

"I'm Julia," I said. And I'm a Financial Fuck-Up.

"Hiiiii Julia. Tim Harvey."

He smiled and I noticed he'd lost a lot of teeth. The few still standing had turned gray-brown. Umber. Like Nicole's knitted vest. I paid him and he refused a tip. We shook hands tightly instead.

"Remember me . . ." he said in a voice twangily heartwrenching as any mega-millioned country-crooner.

"I'll never forget you," I promised and sprang from the car to sob at the foot of the bed for hours.

In my $125/night at the Radisson. Deep in the Midwest.

Where the skin was as pale as the lager-on-tap.

Grieving for the dead people. Sans closure . . .

"Maybe I should get a cab and leave."

"Mom, don't be ridiculous!"

"Don't you think I'd have bought a Republican outfit if I could afford to?!"

Kate's eyes soften and she reaches for my hands.

She clasps them tightly. I look down.

Mine tan wizened rednailed. Hers young sweet freeee.

"It means a lot to me that you're here," she whispers. "I'm very glad you came."

"I'm very glad I came too. I'm very proud of you and I love you very much. I think I'm menopausally over-reacting to Natasha."

Kate smirks sardonically. Not young sweet freeee.

"Remember, Mom, Natasha spelled backwards Ah Satan."

I tamp my butt and we hug and rejoin our table.

Our server, a thin ponytailed many-earringed chap, sidles over to recite Les Specialties and indulge in wine-selection discourse.

Kate and I exchange a knowing glance and order.

"What were OJ's last words to Nicole?" she whispers conspiratorially as he moves on.

"Your waiter will be right with you . . ."

Heard any good jokes lately? Pee Wee Herman inquired.

I know the lighted-match one, said Richard Pryor.

A message from one of those girls:

What's a leettle taco? A taceeto.

What's a leettle burro? A burreeto.

What's a leettle judge? Judge E-E-Ito.

What's the deeff 'tween OJ and Chris Reeve-o?

OJ's gonna walk. No sheeto . . .

"So Michael Jackson took The Glove off to attack The Other and then invoked the sacred names of SKG's principals and Mike Milken. 'Some of my best friends are Jews.' Who could cause anti-Semitism if it didn't already exist."

SKG. The Three SchlAmigos. Starring The Spielberg.

"Chee eeesss lyeen'," I told Todd during SS's Academy Award acceptance speech when he claimed he'd never held a friend's statue. "Sanctimonious little bar mitzvah boy," I snarled as he dribbled tears. *Schindler's List*. My gentile friends loved it.

My father said he cried.

"Oh, I have to run to see the movie about The Good Nazi!" I spat at Fanny and Zoe in the middle of a particularly nasty writer's block. "I read the book!"

Harumph. DreamWorks.

THE DEAL IN SEARCH OF A STORY.

Although the Jackson/Presley informercial costarring That Serious Journalist What's-er-Name waaas close. History is just what someone writes it is, her boss, RitcherrrdNicks!Unnn pronounced and she transcribed . . .

"Right up there with Barry Scheck," Frankie counters.

"Mayhap the gloves were switched and OJ tried Michael's discarded one by mistake. That's why it was so small . . . ?"

We giggle.

"Christopher Darden's IQ's inversely proportionate to what he imagines the size of his dick is and he's a good reason to abandon affirmative action. This dude should never have been allowed to attend law school, never mind stand up in court," I needle.

"I hate this conversation. Affirmative action covers women too!"

"Right. I benefited from affirmative action, *You* benefited . . . I don't *wanna* be nice to the lawyers!"

Flea Bailey hopefuls sprinkle the InfernoBand, exuding confidence characteristic of legaleagles who know 99 percent of their clientele are guilty and most often get paid in cash.

Hundreds delivered in brown envelopes by messenger. Color men for The Trial, which Those ExtraLarge Boys have converted into another sporting event, another war, the hideous state of Ron's and Nicole's corpses notwithstanding.

The Population's capacity for gorging on InfernoGarbage without gagging seemed to be growing exponentially.

Hell, it took almost a decade of heavy InfernoTation for The Population to turn against the Vietnam War, but The Population was already rent asunder.

It — We — never recovered.

Hawks/Doves Black/White Young/Old Rich/Poor Men/Women.

I've been inciting Those Girls. If OJ walks we riot.

Overturn 735Is. Incinerate 7-11s. Abscond with AK47s.

"Let's hire a hit man to shoot him as he's walking down the courthouse steps," one of those girls suggested at Dad's memorial, displaying some white middle class *female* rage.

Yo Yo Yo. O O O. Suck *this*!

"I'm very poor," I laughed, "but you can put me down for $50. Hit *woman*, though."

"If such a species exists anywhere but the movies . . ."

"A fucked-up sabra from Israeli intelligence," I joke to Frankie in my kitchen some weeks after my return.

"Jools, not a Jew."

"I didn't even *think* of that!"

"You should because —"

"*They* will!"

"Race over gender."

"Only *white* women can afford gender over race."

"So much for Marcia Clark's voir dire."

"I hear she's dating Alan Greisman, X-Mr. Sally Field."

"What is she, forty? She's just a kid. She doesn't know any better. She'll learn . . ."

"$41,000 for dental work," I smile, bonding with my bonding. "I know a thing or two about dental distress."

I had my reasons.

What did She just say?

Did He just *do* me that way?

Like Marcia. Anita. Hillary.

Polly Klaas and Susan Smith.

The murdered and the murderers.

"I hate that our comeuppance is The Motherfucker walks!" Frankie sputters angrily.

"Whilst Heidi Fleiss and her entire family do time."

My country t'is of thee/Sweet land of perjury . . .

A message from one of those boys:

Hugh Grant is Joey Buttafuoco . . .

Three etc. and I ClickCher aimlessly.

BlackPOP/WhiteFLASH for a while.

Speed, last summer's must-miss sleeper's on SHO.

I punch my pillows and settle in for cheapthrills.

"Why does Bill Pullman have a career?" Todd comments when I report my sleepless in Sanctuary nocturnal commissions. My sins-of-omissions.

"Because Kathie Lee Gifford does?" Beeep. Good-answer.

WHY ARE THEY ALL NAMED MICHAEL? Ruby had titled her favorite painting years ago, a boldly oversized vivaciously colored opus featuring overlapping scenes of crucifixion.

"How ahead of time are you?" I crackwise during a rare phone visit, referring to InfernoNews of the day: MikeOvitz's bolt from CEO/CAA to President/Disney=CapCitiesABC, Michael Eisner's $19 Billion Small World.

TheFinalSolution.

Number-Two-to-the-x-*more-than-equals*-what-Number-One-used-to-be in the escalating My Dick is Bigger InfernoWar.

A moot point in an era of penile implantation.

Too late in the day for service, my electric gate suffers a priapic nervous breakdown, open-shut open-shut, like Hannibal's beak.

It takes me an hour to find the manual switch.

POWER OFF

POWER ON

BluppBlupp. CRACKERS.

BluppBluppBluppBlupp.

ONCE UPON A TIME

A pugnacious pre-pubescent Sum Total of matter intelligence and spirit pranced playfully among and between the universes. She had no time or space compulsions and frankly she was becoming restless — a nervous state-of-boredom — drifting through the millennia with nothing to do.

Wafting aimlessly through an eon she checked out, permitting herself to hear harmonic convergence between the whoosh of a ballot dropping into a garbage can in a recently-democratized demilitarized-zone and the hypnotic blupp-bluppblupp of a computer keyboard as Shari Fennig's daughter, Dezzylieu, typed her access code:

Too bee oar knot 2 B.

SumTotal hadn't bothered to listen to any cosmic reverberation forever, let alone EarthNoise, about which there was always nefarious gossip among the nebulae.

"If they wail through the galaxies and I don't hear them, do they even exist, never mind make a sound?" was her point of view.

And then SumTotal banged into a wall built of the screams of billions and billions of starving babies. Oy gevalte, they wailed. Oy gevalte! Bolted from torpor, suddenly motivated, she drafted her considerable consciousness to respond personally. En Masse.

Who's to account for the maternal instinct?

She opted too bee.

Midnight, December 25, but skeleton staff were handling transportation, not paying attention, so she materialized a chocolate Labrador Retriever situated in the creche of a nativity scene outside the Mormon Temple on Santa Monica Boulevard, Beverly Hills, California, 90210.

Further, upon close personal inspection, she found herself endowed — encumbered, more precisely — with a penis.

Uh-oh. Dog boy-ness. Boy-dogness.

Is this Rwanda-Herczegovina? he wondered, referring to the soulfoul sounds that had captured his imagination and knew from the profusion of energy-sucking lights and lush topography it wasn't.

He'd landed in Hollywoodland, where he catapulted from the creche to the crucible/crux of global household iconism in a single short year. Less than a hiccup in SumTotal terms and still he lingered long after he wanted to leave.

He named himself CRACKERS (an acronym for Cosmic

Regenerative Alphawave Creation of Knowledge Ergo Rewarding Searches) to remember who she was. When things got bad, he sang Can We All Get Along to the tune of *We Shall Overcome*.

Not a tune for the cosmos, but definitely a melody for man.

Metamorphosed into tangible form, CRACKERS acquired some fatal flaws. The worst was a conscience, located on his left hindquarters, where his Achilles tendon would be if he were human, as he'd intended.

"People," was the last thing he said to me. "Let me tell you about people . . ."

THAT'S A PRETTY SOFT EXIT . . .

"Whozzat?"

IT'S ME. QUARK! THE TOP DOG, SO TO SPEAK.

"I'm losing it. I gotta get out more."

YOU'RE TOO CYNICAL TO BE AROUND PEOPLE.

"Quark, I just don't wanna blow an opportunity like the Clintons. Who blew it for everyone."

THAT'S WHAT I MEAN. YOU'RE TOO CYNICAL.

"Then Quark, quick, tell me about Dgo, I'm forgetting."

He evaporates, another figment of imagination.

Comedy's easy. Writing is hard. Chill, Jools.

Hard is eighteen-hour days in a coalmine.

But I'm frustrated I'll admit. Dizzy from aggravation.

A mantra à la Todd.

"Ommmm-Grrrr. Ommmm-Grrrr. Ommmm-Grrrr . . .

"OMMMM-GRRRR. OOOMMMMM. GRRRRR . . ."

"Mom, what the *hell* are you *doing*?!"

"Contemplating my novel, tentatively titled . . .

"*Memo to Jack Kevorkian*:

Under No Circumstance May Irwin Golden Perform The Autopsy . . ."

Kate's mouth twitches with annoyance.

Ignoring me, she peers over my shoulder and reads.

"Jools, this doesn't suck!"

"B+ isn't *good enough* for a Zimmerman," I reply.

"Don't be ridiculous, Mommy, you're not a *Zimmerman*!"

"Seems like an awfully long drive just to cross a road," I complain. "Was it five years? Five minutes?"

"What's the difference?"

Scroll. Scroll. Scroll. Silent. Sooo silent.

"It doesn't suck," I say. "I might have to puke."

Kate smiles reluctantly.

"Welcome home, Mom. Which backwards is . . . Mom . . ."

Kate. My best teacher. My favorite friend.

What goes around comes around.

Said The Don.

Who did. Whoop dee doo.

Who's The Don? Dad asks and Tanya says.

Who cares?

Is OJ gonna testify? he persists and she laughs.

Oh put a *sock* in it!

Go Fuck Yourself.

IT WAS MARCH

Okay I Will.

THE DAY BEFORE

I Will.

THE DAY BEFORE

I Will.

pace pace . . .

Didja Come?

Well.

Didja?

puff puff . . .

More

Or

Less

Is

More

ooh ooh . . .

MEMO FROM JOOLS
TO: THOSE BOYS AND THOSE GIRLS
SUBJECT: ACKNOWLEDGMENTS

I'm so very grateful for your editorial, financial, emotional, and moral support, but there will be no list of names. You know who you are and you know that I love you.

After careful consideration, however, I've decided that just because I'll never eat lunch in this town again doesn't mean you shouldn't.

Doff of the cap to those who no longer require sustenance: Ludwig van Beethoven, David Begelman, Eazy-E, Wolfgang Amadeus Mozart, and most of all, Lenny Bruce.

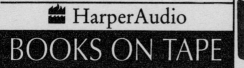